*Longman Exam Guides*
*Bookkeeping and Accounting*

# Longman Exam Guides

*Series Editors:* **Stuart Wall and David Weigall**

*Titles available:*

Bookkeeping and Accounting
Business Law
Economics
English as a Foreign Language: Intermediate
English Literature
Monetary Economics
Office Practice and Secretarial Administration
Pure Mathematics
Secretarial Skills

*Forthcoming:*

Accounting: Cost and Management
             Financial
             Standards
Biology
British Government and Politics
Business Communication
Business Studies
Chemistry
Commerce
Computer Science
Electronics
Elements of Banking
English as a Foreign Language: Preliminary
                                    Advanced
French
General Principles of Law
General Studies
Geography
Mechanics
Modern British History
Physics
Quantitative Methods
Sociology
Taxation

Longman Exam Guides

# BOOKKEEPING AND ACCOUNTING

*David Floyd*

**LONGMAN**
London and New York

**Longman Group Limited**
Longman House, Burnt Mill, Harlow
Essex CM20 2JE, England
*Associated companies throughout the world*

*Published in the United States of America*
*by Longman Inc., New York*

© Longman Group Limited 1986

*First published 1986*
*Second impression 1986*

**British Library Cataloguing in Publication Data**

Floyd, David, *1947–*
    Bookkeeping and accounting.—(Longman exam
    guides)
    1. Accounting
    I. Title
    657      HF5635
    ISBN 0-582-29692-7

**Library of Congress Cataloging in Publication Data**
Floyd, David 1947–
    Bookkeeping and accounting.
    (Longman exam guides)
    Includes index.
    1. Bookkeeping.      2. Accounting.      I. Title.
II. Series.
HF5635.F588   1986      657      85–23982
ISBN 0–582–29692–7

Printed and Bound in Great Britain at
The Bath Press, Avon

# Contents

# Editors' Preface

Much has been said in recent years about declining standards and disappointing examination results. While this may be somewhat exaggerated, examiners are well aware that the performance of many candidates falls well short of their potential. Longman Exam Guides are written by experienced examiners and teachers, and aim to give you the best possible foundation for examination success. There is no attempt to cut corners. The books encourage thorough study and a full understanding of the concepts involved and should be seen as course companions and study guides to be used throughout the year. Examiners are in no doubt that a structured approach in preparing for and taking examinations can, together with hard work and diligent application, substantially improve performance.

The largely self-contained nature of each chapter gives the book a useful degree of flexibility. After starting with Chapters 1 and 2, all other chapters can be read selectively, in any order appropriate to the stage you have reached in your course. We believe that this book, and the series as a whole, will help you establish a solid platform of basic knowledge and examination technique on which to build.

*Stuart Wall and David Weigall*

# Acknowledgements

My thanks go to my parents for their assistance and to my wife for her encouragement and patience.

We are grateful to the following for permission to reproduce copyright material:

Apricot Computers PLC; Barclays Bank PLC; James Beattie PLC; The Boots Company PLC; Alfred Gilbert & Son Ltd; Midshires Building Society; The Society of Company and Commercial Accountants;

and the following Examinations Boards for permission to reproduce past examination questions:

The Associated Examining Board; Association of Accounting Technicians; Joint Matriculation Board; London Chamber of Commerce and Industry; Royal Society of Arts Examination Board; University of Cambridge Local Examinations Syndicate; University of London School Examinations Board; University of Oxford Delegacy of Local Examinations.

Any answers or hints on answers given are the sole responsibility of the author and have not been provided by the exam boards.

*To Emily and Laura*

# Chapter 1

# The examinations

This book aims to help you if you are studying for a qualification or an examination which includes at least some *Bookkeeping* or *Financial Accounting* as content. For example, you may be attending an accounting course which is being run at a local college and which has an externally set examination, such as a foundation or level one course of the Accounting Bodies, or a GCE 'O' or 'A' level in Accounting. You could be a student on a Business Studies course such as BTEC National, which includes accounting as a subject or module. You might have decided to study accounting purely as a matter of interest, or to improve your job prospects; perhaps you plan to follow a career in accountancy and expect to study the subject at a high level. Regardless of the nature of your course, your reasons for studying accounting, or your background as a student, you should find that this book will help to prepare you for your bookkeeping and accounting examinations and assignments.

The book concentrates on the 'how' and the 'why' of bookkeeping and accounting. It provides appropriate examples and illustrations, and suggests answers (and provides relevant workings) to a range of questions which have been selected from recent examination papers. The chapter topics are taken from the major bookkeeping and accounting syllabuses. These include:

Accounting Technician and First-level Professional syllabuses
GCE/CSE Accounting and GCE Advanced-level Accounting syllabuses
Royal Society of Arts Bookkeeping Stage I and Accounting Stage II
London Chamber of Commerce and Industry Bookkeeping syllabuses
   (Elementary and Intermediate levels)
BTEC National level modules – Numeracy and Accounting, and
   Accounting 2
CPVE Preparatory-level Bookkeeping module.

A syllabus coverage guide is given. Each major topic included in the book is listed against the relevant syllabuses, to indicate whether or not the chapter content is featured on the given syllabus. Please note that the table is intended as a *guide* only: syllabuses may be open to some interpretation as to their precise content, and each year new syllabuses may be introduced or existing syllabuses may be altered.

## SYLLABUS COVERAGE CHART

| TOPIC | Foundation and 1st level professional | Accounting Technicians levels 1 and 2 | RSA Bookkeeping Stage I | RSA Accounting Stage II | LCCI Elementary Bookkeeping |
|---|---|---|---|---|---|
| Accounting concepts | √ | √ | | | |
| Source documents | √ | √ | √ | √ | √ |
| Books of original entry | √ | √ | √ | √ | √ |
| VAT records | √ | √ | √ | √ | |
| Ledger accounts | √ | √ | √ | √ | √ |
| Division of the ledger | √ | √ | √ | √ | √ |
| Control accounts | √ | √ | √ | √ | |
| Trial balance | √ | √ | √ | √ | √ |
| Errors and suspense account | √ | √ | | √ | √ |
| Petty cash book | √ | √ | √ | √ | √ |
| Cash book | √ | √ | √ | √ | √ |
| Bank reconciliation | √ | √ | √ | √ | √ |
| Prepayments and accruals | √ | √ | √ | √ | √ |
| Provision for depreciation | √ | √ | | √ | √ |
| Provision for bad debts | √ | √ | | √ | √ |
| Working capital | √ | √ | | √ | |
| Simple final accounts | √ | √ | √ | √ | √ |
| Manufacturing accounts | √ | √ | | √ | |
| Departmental accounts | √ | √ | | | |
| Income and expenditure accounts | √ | √ | √ | √ | √ |
| Partnership accounts | √ | √ | | √ | √ |
| Limited company accounts | √ | √ | | √ | |
| Shares and debentures | √ | √ | | √ | |
| Incomplete records | √ | √ | | √ | |
| Forecast final accounts | √ | √ | | | |
| Funds flow statements | √ | √ | | | |
| Accounting ratios | √ | √ | | √ | |

| LCCI Intermediate Bookkeeping | GCE O-level Accounting | GCE A-level Accounting | BTEC National Numeracy & Accounting | BTEC National Accounting 2 | CPVE Preparatory Bookkeeping | Scottish Cert. of Ed'n. O and H grades Accounting | SCOTVEC Nat. Cert. Accounting Modules |
|---|---|---|---|---|---|---|---|
|  | ✓ | ✓ | ✓ | ✓ |  | ✓ | ✓ |
| ✓ | ✓ | ✓ | ✓ | ✓ | ✓ | ✓ | ✓ |
| ✓ | ✓ | ✓ | ✓ | ✓ | ✓ | ✓ | ✓ |
|  | ✓ | ✓ | ✓ | ✓ | ✓ | ✓ | ✓ |
| ✓ | ✓ | ✓ | ✓ | ✓ | ✓ | ✓ | ✓ |
| ✓ | ✓ | ✓ |  | ✓ |  | ✓ | ✓ |
| ✓ | ✓ | ✓ | ✓ | ✓ |  | ✓ | ✓ |
| ✓ | ✓ | ✓ |  | ✓ |  | ✓ | ✓ |
| ✓ | ✓ | ✓ | ✓ | ✓ | ✓ | ✓ | ✓ |
| ✓ | ✓ | ✓ |  | ✓ | ✓ | ✓ | ✓ |
| ✓ | ✓ | ✓ | ✓ | ✓ |  | ✓ | ✓ |
| ✓ | ✓ | ✓ | ✓ | ✓ |  | ✓ | ✓ |
| ✓ | ✓ | ✓ | ✓ | ✓ |  | ✓ | ✓ |
| ✓ | ✓ | ✓ | ✓ | ✓ |  | ✓ | ✓ |
| ✓ | ✓ | ✓ |  | ✓ |  | ✓ | ✓ |
|  | ✓ | ✓ |  | ✓ |  | ✓ | ✓ |
| ✓ | ✓ | ✓ | ✓ | ✓ | ✓ | ✓ | ✓ |
| ✓ | ✓ | ✓ |  | ✓ |  | ✓ | ✓ |
| ✓ | ✓ | ✓ |  | ✓ |  | ✓ | ✓ |
| ✓ | ✓ | ✓ |  | ✓ |  | ✓ | ✓ |
| ✓ | ✓ | ✓ |  | ✓ |  | ✓ | ✓ |
|  | ✓ | ✓ |  | ✓ |  | ✓ | ✓ |
|  | ✓ | ✓ |  | ✓ |  | ✓ | ✓ |
| ✓ | ✓ | ✓ | ✓ | ✓ |  | ✓ | ✓ |

# Chapter 2

# Examination techniques

## TYPES OF EXAMINATIONS IN BOOKKEEPING AND ACCOUNTING

## PUBLIC EXAMINATIONS

The public examinations of the different examining bodies will differ in their structure, in the type of questions asked, and in the time allowed for their completion. Your teacher will explain the exact requirements of your examining board and examination paper.

There are several different styles of question found in these examinations. *Computational* questions, i.e. number-based questions, are commonly set. Such questions may ask you to construct final accounts from given information, to make adjustments and to correct errors, or to analyse a set of accounts. Figure-work and 'number-crunching' are associated with this type of question. These computational questions are usually supported by additional questions which are in another format: either *essay* questions (and there is a growing trend to include these descriptive questions in examinations), or *short-answer* or *multiple choice* questions.

### Computational questions

These questions vary in difficulty and in the precise demands they make on candidates. They can be short in length, involving for instance the construction of a single ledger account, where adjustments have to be made for prepaid or accrued items. Other questions may be very extensive and detailed, requiring the use of a number of accounting concepts or procedures to solve the problem. An example of a complicated computational question is where final accounts must be constructed from incomplete records. A computational question may test a candidate's ability to handle numerical information, to apply relevant accounting principles, and to organize the information using an acceptable layout.

### Essay questions

We have already mentioned that many examining boards set questions which make their candidates *write* about some aspect of accounting, as an alternative to constructing the relevant accounts. An essay question will normally refer to a particular aspect of accounting theory: for example, you may be asked to write an essay on the advantages and limitations of one method of calculating depreciation.

## Short-answer and multiple choice questions

Many of the public examinations have a separate section on the examination paper (or a completely separate examination paper) devoted to short-answer or multiple choice questions. These questions are also increasing in popularity. There are two main types of question.

1.  Short-answer questions.
    As the name implies, these are questions which are not detailed, and which take only a short time to answer. Candidates are given guidance on how long the answer should be, either through information at the start of the question (such as 'Complete sentences are not required as answers . . .'), or by having to answer the questions on the examination paper itself. In the latter case, the examination paper also serves as an answer book, containing blank lines after each short-answer question.

2.  Multiple choice questions (or 'items').
    Each question usually consists of a sentence which poses a problem: this is called the *stem*. A number of alternatives, often four, are given as possible answers. Only one of these – the *key* – is the correct answer. Your task is to identify which of the alternatives is correct. There are several variations found in practice, but they all ask you to either select an answer or to give an answer in a few words.

## ASSIGNMENT-BASED COURSES

Some students will be studying bookkeeping or accounting as a subject or module on a Business Studies course such as the BTEC National Course of the Business and Technician Education Council. The course may not include an externally set national examination in bookkeeping or accounting. There may, however, be an *internally set* examination paper, and therefore this chapter with its advice on examination technique is still important.

Even if the course is entirely *assignment-based*, such as BTEC National, it is possible that several of the accounting assignments will be similar to questions commonly met in traditional examinations. Where the assignments are more general and 'problem-solving' in approach, students will be required to recall and to apply accounting concepts and principles, *and* to use their knowledge of other business-related disciplines (such as Law or Economics). Although the more general problem-solving assignments lie outside the scope of this book, the *accounting* knowledge required can be developed by practising many of the questions presented in this book.

## TECHNIQUES FOR TAKING AN EXAMINATION

The purpose of these various examinations is to test, at different levels of understanding, your ability to recall and apply accounting techniques and principles and to evaluate given accounting information. You will be required to use a variety of skills, mainly in the areas of *computation, communication* and *manipulation*.

## Computation

At a basic computational level, you have to be able to add up a list of numbers. You will usually be required to undertake further and more complicated calculations, such as working out various accounting ratios; here, an understanding of ratios and percentages is important. Although the emphasis in the examinations is on knowing the accounting principles and procedures, we cannot avoid the fact that you, as a candidate, must be able to handle numbers. If you are reasonably numerate, this is an advantage. If you are not very numerate, then you will need plenty of practice.

Most examining bodies allow the use of calculators in the examination (check with your teacher whether this applies to your course). Calculators can be very useful in an examination, but candidates still have to understand the procedures involved in calculations. There is also a risk of relying too much on the answer shown on the calculator; for instance, this answer may be incorrect simply because we have pressed a wrong button! Each answer needs checking by estimating mentally what it should be before the calculator is used. This acts as a double check.

Examination questions normally require all calculations and workings to be shown. There is a tendency to forget this when a calculator is being used. It is advisable to get into the habit of displaying *all numerical workings* associated with computational questions. By doing this at all times, the habit will be firmly established by the time of the examination.

## Communication

Communication skills are also important. If your written English is weak, this will be a disadvantage because you have to communicate your thoughts clearly and legibly. Time spent improving your written English and communication skills will be time well spent, and any improvement gained will be beneficial (and not only for the purposes of taking an accounting examination).

## Manipulation

It is often insufficient merely to recall *how* to debit or credit, or to identify *which* accounts are involved, because you may be required to show a fuller and deeper understanding of the accounting principles involved. You will often have to 'manipulate' the information provided in order to answer the question.

The use of a descriptive textbook which contains worked examples and illustrations will help you to appreciate the linkages between the various accounting principles. It is often advisable to use more than one textbook when studying accounting principles and concepts, because different books use different approaches and provide different examples.

## Revision

Planned revision is most important. The teacher should have covered the whole syllabus, because there are often compulsory questions on the examination paper. Even where there is a choice of questions on the paper, this choice is usually so limited that your chances of failing the examination become much higher if you try to 'cut corners' when revising.

When revising, it is important to bear in mind the format of the examination paper. Here are some questions that you need to be able to answer:

How many papers – one or two? How many sections within the paper(s)? What choice is there? What is the total time allowed? Is reading time allowed? Are calculators (and dictionaries) permitted? Is accounting paper provided? If so, of what type?

## Mark allocation

Before the examination, you can calculate an approximate 'minutes per mark' guide. Many of the examinations contain questions which are weighted differently in terms of their marks. Other things being equal, you should spend less time in answering a question which receives, say, 10 marks than in answering a question which has 20 marks allocated to it.

Here is an example of how to calculate a 'minutes per mark' guide. We shall assume that the examination consists of two papers. Paper 1 contains fifty objective (multiple choice) items, and the time allowance is one and a quarter hours. Paper 2, which is worth 70% of the total marks, contains computational and essay questions, and has a time allowance of two and a half hours.

The time allocation on Paper 1 (50 questions) is 75 minutes. By dividing the number of questions into the time allocation, it becomes clear that you have one and a half minutes to answer each question. This gives some guidance regarding the pace you need to sustain when answering the questions: for example, have the first ten questions taken approximately 15 minutes (10 questions at $1\frac{1}{2}$ minutes each) to answer?

The calculation is equally important for the second paper. You have two and a half hours – 150 minutes – to answer questions totalling 70 marks. Allowing 10 minutes for settling down and reading the questions so that you can work out which to answer and in which order (you may want to allow longer in practice), you are left with 140 minutes for 70 marks, or 2 minutes per mark. As a rough guide, therefore, a question on Paper 2 which is worth 18 marks should take approximately 36 minutes to answer. If you are still working on this question after, say, 46 minutes, you must consider whether it is more advisable to move on and attempt another question.

You should remember (and this is a most important point) that you can still obtain most of the marks for one of these longer questions even if you do not get it completely correct or completely finished. The time pressure in these examinations is quite severe, and dwelling too long on any one question can lead to a candidate losing marks (through lack of time) on all the other questions.

## Before entering the examination room

The first piece of advice must be to revise thoroughly, and the second, to become familiar with the nature of the examination paper itself. The next task is to come to the examination room fully prepared and equipped, with pens, ruler, calculator (if allowed) and other optional items such as blotting paper. Blue or black are regarded as the most appropriate pen colours to use.

## The examination room

If you can discover which room is to be used for the examination, it may be possible to check the room in advance. This would mean that 'on the day' it will not be a totally new room and new experience. You should arrive early on the day, which will give you more time to compose yourself, and to choose a desk, where choice is allowed. This can be quite important: on a hot day, for example, it is advisable to avoid sitting by a window and being adversely affected by the sun. It is also advisable to position yourself where you can see the clock and also see the invigilator. This means that you can be more easily seen should you need to attract attention.

## THE EXAMINATION PAPER

### General points

1.  There may be *reading time* allowed at the start of the examination. If there is reading time allowed, you should take full advantage of this, even if it only results in settling nerves. It is likely, however, that the examination paper will not contain any formal reading time, and you must therefore allow for this in the total time allocation.
2.  You should re-check the *structure* of the paper. There is always the possibility that the examining board has altered the structure, and that this has been overlooked. If there is a choice on the paper, a decision on which questions to answer should not be made until the questions have been studied thoroughly. You must read each question carefully, because a question may not be what it seems at first glance. Many candidates fail to do themselves justice because they select the wrong question to answer, through failing to read the alternative questions properly.
3.  By careful reading, you can avoid *misinterpreting* a question. If the question contains an apparent key word or phrase, such as 'profit' or 'working capital', you still need to ensure that the question is testing these concepts. Some examination papers are constructed in a very clear way, containing a 'REQUIRED' section at the end of each question. It is this section which identifies the true nature of the question. Even then the earlier content of the question still requires careful study to ensure that you have understood the various items, notes and concepts.
4.  We can now apply the principles which allow *examination time* to be managed most efficiently. How many marks are there for the question you are now attempting? How long, in very approximate terms, should it take you to answer? The exact wording of the question may give some guidance. If it asks candidates to 'Explain briefly', you need to do that and to avoid writing detailed answers simply because the question is on a topic which you know in great detail. If another question asks you to 'List' items, you must again do that: a list of items is required, and not a detailed essay.

| | |
|---|---|
| **Answering computational questions** | You should now be in a position to establish:<br>(a) what is the nature of the problem;<br>(b) how you should present the answer (in account or in non-account form).<br>Examiners will test whether you can display answers in an appropriate accounting format; for example, as a ledger account or as a set of final accounts. |
| Workings | With computational questions, you have to carry out some calculations. You are therefore going to have some 'rough work' as a result of answering these questions. Examiners expect to see workings, and therefore you need to show these so that the examiner can see how you have arrived at a final figure for (say) depreciation or a bank overdraft. Many examination boards state on the paper that all workings must be shown.<br><br>You have nothing to lose, and much to gain, by displaying workings. If a simple arithmetical error has been made in arriving at a final figure for the answer, some (or even most) of the marks for that calculation can still be awarded if the working can be checked by the examiner. If no workings and calculations are shown then no marks can be awarded for that part of the question.<br><br>You need therefore to *display all workings*, and to have a clearly identified and labelled 'rough work' section for each of the computational questions. |
| **Answering essay questions** | There is also a very good reason for having a 'rough work' section at the start of an essay answer. This is to ensure that you plan your answer. An essay answer is an important way of communicating your thoughts on an aspect of accounting to another person: the examiner. If you are asked to verbally explain something, perhaps involving the giving of directions to someone in the street who is lost, you typically stop and think, and then give the answer. Time and time again, however, examination candidates do *not* stop to think before they start to write their answers. The result is often an answer that is both badly constructed and badly written. |
| Planning the essay | Time spent planning an answer is not wasted. The first task in planning the answer is to read the question very carefully. Once this has been done, misinterpretation should be avoided and you can start constructing the plan. The plan will contain a note of the key points which are to be included in the answer. When the essay is finished, this record of the key points can act as a checklist to ensure that no points have been omitted.<br><br>As well as identifying the 'what' in terms of accounting content, the plan will also have to include the 'where'. Where do the various points of content go in the answer: in the introduction, in the body of the answer, or in the conclusion? |
| 1. What to put in the introduction | The introduction should be brief and to the point. You could include relevant definitions here, especially where the essay asks you to |

'Define', 'Explain' or 'Describe'. For example, to answer a question which asks 'Why is the calculation of the working capital ratio important to a business?', you can define working capital, demonstrate how it is calculated and present the ratio itself in the introduction.

| 2. What to include in the body of the answer | Your plan should include a note of the major points to be included in the answer. These points – perhaps a series of advantages and disadvantages asked for by the question – should be grouped together in a logical fashion by using paragraphs, or by numbering the points. |
|---|---|

| 3. What to put in the conclusion | All essays need a beginning, a middle and an end, in that order! Some form of conclusion is therefore required. This may not amount to much more than a quick restatement of the key points already made in the body of the essay. In this case you should keep it brief, since extra marks will not be gained for mere repetition. If the essay title is in the form of a question, you must offer an answer; if there is no obvious right or wrong answer to the question, then you can usefully summarize the 'pros and cons' of the various arguments in the conclusion. |
|---|---|

| **Towards the end of the examination** | You will, hopefully, have some examination time left when you finish answering the final question. This time should be used effectively. Candidates have been working under considerable stress, for a long time. It is only to be expected that one or two errors have crept into the work, not necessarily from a lack of knowledge, but simply as a result of examination pressure. |
|---|---|

These final minutes give you the opportunity to re-read and re-check your answers and calculations. You can check against the rough work, whether it be in the form of calculations or an essay plan. This may well result in several errors or omissions being identified and rectified.

The four areas to which time should be allocated during the examination are therefore:

Read (and select)
Plan
Answer
Check

The majority of time must be spent in answering the question, but this time is used more efficiently if you devote some time to the other areas.

| **SUMMARY** | These examinations, whatever the form they take, test both your knowledge of bookkeeping or accounting principles and your ability to communicate that knowledge. Handwriting and the way answers are presented can make the difference between passing and failing the examination. Essays need to be organized sensibly, and written neatly and legibly. Numerical answers must also be neat: you should not over-write numbers, but rather delete them and write them again. You must also keep the numbers in line where appropriate, and ensure that the numbers are written as clearly as words. Throughout any course, you should regularly check your understanding of the key principles |
|---|---|

and concepts involved. In bookkeeping or accounting courses, this tends to be done almost automatically, due to the number of exercises that are completed in class, or as assignments or homework. To support this regular revision process, Chapters 3 to 16 contain recent examination questions set by various examining boards, supported by detailed or outline answers together with the relevant workings.

# Chapter 3

# Accounting: background and key concepts

## A. GETTING STARTED

The first part of the chapter looks closely at the *documents* which act as the record for business transactions, and as the basis for recording these business transactions in the books; notably the Books of Original (or Prime) Entry such as the Sales Book or the Purchases Book. These and the other books of original entry, together with the important business documents which lie behind them, are commonly found on accounting syllabuses, and many of the descriptive questions are based on them.

The second part of the chapter covers the *concepts* which underlie financial accounting: again, this area of work is commonly found on syllabuses, and is descriptive by nature. An important part of a typical answer on accounting concepts involves giving *examples* of the concepts: these examples should be easier to understand once you have completed the syllabus.

The third and final part of this chapter explains the distinction between *capital expenditure* and *revenue expenditure*. This distinction is quite easy to learn, but its application is vitally important when you construct final accounts.

A variety of questions are presented later in the chapter. These questions are typical of the ones normally asked on these topics: they are often essay-based, and usually refer to actual accounting or business situations. They may require you to provide appropriate examples to help illustrate the accounting principles involved.

## B. ESSENTIAL PRINCIPLES

### SOURCE DOCUMENTS

With *source documents*, it is important to remember that we are concerned with credit transactions rather than cash transactions. Many firms both buy and sell on credit, so they need to keep detailed records of their creditors (credit suppliers) and their debtors (credit customers).

## The invoice

The most important source document is the *invoice*. It is made out by the seller of the goods, and is recorded in his books as a Sales Invoice. Since a transaction has a two-fold effect, the seller's sales account (via the Sales Day Book) and the seller's debtor account (via the Sales Ledger) are both affected.

For every sale, there is a purchase: so the seller's sales invoice is forwarded to the purchaser and it can act as a source document for the purchaser. In the purchaser's books, however, it is not treated as a sales invoice; he has bought the goods and therefore it becomes his Purchases Invoice. It is really a mirror image. For the buyer, the dual effect of the transaction is that his purchases account (via the Purchases Day Book) and his purchases ledger – containing the supplier's account – are altered. We shall clarify these various accounts, ledgers and books later in the chapter.

Questions sometimes involve VAT or trade discount, both of which appear on invoices. The treatment of *Value Added Tax* in accounts is dealt with in the following chapter. *Trade Discount*, unlike cash discount, is not entered in the ledger (though it may be recorded by way of note in the relevant day book), but is deducted on the invoice.

## Credit and debit notes

The issue of a *credit note* by a creditor tells us that the creditor has credited (thus the name) his customer, the debtor, with the value of the credit note. Credit notes are therefore associated with a reduction in the amount that the debtor owes to the creditor. This reduction may be due to returns made by the debtor, or perhaps because the debtor was overcharged in the first place.

The issue of a *debit note* by a creditor has the opposite effect. Again, it is issued by the creditor to the debtor, but this time its purpose is to inform the debtor of an increase in the amount owed to the creditor (perhaps there was an undercharge originally made). It is called a debit note because the supplier makes a debit entry in his debtor account.

For each of these notes issued by a creditor a 'mirror image' is to be found in the debtor's ledger. When the debtor *receives* a copy of the *credit note*, this means that (as far as the debtor is concerned) he owes the creditor less. The debtor will make a debit entry in the creditor's account in his (the debtor's) purchases ledger. When the debtor *receives* a *debit note*, the debtor will owe the creditor more. The debtor will make a credit entry in the creditor's account in his (the debtor's) purchases ledger.

## BOOKS OF ORIGINAL ENTRY

*Books of Original Entry* link very closely with these source documents. Here, we meet those books of original entry which are directly affected by the issue of invoices and credit and debit notes. Again, some problems are created by this creditor–debtor relationship. Just as the creditor's sales invoice acts as the debtor's purchases invoice, so the entry made in the creditor's *Sales (Day) Book* 'matches' that made by the debtor – from his copy of the invoice – in his *Purchases (Day) Book*. Where returns are involved, the creditor will use his *Returns Inwards (Sales Returns) Book* to record the value of the returns: the debtor will enter this information in his *Returns Outwards (Purchases Returns) Book*.

These books have a common purpose; that is, to keep detail out of the general ledger. The idea is that one large entry will be made in the relevant account – sales, purchases, returns in or returns out – in the general ledger, rather than a series of separate entries being made. The single large entry will match, in total, the value of the individual entries made in the relevant creditor or debtor accounts. It is, therefore, important to remember, first, that only credit sales and purchases are recorded in these books; and second, that these books do not contain credit or debit entries. They are listing devices to obtain that single large total.

## 'Sales' and 'Purchases'

Confusion may sometimes occur because of the common use of 'sales' and 'purchases'. The position is as follows:

| | |
|---|---|
| Sales Account<br>Purchases Account | { accounts proper, kept in the general ledger. |
| Sales Book<br>Purchases Book | { not accounts, but listing devices for credit sales and credit purchases. Creditor and debtor accounts updated as the day books are used: at the end of period, totals posted to sales and purchases accounts. |
| Sales Ledger<br>Purchases Ledger | { contain creditor and debtor accounts: do not contain sales and purchases accounts. |

## The journal

Examination questions often ask you to journalize various situations (usually to correct errors, as with the suspense account in Chapter 9). Layout is very important here, and a narrative description is often required for each entry.

One of the more common areas of Journal use in exams is in recording 'Opening Entries', i.e. details of the opening assets and liabilities of the owner of a business. Section F of this chapter illustrates journal layout and use, in the 'tutor's answer' to question 5 (section D).

## ACCOUNTING CONCEPTS

There are many concepts recognized in financial accounting. We can think of them as a set of accountancy laws or rules, which are obeyed by accountants. It is advisable to learn the principle that each concept represents, and to study relevant examples of each concept in practice.

The number of concepts you may be required to study can vary, according to the syllabus. Some of the more important ones are:
*Materiality*
*Consistency*
*Going Concern*

*Conservatism* (or *Prudence*)
and *Accruals*
Question 6 (section D) identifies five concepts, and the outline answer in section E provides further details.

## CAPITAL AND REVENUE EXPENDITURE

Questions will often provide details of a range of expenditure, and will ask you to identify which is capital expenditure and which is revenue expenditure.

The fundamental distinction between the two types of expenditure is that *capital expenditure* refers to buying, or increasing the value of, fixed assets (items for use over several accounting periods): whereas *revenue expenditure* refers to the day-to-day expenses of running the business, with the benefit from the expense being consumed in the same accounting period.

## Problem areas

One difficulty we may face involves what is often referred to as the *capitalization* of revenue expenditure. This results when a business incurs revenue expenditure on something which becomes a fixed asset (a 'capital asset'); for example, when wages are paid to workmen engaged in building a new extension. This apparent revenue expenditure – the cost of the wages – is not debited to Profit and Loss, because to do so would be to charge against *one* year's profits, a cost associated with an asset which will last *many* years. The revenue expenditure is therefore 'capitalized', being treated as capital expenditure.

A second difficulty we may face is where an item of expenditure is part capital and part revenue. Perhaps a business has not only built and painted an extension, but has repainted the existing premises as well. If total costs are £20 000, of which £1 500 refers to the cost of redecorating the existing buildings, then total cost must be divided in this way:

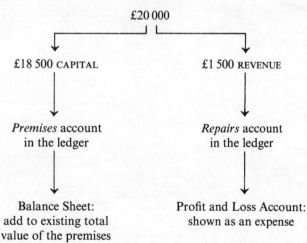

£20 000

| £18 500 CAPITAL | £1 500 REVENUE |

*Premises* account in the ledger

*Repairs* account in the ledger

Balance Sheet: add to existing total value of the premises

Profit and Loss Account: shown as an expense

# C. USEFUL APPLIED MATERIALS

Source documents and books of original entry will vary in layout from business to business, but will contain essentially the same type of information.

**Figure 3.1** illustrates an analysed sales book. The accounts are listed, and new debtor balances are obtained by totalling the 'Old Balance', 'VAT' and 'Debit' columns. The types of goods sold are analysed under headings A to J.

For example, we have sold goods worth £39 (plus £4.24 VAT) to J. Smith and Sons. The new balance on this account is therefore £169.74: Smith and Sons have bought our type 'B' goods (worth £14) and our type 'I' goods (worth £25).

**Figure 3.2** shows how a computer-based accounts system can be used for invoicing. It is an example of screen layout, where product and price details are displayed for acceptance (if correct).

*Figure 3.1    Analysed Sales Day Book*
Courtesy: Kalamazoo Business Systems

## Sales Day Book

Page SDB/180

| Date | Ref. No. | | VAT | | Debit | | Credit | | Balance | | Old Balance | | Account |
|---|---|---|---|---|---|---|---|---|---|---|---|---|---|
| | | Brought Forward | | | | | | | | | | | |
| Sept 18 | 1174 | Goods | 4 | 24 | 39 | 00 | | | 169 | 74 | 126 | 50 | J. Smith & Sons |
| Sept 18 | 1175 | Goods | 7 | 71 | 133 | 50 | | | 351 | 39 | 210 | 18 | Church Mfg. Co. |
| Sept 18 | 1176 | Goods | 9 | 02 | 125 | 29 | | | 474 | 52 | 340 | 21 | Johnson & Johnson |
| Sept 18 | 1177 | Goods | 6 | 02 | 75 | 25 | | | 160 | 45 | 79 | 18 | Brown & Webb |
| Sept 18 | 1178 | Goods | 13 | 62 | 85 | 15 | | | 233 | 77 | 135 | 00 | Modern Furniture Ltd. |
| Sept 18 | 1179 | Goods | 4 | 15 | 75 | 30 | | | 217 | 87 | 138 | 42 | Horizons Ltd. |
| Sept 18 | 1180 | Goods | 8 | 48 | 76 | 90 | | | 222 | 88 | 137 | 50 | Black Bros. |
| Sept 18 | 1181 | Goods | 2 | 36 | 43 | 70 | | | 125 | 67 | 79 | 61 | Smith Forge Ltd. |
| Sept 18 | 1182 | Goods | 17 | 40 | 175 | 62 | | | 209 | 26 | 16 | 24 | Johnson Hardware |
| Sept 18 | 1183 | Goods | 7 | 78 | 164 | 60 | | | 189 | 58 | 17 | 20 | Jenkins & Peters |
| Sept 18 | 1184 | Goods | 18 | 09 | 241 | 91 | | | 260 | 00 | – | – | Adams & Co. Ltd. |
| Sept 18 | 1185 | Goods | 11 | 33 | 161 | 84 | | | 203 | 17 | 30 | 00 | Benton Bros. Ltd. |
| Sept 18 | 1186 | Goods | 8 | 26 | 117 | 48 | | | 225 | 74 | 100 | 00 | Northern Petroleum |
| Sept 18 | 1187 | Goods | 16 | 03 | 177 | 26 | | | 216 | 57 | 23 | 28 | Abbott & Sons Ltd. |
| Sept 18 | 1188 | Goods | 11 | 54 | 156 | 36 | | | 247 | 40 | 79 | 50 | Jenkinson & Smith |
| Sept 18 | 1189 | Goods | 6 | 67 | 66 | 70 | | | 146 | 77 | 73 | 40 | Ward & Co. Ltd. |
| | | | 152 | 70 | 1915 | 86 | | | 3654 | 78 | 1586 | 22 | |
| | | | | | | | | | | | 152 | 70 | |
| | | | | | | | | | | | 1915 | 86 | |
| | | | | | | | | | | | 3654 | 78 | |

*Figure 3.2   Computer screen display from an 'Invoicing' package*

Courtesy: ACT (UK) Ltd

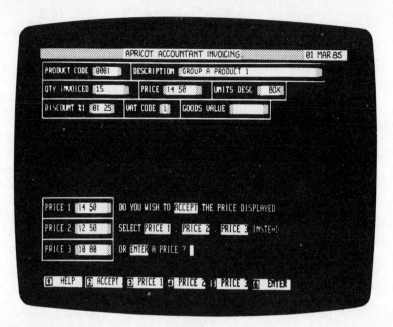

| A | | B | | C | | D | | E | | F | | G | | H | | I | | J | |
|---|---|---|---|---|---|---|---|---|---|---|---|---|---|---|---|---|---|---|---|
| | | | | | | | | | | | | | | | | | | | |
| | | 14 | 00 | | | | | | | | | | | | | 25 | 00 | | |
| 59 | 25 | | | | | 74 | 25 | | | | | | | | | | | | |
| | | | | | | | | | | 25 | 14 | 100 | 15 | | | | | | |
| | | | | 75 | 25 | | | | | | | | | | | | | | |
| | | | | 85 | 15 | | | | | | | | | | | | | | |
| 14 | 10 | | | | | 14 | 30 | | | 46 | 90 | | | | | | | | |
| | | 47 | 60 | | | | | 29 | 30 | | | | | | | | | | |
| 29 | 45 | | | | | | | 14 | 25 | | | | | | | | | | |
| 97 | 16 | | | 24 | 36 | | | | | | | 54 | 10 | | | | | | |
| | | | | | | | | | | 15 | 26 | | | | | 45 | 24 | 104 | 10 |
| 179 | 52 | | | | | 52 | 14 | | | | | 10 | 25 | | | | | | |
| | | 129 | 45 | | | | | 24 | 24 | | | | | 8 | 15 | | | | |
| | | | | 17 | 94 | | | | | | | 5 | 27 | | | | | 94 | 27 |
| | | 154 | 14 | | | | | | | 23 | 12 | | | | | | | | |
| 132 | 17 | | | | | 24 | 19 | | | | | | | | | | | | |
| | | 13 | 35 | | | | | 30 | 00 | | | | | 23 | 35 | | | | |
| 511 | 65 | 358 | 54 | 202 | 70 | 164 | 88 | 97 | 79 | 110 | 42 | 169 | 77 | 31 | 50 | 70 | 24 | 198 | 37 |
| | | | | | | | | | | | | | | | | | | | |
| | | | | | | | | | | | | | | | | | | | |
| | | | | | | | | | | | | | | | | | | | |

## D. RECENT EXAMINATION QUESTIONS

Questions **1**, **2** and **3** are multiple choice or short answer (sentence completion), and they should take about five minutes to complete.

Question **4** is on source documents: it is quite difficult because it also tests your ability to record information in the ledger.

If accounting concepts are on your syllabus, attempt question **6**, which is an essay-type question on this topic.

*The answer to question **5** (using the Journal to record opening entries) is given in section F, 'A tutor's answer'.*

---

**Objective questions**

**1** A credit note received from a supplier would be recorded in:
A the cash book
B the journal
C the returns inwards book
D the returns outwards book
(AEB Specimen Accounting O level Paper, 1980)

**2** Which of the following concepts distinguishes and separates the business from the owner?
A The cost concept
B The dual aspect concept
C The business entity concept
D The money measurement concept
(AEB Specimen Accounting O level Paper, 1980)

**3** Write in the spaces below whether the following transactions of Salford Engineering Co. Ltd are CAPITAL or REVENUE expenditure.
(a) Purchase of motor van . . . . . . . . . . . . . . . . . . . . . . . . . . . . . . . . .
(b) Yearly premium to insure motor van . . . . . . . . . . . . . . . . . . . . .
(c) Cost of rebuilding factory wall damaged by frost . . . . . . . . . . . .
(d) Purchase of freehold land . . . . . . . . . . . . . . . . . . . . . . . . . .
(e) Cost of building extension to factory. . . . . . . . . . . . . . . . . . . . . .
(f) Cost of painting new extension. . . . . . . . . . . . . . . . . . . . . . . .
(g) Legal costs on acquiring land for the extension . . . . . . . . . . . . . .
(h) Repainting extension four years after completion . . . . . . . . . . . .
(j) Cost of repairs to motor van . . . . . . . . . . . . . . . . . . . . . . . . . .
(k) Repairing roof of extension . . . . . . . . . . . . . . . . . . . . . . . . . . .
(JMB Bookkeeping and Accounting O level, June 1983)

---

**Essay and computational questions**

**4** Study the following commercial documents:
*REQUIRED:*
(i) Fully explain the meaning and/or purpose of the items marked with the letters (*a*) to (*m*). In your answer indicate the source of item (*e*).
(ii) State the recommended retail price including VAT of:
    (*a*) a sleeping bag;
    (*b*) a pair of walking boots.
(iii) Post the two documents to the personal accounts only in the ledgers of Ace Army & Navy Stores and Malletts Stores, clearly heading each ledger with the name of the firm.

## (a) INVOICE                                    No. 1134

VAT Reg. No.
834 1567

### ACE ARMY & NAVY STORES
#### (b) WHOLESALERS
15 Broad Street
Malvern MA1 2PF

1 March 1983

(c) To: Malletts Stores
31 High Street
Kidderminster KA2 5SA

(d) Your Order No. 137
Despatched by Road Services

| Quantity | Description | (e) Unit price | Total price | (f) Trade discount | (g) Net |
|---|---|---|---|---|---|
| | | £ | £ | | £ |
| 10 | Sleeping Bags | 15.00 | 150 | 20% | 120 |
| 12 pairs | Walking Boots Size 8 | 20.00 | 240 | 25% | 180 |
| | | | | | 300 |
| | | (h) VAT @ 10% | | | 30 |
| E. & O. E. | | (i) TOTAL | | | 330 |

---

### (j) CREDIT NOTE                          No. 86
### ACE ARMY & NAVY STORES
### WHOLESALERS
15 Broad Street
Malvern MA1 2PF

8 March 1983

To: Malletts Stores
31 High Street
Kidderminster KA2 5SA

|  | £ |
|---|---|
| (k) 2 pairs Walking Boots—wrong size @ £20 each | 40.00 |
| Less 25% Trade discount | 10.00 |
| | 30.00 |
| Add 10% VAT | 3.00 |
| (m) TOTAL | 33.00 |

(l) E. & O. E.

(RSA I Bookkeeping, March 1983)   (26 marks)

**5** On 1 June 1984 T. Jones had the following assets and liabilities:

Freehold Premises, £25 000; Mortgage on Premises, £12 500; Motor Vehicle, £2 700; Amount owing on motor vehicle, £1 400; Fixtures and Fittings, £2 000; Stock, £2 750; Debtors, £1 580; Bank overdraft, £920; Unpaid electricity bill, £72.

On 1 April 1984 Jones had paid rates £180 for the half-year ending 30 September 1984 and on 1 February 1984 had paid one year's insurance premium £60.

You are required to prepare an Opening Journal Entry as at 1 June 1984 showing clearly the Capital of Jones at that date.

(12 marks)

(RSA I Bookkeeping, June 1984)

**6** Financial statements are normally prepared upon the basis of a number of accounting concepts.

*REQUIRED:*

State what you understand by each of the following accounting concepts, and how they are applied in the preparation of financial statements:

(i)   entity; (4 marks)
(ii)  going concern; (3 marks)
(iii) accruals (or matching); (4 marks)
(iv)  conservatism (or prudence); (4 marks)
(v)   consistency. (4 marks)

(Total 19 marks)

(AAT Accounting 2, June 1984)

---

**E.   OUTLINE ANSWERS**

**1** Credit notes from a supplier are recorded in the customer's returns outwards book (D), because the credit note is associated with returns made by the customer.

**2** Alternative (C) is correct: (A) refers to valuing items at cost, (B) to double entry, and (D) to the fact that financial accounting is concerned with items measured in monetary units.

**3** The capital items are (a), (d), (e), (f) and (g); the last two involve capitalization of revenue expenditure.

**4**(i) (a) document informing customer of goods and amount owed; (b) the supplier of these goods; (c) customer (retailer); (d) retailer's request for goods; (e) price of single item; (f) reduction for being 'in the trade' or bulk buying; (g) total price less trade discount; (h) tax based on net invoice value; (i) amount owed by customer; (j) document recording customer returns; (k) items returned; (l) 'errors & omissions excepted' (any wrong information entered, no liability on the creditor's part); (m) value of credit note, deducted from amount customer owes.

(ii) Bags, £15 + £1.50 VAT = £16.50: boots, £20 + £2 VAT = £22.

| (iii) | Ace's books (Sales ledger)<br>Mallets' a/c | | Mallet's books (Purchase ledger)<br>Ace's a/c | |
|---|---|---|---|---|
| | £ | £ | £ | £ |
| | Sales 330 | Returns 33 | Returns 33 | Sales 330 |

**6** Each concept is worth 3 or 4 marks, so very detailed answers are not required. Key points for each concept are:

(i)   We are interested in the business records and not the owner's personal financial records; e.g. depreciation of owner's private car is not recorded in the business books, whereas depreciation of business-owned vehicles will be.

(ii)   We assume a business will carry on indefinitely, with accounts being prepared on this basis (e.g. new fixed assets; it may be planned to write these off over the next 20 years).

(iii)   Matching items to the period to which they refer: e.g. closing unpaid expense recorded in this year's profit and loss a/c; even though unpaid, the expense has been incurred this period.

(iv)   Where a choice exists, accountants tend to understate profits rather than risk overstating; losses (items leading to loss, e.g. expenses) overstated, where judgements have to be made.

(v)   Where more than one method exists (e.g. depreciation methods), use the method already in existence, unless good reason to change.

## F. A TUTOR'S ANSWER

Here is the suggested answer for question **5**. The answer demonstrates an acceptable layout for the Journal. Debit balances are listed, then credit balances are listed and indented. The narrative is then given.

### The Journal

| 1984 | | £ | £ |
|---|---|---|---|
| 1 June | Premises | 25 000 | |
| | Fixtures and fittings | 2 000 | |
| | Motor vehicles | 2 700 | |
| | Stock | 2 750 | |
| | Debtors | 1 580 | |
| | Rates | 120 | |
| | Insurance | 40 | |
| | Mortgage | | 12 500 |
| | Vehicle loan | | 1 400 |
| | Electricity | | 72 |
| | Bank | | 920 |
| | Capital | | 19 298 |
| | Assets and liabilities<br>of T. Jones at this date | 34 190 | 34 190 |

**Workings**

(1) Assets = Dr balances and liabilities = Cr balances
(2) Rates: £180 for 6 months = £30 per month
    At 1 June, 4 months prepaid = 4 × £30 = £120
(3) Insurance: £60 per annum = £5 per month
    At 1 June, 8 months prepaid = 8 × £5 = £40
(4) The capital a/c balance is not given. We use the 'Accounting equation'
$$\text{CAPITAL} = \text{ASSETS} - \text{LIABILITIES}$$

---

## G. A STEP FURTHER

Many records are now held on computers: even small businesses are using computers more and more, to assist in recording, storing and analysing items of information. It would be quite helpful, if you are not familiar with the operation of computers or with the advantages which arise from their use in business, to spend some time studying this area. Many computer books are on the market, and most contain at least one chapter devoted to their practical use in business. A book such as *You and the Computer: a course in computer literacy* by West and Lloyd, published by Edward Arnold, will provide a good background. Should you wish to read about how bookkeeping records are computerized, Whitehead's *Bookkeeping Made Simple* (Heinemann 'Made Simple' series) contains a chapter outlining how this is done (Ch. 33).

Here is an indication of some textbook sources for this and the other topics covered in the chapter:

**SOURCE DOCUMENTS AND BOOKS OF ORIGINAL ENTRY**

Castle and Owens, *Principles of Accounts* (7th edn) (M & E Handbooks). Ch. 6: Subsidiary books and sources of information; Ch. 10: The Journal.

Garbutt, *Carter's Advanced Accounts* (7th edn) (Pitman). Ch. 01: on basic principles.

Whitehead, *Success in Principles of Accounting* (John Murray). Units 9, 12, 13 and 16: on the Journal; Units 10 and 11: on Day Books.

**CONCEPTS OF ACCOUNTING**

Eve and Forth, *Accounting: an Insight* (Pitman). Ch. 1.

Wood, *Business Accounting 1* (4th edn) (Longman). Ch. 10.

Wood, *Business Accounting 2* (4th edn) (Longman). Ch. 25.

**CAPITAL AND REVENUE EXPENDITURE**

Etor and Muspratt, *Keep Account* (Pan 'Breakthrough' series). Ch. 9.

Whitehead, *Bookkeeping Made Simple* (Heinemann 'Made Simple' series). Ch. 9.

# Chapter 4

# Principles of double entry (1)

## A.  GETTING STARTED

The purpose of this chapter is to concentrate on the *Ledger*: the various types of accounts that are kept in the different ledgers which are used by businesses. Expense accounts, revenue accounts, asset accounts and liability accounts are considered in this chapter. The next chapter will examine the nature of the Trial Balance, and introduce us to simple final accounts. Complications such as prepayments and accruals, and the effect of errors, are held back to later chapters.

What existing knowledge should you have in order to study the content of this chapter effectively? Questions tend to be based on constructing, balancing or interpreting accounts (often those of debtors or creditors). We shall explain how we decide whether an account needs to be debited or credited, how an account is balanced, and in which ledger it is to be found. To study these items you will therefore need to understand the purpose and function of source documents and the books of original entry.

## B.  ESSENTIAL PRINCIPLES

### DECIDING WHETHER TO DEBIT OR CREDIT AN ACCOUNT

Because every transaction will have a dual effect, two accounts will be used to record its effect. Your task is to work out the answer to two problems:

(a)  which two accounts are involved; and

(b)  which account is debited and which is credited.

### Which accounts are involved

Here are some examples of possible transactions and the two accounts involved:

(i)  Wages paid by cheque, £100.

The value of *wages* is affected, and the *bank* balance is also affected. These are therefore the accounts involved.

| | |
|---|---|
| (ii) Paid creditor by cheque, £100. | Again, the *bank* balance alters (so the bank account is affected), and the *creditor's* position in relation to the business is also affected. |
| (iii) Cash sales, £100. | The values of *sales* and *cash* are affected, so these accounts are updated. |
| (iv) Sold goods on credit to A. Lee, £100. | Here, sales are affected so the *sales* account is used. Lee's position with the business is also affected, so *Lee's* account is updated. |
| (v) Sold goods to A. Lee for £100, Lee paying by cheque. | Again, *sales* account is used because sales alter; but the other area affected is the *bank* account, and not Lee's account. |

In (v) above, the position of Lee in relation to the business has not altered, and so his account is not used. This is quite a common trick of examination questions, so be careful to identify the areas which are affected by the transaction, and to ignore those areas which are not affected. In this example it does not really matter to the business who made out the cheque, assuming of course that it does not 'bounce'. What matters to the business is that the value of sales has increased, and that its bank balance has increased.

## Which account to debit, and which to credit

Once it is established which two accounts are involved with the transaction, the next problem is to identify which of these accounts to debit and which to credit. There are two popular methods for working out whether to debit or credit an account. If you take the trouble to study and learn *both* methods, you can use your knowledge of both to double-check your answer.

## Method 1

The first method is to see whether the account is *receiving* value or *giving* value. The rule is:

Debit (Dr) the account RECEIVING value
Credit (Cr) the account GIVING value

To illustrate this, we can use the transactions outlined in (i) to (v) above.

### (i) **Paid wages by cheque, £100**

| | |
|---|---|
| Wages are received (the business has received the value of work done to earn these wages), so this account is debited. | The bank gives value, so the bank account is credited. |

### (ii) **Paid creditor by cheque, £100**

| | |
|---|---|
| The creditor receives the value of the cheque, so the creditor's account is debited. | The bank gives value and so the bank's account in the business's books is credited. |

### (iii) **Cash sales, £100**

| | |
|---|---|
| Cash is received, so the cash account is debited. | Sales are given, so the sales account is credited. |

### (iv) Sold goods on credit to A. Lee, £100

| | |
|---|---|
| Lee receives value, so Lee's account is debited. | Sales are given, so the sales account is credited. |

### (v) Sold goods to A. Lee, £100, Lee paying by cheque

| | |
|---|---|
| A cheque is received, so the bank account is debited. | Sales are given, so the sales account is credited. |

In (v) above, note that Lee has given the cheque, but we are interested only in the areas (accounts) affected by the transaction, and Lee's 'net indebtedness' to the business has not altered.

**Method 2**

The second method is to identify whether the account involved represents an asset, a liability, an expense or a revenue (income, or a gain).

If the account is an asset or a liability, the rules are:

| Asset a/c | | Liability a/c | |
|---|---|---|---|
| Dr | Cr | Dr | Cr |
| INCREASE | REDUCTION | REDUCTION | INCREASE |

If the *asset* value is increased by a transaction, the account is therefore debited; if the asset value is reduced, the account is credited. The opposite occurs for a *liability*, as we can see above.

If the relevant account represents an *expense*, it is debited. This is sometimes difficult to understand: following our previous method 1, the business has *received* the value of the expense, so debit the account. Similarly, if the relevant account represents a *revenue*, it is credited.

We can again use the same transactions to demonstrate method 2:

### (i) Paid wages by cheque, £100

| | |
|---|---|
| Wages represent an expense to the firm, so the account is debited. | The asset of the bank decreases (cheque paid out), so the bank account is credited. |

### (ii) Paid creditor by cheque, £100

| | |
|---|---|
| Liability reduced, so creditor account debited. | Asset reduced, so bank account credited. |

### (iii) Cash sales, £100

| | |
|---|---|
| Asset of cash increased, so the cash account is debited. | Sales represent revenue, so the sales account is credited. |

### (iv) Sold goods on credit to A. Lee, £100

| | |
|---|---|
| Lee is a debtor, an asset: the asset increases in value, and so Lee's account is debited. | Sales = revenue, so the sales account is credited. |

### (v) Sold goods to A. Lee for £100, Lee paying by cheque

| | |
|---|---|
| The firm's bank balance (asset) increases, so the bank account is debited. | Sales account is credited. |

Using *both* these methods should ensure that you select the appropriate accounts, and debit or credit them correctly.

| Value Added Tax (VAT) | An area of double entry that may affect you involves accounting for VAT. VAT is recorded on invoices, debit and credit notes, and – unlike a trade discount – it must be recorded in the accounts. |
|---|---|

An area of double entry that may affect you involves accounting for VAT. VAT is recorded on invoices, debit and credit notes, and – unlike a trade discount – it must be recorded in the accounts.

The books of original entry act as a base for analysing amounts receivable or payable by the business. The sales book will record the net value of sales (i.e. sales less trade discount) in one column, and the value of VAT (based on price less any trade and cash discount) in a separate column. The VAT total is posted to the credit of the VAT account, while total sales go to the sales account. Debtors are debited with the value of the sale, including the VAT percentage.

Similarly, the purchases book is analysed to produce a total for VAT (posted to the debit of the account) and for net purchases (debited to the account), with creditors being credited with the total gross purchases (i.e. net purchases plus VAT).

There are a number of complications with VAT. One is due to the fact that on some occasions a firm can recover VAT; and on other occasions it cannot. The balance on a VAT account represents what the firm owes to HM Customs and Excise, assuming a credit balance on the account. If there is a debit balance on the account, then HM Customs and Excise is no longer a creditor, but rather a debtor to the business.

## BALANCING ACCOUNTS

The steps involved in balancing are:
(a)  Total both sides.
(b)  Calculate the difference (i.e. the balance).
(c)  Record the balance on the smaller side, to get the totals to agree.
(d)  Insert the totals on both sides.
(e)  Bring down the balance.

Sometimes, both sides of the account will agree, and in such a situation all we have to do is to enter the totals.

We have assumed that the balance will be carried down to the next period. This will be so with all assets and liabilities. Expense and revenue accounts are kept so that profit can be calculated, and therefore these balances may be transferred to the trading or profit and loss accounts.

## THREE-COLUMN LEDGER ACCOUNTS

Many of the questions on ledger accounts require you to construct or to interpret the accounts in the traditional, two-sided, format. A modern alternative is to ask you to either draw up or to interpret a *three-column account*. This is an account which will have columns for debit, credit and balance, a 'running balance' being kept by updating the balance column each time a debit or credit entry is made. The layout is associated with mechanized accounting systems, and is widely found in practice. The account illustrated in section C and the answer in section F both demonstrate the three-column layout.

# DIVISION OF THE LEDGER

We introduced the idea of the division of the ledger in the last chapter. The major division is:

Cash Book : contains cash and bank accounts
Sales Ledger : contains credit customer accounts
Purchases (or : contains credit supplier accounts
Bought) Ledger
General Ledger : contains all other accounts

Sometimes the general (or nominal) ledger has certain accounts, such as the capital account and some asset accounts, removed into a separate *Private Ledger*, which will be under the control of the owner rather than an employee.

# C. USEFUL APPLIED MATERIALS

The increasing use of mechanized and computerized accounting systems has led to changes in the appearance of accounts. The three-column layout of a ledger account has been described in the last section. Here is an example of an account being kept using a three-column layout.

| Name | ANDERSON & Co. | | | | | | Account No. | A14 | |
|------|------|------|------|------|------|------|------|------|------|
| Address | High Street, BARCHESTER | | | | | | Credit Limit | £400 | |

| Date | Ref/Chq. No. | Details/Name | | Debit | Discount | VAT | Credit | Balance | |
|------|------|------|------|------|------|------|------|------|------|
| Nov 15 | | Bal. B/Fwd | | | | | | 524 40 | ·A |
| Nov 14 | 4009 | Goods | Anderson & Co | | | 6 44 | 67 40 | 601 84 | · |
| Dec 3 | 4417 | Goods | Anderson & Co | | | 4 18 | 41 48 | 644 83 | · |
| Dec 15 | 579 | Anderson & Co. | | 524 40 | | | | 120 43 | ·AB |
| Dec 21 | 4524 | Goods | Anderson & Co | | | 8 10 | 81 00 | 209 53 | · |
| Dec 28 | 4691 | Goods | Anderson & Co | | | 2 07 | 20 70 | 232 30 | · |
| Jan 3 | 4411 | Goods | Anderson & Co | | | 4 74 | 44 42 | 314 46 | · |
| Jan 11 | 4904 | Goods | Anderson & Co | | | 1 55 | 15 46 | 334 49 | · |
| Jan 12 | 4991 | Goods | Anderson & Co | | | 6 70 | 67 00 | 408 14 | · |
| Jan 14 | 668 | Anderson & Co. | | 120 43 | | | | 284 74 | · |

*Fig. 4.1   Creditor account Anderson & Co.*

Courtesy: Kalamazoo Business Systems

**Figure 4.1** is a creditor's account (Anderson and Co.) which could be found in a purchases ledger. Our credit limit – £700 – is recorded, together with the account number (A17). In addition to the three columns described earlier, a fourth column is used, to record the amounts of VAT paid as part of the total price.

## D. RECENT EXAMINATION QUESTIONS

Questions **1**, **2**, **3** and **4** are of a multiple choice or short answer type, and should take about six minutes to complete.

Question **5** provides you with a series of transactions, and tests your knowledge of both ledger accounts and books of original entry.

Questions **6–9** are based on personal accounts; specifically debtors and creditors. Question **6** asks you to interpret (and rewrite) personal accounts, and questions **7** and **8** make you construct personal accounts from given information.

*Question 9 is answered in detail in section F.*

**Objective questions**

**1** The difference in amount between the two sides of a customer's account is the . . . . . .

(London Board Principles of Accounts O level, January 1983)

**2** Which one of the following is a 'nominal account'?
A Carriage outwards account
B Machinery account
C J. Smith's account
D Drawings account

(AEB Specimen Accounting O level paper, 1980)

**3** Which one of the following accounts would be found in the sales ledger?
A Sales
B Returns inwards
C E. Owen, a customer
D H. Kean, a supplier

(AEB Specimen Accounting O level paper, 1980)

**4** The accounting system of a firm of office equipment suppliers includes the use of the usual subsidiary books and three ledgers: sales, purchases and general. If a typewriter were purchased on credit for later resale, the subsidiary book and ledger(s) to be used for recording this transaction should be
A journal and general ledger
B journal, general and purchases ledgers
C purchases day book and general ledger
D purchases day book, general and purchases ledgers

(AEB Specimen Accounting O level paper, 1980)

**5** D. Parker, a wholesaler in the grocery trade, keeps his business
accounts by the double-entry system, with the usual full set of books.
Some of the transactions and events which occurred in his business are
listed below. You are asked to show for each of them the appropriate
book of first entry and the accounts which will receive the debit and
credit entries, with the amounts. The form in which your answer must
be presented is indicated by this answer to item (a).

| Item | Book of first entry | Accounts debited and amount | Accounts credited and amount |
|------|---------------------|-----------------------------|------------------------------|
| (a)  | Cash Book           | Wages £220                  | Cash Book (Cash column) £220 |
| (b)  |                     |                             |                              |
| (c)  |                     |                             |                              |
| etc. |                     |                             |                              |

(a)  Paid wages in cash, £220.
(b)  Bought goods on credit from Adams and Co. (list price £460,
     trade discount 25%).
(c)  Accepted a cheque for £234 from a customer, J. Abel, in full
     settlement of his debt, £240.
(d)  Wrote off as irrecoverable a debt of £96 owing by T. Black.
(e)  Returned faulty goods to Adams and Co. (list price £68, trade
     discount 25%).
(f)  Sent a credit note to D. Young, a customer, in respect of an
     overcharge, £31.
(g)  Made a contra transfer from Sales Ledger to Bought Ledger in
     respect of £79 owing by P. Johnson in his Sales Ledger account.
(h)  Paid surplus cash into bank, £562.
(i)  The bank notified D. Parker of bank charges, £27.
(j)  The year-end trial balance showed: debits total £218 971; credits
     total £219 029. Opened a Suspense Account as a temporary
     measure.
(k)  At year-end, made the necessary transfers from Purchases
     Account (£282 640) and Sales Account (£365 420).
(l)  At year-end, entered the closing stock £21 290.

(24 marks)

(Oxford Board Principles of Accounts O level, Summer 1984)

**6** The following ledger accounts appear amongst many others in the
books of R. Cope:

| T. Brown (credit limit £500) | | Dr £ | Cr £ | Balance £ |
|---|---|---|---|---|
| December 1 | Balance | .. | | 250 |
| 4 | Sales* | ..110 | | 360 |
| 9 | Returns | .. | 20 | 340 |
| 10 | Bank | .. | 245 | |
| | Discount | .. | 5 | 90 |

| R. Fisher | | Dr | Cr | Balance |
|---|---|---|---|---|
| | | £ | £ | £ |
| December 1 | Balance | .. | | 150 |
| 8 | Purchases .. | | 450 | 600 |
| 9 | Cash | ..150 | | 450 |

(i) Study the above accounts and answer the following questions:
    (a) Which of the accounts is that of a customer?
    (b) What is the significance of the entry 'credit limit £500'?
    (c) Why is there no credit limit written on R. Fisher's account?
    (d) What is the name of the document associated with the entry marked *?
    (e) What is the rate of cash discount allowed to T. Brown?
    (f) Which entry would be associated with a credit note?
    (g) Which of the accounts would appear in a creditors' ledger?
    (h) What is an advantage of writing out accounts in three column form?

(ii) Write up T. Brown's account in the traditional form.    (13 marks)

(London Board Principles of Accounts O level, June 1984)

**7** On 1 January 1982, J. Brown owed White and Co. £572.85. On 31 December 1982, he owed them £618.25. In the intervening 12 months, Brown had sent cheques totalling £4 527.60 to White and Co.; White and Co. had allowed him £72.45 for cash discount and £116.44 for faulty goods returned.

    You are asked to prepare an account headed 'J. White and Co. Account' which will be a summary of the White and Co. Account in J. Brown's ledger for 1982, including Brown's gross purchases (i.e. before deducting returns) from White and Co. in 1982.    (12 marks)

(Oxford Board Principles of Accounts O level, Summer 1983)

**8** R. Farrier buys goods from B. Smith and also sells goods to him. Farrier keeps an account for Smith in his Sales Ledger and also another account for Smith in his Purchases Ledger.

    Smith's account in the Sales Ledger on 1 April 1983 had a debit balance of £180 and on the same date there was a nil balance on his account in the Purchases Ledger.

    The following information related to transactions during April:

April  5      Goods sold on credit to Smith £200 less 10% trade discount.

       8      Received invoice from Smith for £145 for goods supplied.

       9      Received cheque from Smith in settlement of the balance outstanding at 1 April less 5% cash discount.

     15      Sent Smith a credit note for £25 for goods returned by him.

     22      Received a credit note from Smith for £10 for packing cases returned to him.

<blockquote>
30         Balance of Smith's account in the Purchases Ledger transferred to his account in the Sales Ledger.
</blockquote>

You are required to open the two accounts for Smith (clearly indicating in which ledger they would be found) commencing with the opening balance where appropriate and then to make the entries which result from the above transactions. Finally, the two accounts are to be balanced as at 30 April 1983.

Pay special attention to dates and details.        **(14 marks)**

(Cambridge Board Principles of Accounts O level, Summer 1983)

**9** On 7 November 1983, C. Pepper had a creditor, Brian Terry, in his books. On that date the credit balance on Terry's Account was £800. The following transactions took place during the month of November:

| | |
|---|---|
| 9 November | Purchases from Terry, £680 |
| 16 November | C. Pepper returned goods to Terry, £40 |
| 23 November | C. Pepper paid Terry (by cheque) the amount due on 7 November *less* $2\frac{1}{2}\%$ cash discount |
| 25 November | Purchases from Terry, £200 |
| 28 November | Purchases from Terry, £180 |
| 30 November | C. Pepper paid Terry (by cheque) for the goods retained from those purchased on 9 November and qualified for a $2\frac{1}{2}\%$ cash discount. |

*REQUIRED:*

You are required to write up the account for Brian Terry as it would appear in C. Pepper's Ledger.

To obtain full marks the personal account should be written up in three column (running balance) form: debit, credit and balance.

**(12 marks)**

(RSA I Bookkeeping, February 1984)

---

**E.  OUTLINE ANSWERS**

**1** The answer is 'balance'.

**2** Carriage outwards, as an expense, is a nominal account; (A). (B) represents a real account; (C) and (D) are personal accounts.

**3** Customers (C) in sales ledger: sales and returns in the general ledger, and suppliers in the purchases ledger.

**4** (D); purchase day book to record the credit purchase; creditor a/c in the purchases ledger, and purchases a/c in the general ledger.

**5**

| | | |
|---|---|---|
| (b) | Purchases book: | Dr purchases and Cr Adams £345 |
| (c) | Cash book: | Dr bank £234 and discount allowed £6, Cr Abel £240 |
| (d) | Journal: | Dr bad debts and Cr Black £96 |
| (e) | Returns Outward book: | Dr Adams and Cr returns outwards £51 |
| (f) | Sales book: | Dr sales and Cr Young £31 |

| | | (g) | Journal: | Dr Johnson (PL) and Cr Johnson (SL) £79 |
|---|---|---|---|---|

(g) Journal:      Dr Johnson (PL) and Cr Johnson (SL) £79

(h) Cash book:      Dr bank and Cr cash £562

(i) Cash book:      Dr bank charges and Cr bank £27

(j) Journal:      Dr Suspense £58 (£219 029–£218 971)

(k) Journal:      Dr sales £365 420 & Trading £282 640; Cr purchases £282 640 and Trading £365 420

(l) Journal:      Dr stock and Cr Trading £21 290

**6**

(i)   (a) Brown (Cope is selling to him)

     (b) maximum amount Brown can owe at any one time

     (c) Cope does not allow Fisher credit (the reverse applies)

     (d) Sales invoice

     (e) 2% (£5 as a percentage of £250)

     (f) December 9 returns

     (g) Fisher

     (h) amount of the balance is immediately seen

(ii)

*T. Brown account*

| | | £ | | | £ |
|---|---|---|---|---|---|
| 1 Dec | Balance | 250 | 9 Dec | Returns | 20 |
| 4 Dec | Sales | 110 | 10 Dec | Bank | 245 |
| | | | | Discount | 5 |
| | | | | (Balance | 90) |

**7**

*J. White & Co. account*

| | £ | | £ |
|---|---|---|---|
| Bank | 4 527.60 | Balance b/d | 572.85 |
| Discount | 72.45 | PURCHASES | 4 761.89 |
| Returns | 116.44 | | |
| Balance c/d | 618.25 | | |
| | 5 334.74 | | 5 334.74 |

Purchases calculated once all the information is entered in the a/c. Credit opening balance (liability); record closing balance on the debit side above the totals; White receives money (and discount recorded on the same side) and returns.

**8**

## B. Smith account (SALES ledger)

| 1983 | | £ | 1983 | | £ |
|---|---|---|---|---|---|
| 1 April | Balance b/d | 180 | 9 April | Bank | 171 |
| 5 April | Sales (200–20) | 180 | | Discount (5% of 180) | 9 |
| | | | 15 April | Returns | 25 |
| | | | 30 April | Transfer from PL | 135 |
| | | | | Balance c/d | 20 |
| | | 360 | | | 360 |
| 1 May | Balance b/d | 20 | | | |

## B. Smith account (PURCHASES ledger)

| 1983 | | £ | 1983 | | £ |
|---|---|---|---|---|---|
| 22 April | Returns | 10 | 8 April | Purchases | 145 |
| 30 April | Transfer to SL | 135 | | | |
| | | 145 | | | 145 |

## F. A TUTOR'S ANSWER

Question **9** has been selected to demonstrate the three-column ledger account layout. B. Terry is a creditor, and therefore his account is kept in the purchases ledger.

### PURCHASES LEDGER

| B. Terry account | | Dr | Cr | Balance |
|---|---|---|---|---|
| 1983 | | £ | £ | £ |
| Nov 7 | Balance b/d (Cr) | | | 800 |
| 9 | Purchases | | 680 | 1 480 |
| 16 | Returns outwards | 40 | | 1 440 |
| 23 | Bank | 780 | | |
| | Discount received | 20 | | 640 |
| 25 | Purchases | | 200 | 840 |
| 28 | Purchases | | 180 | 1 020 |
| 30 | Bank | 624 | | |
| | Discount received | 16 | | 380 |

**Workings**

(1)   Purchases credited (Terry gives value): bank/discount and returns debited (Terry receives value). Alternatively, purchases increase Terry as a liability (creditor) so credit them to the account: bank/discount and returns reduce the liability, so they are debited.

(2)   On the 23rd: $2\frac{1}{2}\%$ of £800 $= \dfrac{2\frac{1}{2}}{100} \times \dfrac{800}{1}$

(3)   On the 30th: $2\frac{1}{2}\%$ of £640 (£680 less £40 returns).

---

## G.   A STEP FURTHER

We have already mentioned that, in reality, more and more businesses keep their accounts using either mechanized or computerized systems. Also, in practice, there are many areas of accounting – such as wages and taxation – which can involve complicated calculations in a number of different accounts. Many computer-based 'packages' are available to help businesses carry out their bookkeeping function, and you should find it both interesting and useful to see some of this software in operation. Local colleges often have courses which include the demonstration of computer software, and many of the major high street shops also display these packages. In this book you will find examples and illustrations of computerized (and mechanized) accounting packages.

At this level of financial accounting, you do not require a detailed knowledge of how amounts of income tax, National Insurance and superannuation are calculated and recorded in the various accounts, but it is useful to have some understanding of these procedures. Many accounting textbooks will explain the nature of these deductions from gross pay, and how they are calculated and recorded. *Business Accounting 1* by Frank Wood (published by Longman) contains such a chapter (Ch. 44 in the 4th edn).

Because we have dealt with two rather different approaches for identifying whether an account is to be debited or credited, it is advisable to study more than one textbook; perhaps one which emphasizes the 'debit the receiver, credit the giver' method, and one which uses the 'increase asset, debit the account . . .' method. Frank Wood's popular *Business Accounting 1* primarily uses the latter approach, whilst many of the other books teach the receiving/giving method.

Here is a selection of books that demonstrate these approaches:

Harrison, *Stage One Financial Accounting* (Northwick). Ch. 3.

Whitehead, *Bookkeeping Made Simple* ('Made Simple' Series). Chs 2 and 3.

Whitehead, *Success in Principles of Accounting* (John Murray). Units 1 and 2.

Frank Wood has also written *Bookkeeping and Accounts* (Longman), which is based at a slightly lower academic level than his *Business Accounting 1*. It contains a similar range of content, and Chapters 3, 4, 5 and 6 explain the double-entry system.

Should your syllabus require you to study the accounting requirements for VAT, you will find that there are several accounting textbooks which have chapters devoted to this topic. Examples are: Ch. 10, *Accounting Made Simple* by Simini and Hingley; Ch. 18 in *Business Accounting 1* (4th edn) by Frank Wood; and Ch. 36 in *Business Accounting 2* (4th edn) also by Frank Wood.

# Chapter 5

# Principles of double entry (2)

## A.  GETTING STARTED

Questions on both the trial balance and final accounts are commonly set. A typical area of questioning on the *trial balance* relates to the correction of errors following its construction, using the Journal and suspense account as the basis for correction. The subject of errors and the trial balance is covered in Chapter 9.

The trial balance is also often used by examiners as a source of information from which the *final accounts* of a business are to be constructed (along with accompanying notes on adjustments). Various chapters, such as those on partnerships (Ch. 13) and limited companies (Ch. 14), will examine this type of question.

In this chapter, we will initially explain how a trial balance is constructed, but not the detail of its limitations, nor how it is affected by the correction of errors. We will also initially limit our study of final accounts to the basic principles. You will have the opportunity to practise constructing the different types of final accounts later in the book. Here we introduce the final accounts, and consider the nature of profit and working capital, together with the major double-entry procedures involved.

To study the content of this chapter, you should have a knowledge of the principles of double entry, as well as an understanding of the difference between capital expenditure and revenue expenditure.

## B.  ESSENTIAL PRINCIPLES

### THE TRIAL BALANCE

The first important point to make about the trial balance is that, like the balance sheet, it is not an account proper. Identifying its purpose helps to explain why this is so. It is the main method used to 'prove' the arithmetical accuracy of the ledger (or various ledgers). Because every debit entry must have a corresponding credit entry to match it, the sum total of debits should equal the sum total of credits. To check that this is so, each account in the ledger is balanced, the balance being noted in the trial balance.

The trial balance has a limited role, and it is important to realize this. There are a range of errors which it will *not* disclose, quite simply because errors can be made even where the debit entry equals the credit entry. Because the trial balance – as an *arithmetical* check – will only identify where unequal debit and credit entries have been made, it cannot identify the fact that, say, a transaction valued at £89 has been posted to the relevant accounts as £98 (Dr = Cr = £98, even though both entries are incorrect). These errors are detailed in Chapter 9. This limitation of the trial balance often forms the basis of an essay question.

## Balances

One easy way of identifying which accounts have which balance is to remember the word **PEARLS**:

| Dr | Cr |
|---|---|
| Purchases | |
| Expenses | |
| Assets | |
| | Revenues |
| | Liabilities |
| | Sales |

The first letter of the word PEARLS should help you recall that Purchases, other Expenses and Assets all have debit balances; and Revenues, Liabilities and Sales have credit balances.

## Complications

There are a number of complications which an examiner may introduce into a question which includes a trial balance.

1. First, one balance may be omitted from the given list of balances. This is usually the balance on the capital account and you are expected to calculate it on the basis of
   TOTAL DEBITS less TOTAL CREDITS = CAPITAL ACCOUNT BALANCE

2. A second complication involves Provision account balances. The nature of provisions, and how the accounts are constructed, is examined in Chapter 7. For the moment, we can think of a 'provision' as a way of reducing an asset value. Since asset accounts will have debit balances, any account which sets out to reduce their value must possess a credit balance. It therefore follows that Provision accounts have credit balances.

## FINAL ACCOUNTS

Following the construction of the trial balance, *final accounts* can be drawn up. When we compare the final accounts, we find these key differences:

| | Trading and P&L | Balance Sheet |
|---|---|---|
| Each has a different *purpose* | acts as a profit or income statement; calculates net profit. | a list of all assets and liabilities. |

| | | |
|---|---|---|
| Each has a different *information source* | expense and revenue a/cs; revenue expenditure. | asset and liability a/cs; capital expenditure. |
| Each has a different *heading* | '. . . for period from . . . to . . .' (profit made over a period of time) | '. . . as at . . .' (balances taken at a particular point in time). |

## THE TRADING ACCOUNT

The purpose of the *Trading Account* is to calculate gross profit, and you will be tested on your knowledge of its operation and its layout. The construction of a typical trading account requires you to carry out a stock adjustment, involving opening and closing stock balances and purchases (as well as possibly returns and carriage).

The most common layout used is where closing stock is shown as a deduction on the debit side of the trading account, rather than on the credit side. The effect is the same – a 'minus debit' has the same effect as a credit entry – and by showing closing stock on the debit side, the very important *Cost of Goods Sold* figure can be displayed.

## Returns

Sales and purchases are shown in their separate accounts at gross value: any returns are recorded in either the *Returns Inwards (Sales Returns)* or the *Returns Outwards (Purchases Returns)* accounts. You will have to calculate net sales and purchases, by deducting the relevant returns: sales less sales returns (returns inwards), and purchases less purchases returns (returns outwards).

Returns inwards are *received* by the business, and are therefore debited to the returns inwards account. Returns outwards are *given* by the business, and are therefore credited to the returns outwards account.

## Carriage

Carriage, like returns, can be 'inwards' or 'outwards'. If the expense of carriage refers to the firm's purchases, then use *carriage inwards*, because purchases come 'inwards'; if to the firm's sales, then use *carriage outwards*, because the sales are going 'outwards'. Note that in both cases we are dealing with an expense to the business, and therefore both accounts have debit balances, and both will reduce profit.

Examiners will test your knowledge of where to record the two carriage account totals. If there is carriage *inwards* in a question, it is added to the purchases total in the trading account. It is an expense directly related to the cost of purchases. On the other hand we need to treat carriage *outwards* as a profit and loss (expense) item, and not as a trading account item.

## THE PROFIT AND LOSS ACCOUNT

The purpose of the *Profit and Loss Account* is to calculate the firm's net profit, by adding revenues other than sales to the gross profit figure, and by deducting the various expenses from this total. You will be tested on your knowledge of what to include, how to adjust items, and how to present the account.

Most of the difficulties associated with profit and loss accounts involve either:

(a)  adjustments as a result of prepayments or accruals;

(b)  the calculation and inclusion of the provisions which are associated with debtors or fixed assets.

Because these are detailed and quite complex areas, Chapters 7 and 8 of the book are devoted specifically to them. One point to emphasize here is that the profit and loss account involves double entry. *Net Profit* is its balance, just as gross profit is the balance resulting from the construction of the trading account. Net profit, like gross profit, is a credit balance: the revenue side is greater than the expense (debit) side.

## Net losses

Some questions will result in a net loss being recorded in the profit and loss account. Where a net loss results from your calculations, it is treated in the opposite way to a net profit. Because it is a debit balance – the debit side of profit and loss will be greater than the credit side – the net loss is first recorded on the credit side of the account, so that the two totals agree.

## The capital account

With a sole trader – a single owner – the capital account is linked to the profit and loss account, and it is possible that you will be asked to construct or update the capital account.

You are often asked why capital is treated as a liability: the business entity concept provides the answer. The accounts are those of the business, which owes capital to the owner, the owner having given value (therefore a credit balance) to the business. The owner can be thought of as the most important liability the business has.

## The drawings account

Most examination questions on final accounts will include an amount for *Drawings*. Because the owner receives the value of the drawings, the drawings account is debited, and the final debit balance is transferred to the debit of the capital account. Should you therefore have to include a balance for drawings in the trial balance, you need to remember that this account has a debit balance.

| *Drawings a/c* | | | *Capital a/c* | | |
|---|---|---|---|---|---|
| £ | | £ | | £ | £ |
| (Individual amounts) | Transfer of total to Capital a/c | X | Total Drawings | X | |
| | X | X | | | |

## THE BALANCE SHEET

Examination questions on the *Balance Sheet* typically test your knowledge of its construction and the various forms in which it presents its information.

**The headings**

We need to group assets and liabilities under their major headings. The classifications are:

| | |
|---|---|
| FIXED ASSETS | assets lasting longer than one accounting period, bought not to resell but to help the business make a profit. |
| CURRENT ASSETS | assets which fluctuate in the short-term, cash or 'near-cash', such as debtors. |
| CAPITAL | the owner's investment and resultant profits made by the business for the owner, and drawings made by the owner out of the business. |
| LONG-TERM LIABILITIES | amounts owed by the business over more than one accounting period. |
| CURRENT LIABILITIES | short-term debts of the business. |

You will have to present balance sheets using various layouts, and the book will introduce these different layouts at appropriate points.

**Working capital**

One layout which is widely used, regardless of the type of business organization, is where the value of the business's *Working Capital* is shown. The calculation of working capital is carried out to check a firm's ability to meet its short-term debts, and is a commonly examined item. You will probably need to know

| | | | |
|---|---|---|---|
| (a) | its *definition/purpose* | : | excess of current assets over current liabilities; to identify the ability of the business to meet its future debts |
| (b) | its *calculation* | : | current assets minus current liabilities |
| (c) | its *display* in a balance sheet | : | current liabilities deducted from current assets. |

**C. USEFUL APPLIED MATERIALS**

Where manual systems are used to record transactions, the production of trial balances and final accounts may take a considerable time. Nowadays, computer-based accounting 'packages' can generate, at a considerable speed, this same information. Trial balances, balance sheets, lists of transactions, and trading statements supported by statistical analyses, are all available as a result of the computer's ability to record, process and present information at great speed.

**Figure 5.1** is an example of a balance sheet which has been generated by a Nominal Ledger software package.

```
                    APRICOT ACCOUNTANT NOMINAL LEDGER
R. B. DUNCAN LTD        BALANCE SHEET           31 JAN 85
                          THIS YEAR                    LAST YEAR
FIXED ASSETS
 PLANT & MACHINERY      5134.25                  4563.48
 MOTOR VEHICLES         9076.16                  8042.33
                                14210.41                  12605.81
 DEPRECIATION                   (3000.00)                 (3200.00)
                                         11210.41                  9405.81
 TRADE INVESTMENTS                        1500.00                  1000.00
 TOTAL FIXED ASSETS                      12710.41                 10405.81
CURRENT ASSETS
 STOCKS                 2015.00                  2639.00
 WORK-IN-PROGRESS        950.00                  1340.00
                                 2965.00                   3979.00
 DEBTORS                15549.52                 10413.17
 BANK AND CASH          11021.90                 14141.98
 TOTAL CURRENT
 ASSETS                 29536.42                 28534.15
CURRENT LIABILITIES
 TRADE CREDITORS         8991.47                  6097.28
 PROVISIONS             2000.00                   1800.00
 DIVIDENDS              1000.00                   1300.00
 TAXATION               2140.00                   2503.00
 TOTAL CURRENT
 LIABLITIES             14131.47                 11700.28
WORKING CAPITAL                  15404.95                 16833.87
CAPITAL EMPLOYED                 28115.36                 27239.68
REPRESENTED BY
 SHARE CAPITAL                    1000.00                  1000.00
 RESERVES                         6000.00                  7000.00
 DEFERRED TAXATION                1000.00                  1755.00
 NET PROFIT BEFORE
  TAX                  12347.32                 11366.39
 PROFIT THIS YEAR       7768.04                  6118.29
                                 20115.36                 17484.68
                                 28115.36                 27239.68
```

Fig. 5.1   Balance Sheet
Courtesy: ACT (U.K.) Ltd

---

**D  RECENT EXAMINATION QUESTIONS**

Questions 1–5 are either multiple choice or sentence completion items. They should take less than 10 minutes to complete.

Question 6 requires you to construct ledger accounts and extract a trial balance: it includes books of original entry as well. Question 7 also involves the trial balance, asking you to construct one from a list of balances. Question 9 involves the construction of a balance sheet and a capital account.

*Question 8 is answered in detail in section F.*

1  Turnover less the cost of sales is the . . . . . . of the business.
(London Board Principles of Accounts O level, January 1983)

2  The cost of goods sold is arrived at by finding the
A  amount of the purchases less returns
B  amount of the sales less returns
C  closing stock plus goods purchased
D  opening stock plus goods purchased less closing stock
(AEB Specimen Accounting O level paper, 1980)

3  . . . . . . is gross profit less total expenses.
(London Board Principles of Accounts O level, January 1983)

4  Working capital is described as:
A  fixed assets less current liabilities
B  total assets less current liabilities
C  current assets less current liabilities
D  current assets less capital
(AEB Specimen Accounting O level Paper, 1980)

5  A credit balance on a sole trader's capital account is:
A  equal to the cash and bank balances of the business
B  the amount the sole trader owes the business
C  the difference between the assets and external liabilities of the business
D  equal to the value of the fixed assets of the business
(AEB Specimen Accounting O level Paper, 1980)

**Essay and computational questions**

6  Mr J. Ockey commenced trading as a wholesale stationer on 1 May 1984 with a capital of £5 000 with which he opened a bank account for his business.
During May the following transactions took place:

| May | 1  | Bought Shop Fittings and Fixtures on credit from Store Fitments Ltd for £2 000 |
| | 2  | Purchased goods on credit from Abel £650 |
| | 4  | Sold goods on credit to Bruce £700 |
| | 9  | Purchased goods on credit from Green £300 |
| | 11 | Sold goods on credit to Hill £580 |
| | 13 | Cash sales paid intact into Bank £200 |
| | 16 | Received cheque from Bruce in settlement of his account |
| | 17 | Purchased goods on credit from Kaye £800 |
| | 18 | Sold goods on credit to Nailor £360 |
| | 19 | Sent cheque to Abel in settlement of his account |
| | 20 | Paid rent by cheque £200 |
| | 21 | Paid delivery expenses by cheque £50 |
| | 24 | Received from Hill £200 on account |
| | 30 | Drew cheques for personal expenses £200 and assistant's wages £320 |
| | 31 | Settled the accounts of Green and Store Fitments Ltd |

*REQUIRED:*

(a) record the foregoing in appropriate books of original entry;

(8 marks)

(b) Post the entries to the ledger accounts;

(8 marks)

(c) Balance the ledger accounts where necessary;

(2 marks)

(d) Extract a Trial Balance at 31 May 1984.

(2 marks)

(Total 20 marks)

(AAT Numeracy and Accounting, June 1984)

**7**

(a) Explain the function and purpose of a trial balance and outline the steps you would take to ascertain how the error may have occurred if the debit and credit totals of the trial balance disagreed.

(b) The following balances were extracted from the books of K. Whitehead on 31 May 1982. You are required to prepare a trial balance. The amount required to balance should be entered as capital.

|  | £ |
|---|---|
| Purchases | 10 000 |
| Drawings | 1 100 |
| Stock 1 June 1981 | 2 000 |
| Returns inwards | 500 |
| Sales | 15 000 |
| Premises | 4 000 |
| Sundry debtors | 3 400 |
| Sundry creditors | 2 300 |
| Discounts received | 500 |
| Discounts allowed | 400 |
| Carriage outward | 100 |
| Carriage inward | 200 |
| Cash in hand | 500 |
| Cash at bank | 2 500 (DR) |
| Machinery | 3 500 |
| Sundry expenses | 300 |
| Provision for depreciation on machinery | 600 |
| Bad debts written off | 350 |
| Provision for doubtful debts | 340 |

(20 marks out of 200)

(JMB Bookkeeping and Accounting O level, June 1982)

**8** W. Watson is the owner of a small retail outlet. He keeps a full set of accounts including books of original entry. A selection of his transactions during 1983 is given below.

(1) Purchased goods for resale on credit from D. Compton £863.

(2) Cash sales £462 (cost price of these goods was £300).

(3) Received £500 from B. Richards (a debtor) on account; paid the full amount into bank.

(4) Bought a motor van, for use in the business, £2 350 on credit from A. Ramsay Motors Limited. The full debt is repayable before the end of the current accounting period.

(5) Paid the window cleaner, out of petty cash, £5 for cleaning the office windows.

*REQUIRED:*

(a) Completion of the following table for each transaction [(2)–(5) above], naming the book of original entry and the immediate or eventual debit and credit entries. The first one has been done for you as an example.

(6 marks)

| | | Book of Original Entry | Debit | Credit |
|---|---|---|---|---|
| (a) | (1) | Purchase day book | Purchases £683 | D. Compton £863 |

Note. State the amount of money involved in each debit and credit entry.

*REQUIRED:*

(b) Completion of the following table for each transaction [(2)–(5) above] indicating how each transaction would affect gross profit, net profit and working capital. Again, the first one has been done for you, as an example.

(10 marks)

| | | Gross Profit | Net Profit | Working Capital |
|---|---|---|---|---|
| (b) | (1) | Purchases − £863 but Stock + £863; therefore no effect on gross profit. | Gross profit no effect; net profit no effect. | Creditors + £863 therefore current liabilities + £863. Stock + £863 therefore current assets + £863. No effect on working capital. |

*REQUIRED:*

(c) An explanation of the importance of working capital.

(2 marks)

(AEB Principles of Accounts O level, June 1984)

**9** After the preparation of the Trading and Profit and Loss Account for the year ended 31 December 1982 the following balances remained on the books of James Mellor.

|                                                    | £       |
|----------------------------------------------------|---------|
| Capital 1 January 1982                             | 128 380 |
| Prepaid expenses                                   | 650     |
| Bank overdraft                                     | 1 360   |
| Net loss for the year ended 31 December 1982       | 280     |
| Loan from a finance company (repayable 1992)       | 5 000   |
| Trade creditors                                    | 1 120   |
| Freehold Premises                                  | 85 000  |
| Expense creditors                                  | 520     |
| Proprietor's drawings                              | 9 000   |
| Trade debtors                                      | 3 400   |
| Cash in hand                                       | 50      |
| Stock-in-trade                                     | 22 000  |
| Furniture & Equipment                              | 16 000  |

You are required to:

(a) Set out James Mellor's Balance Sheet as at 31 December 1982. Your balance sheet should show clearly fixed assets; current assets; long-term liabilities; current liabilities.

(b) Write up the capital account of James Mellor for the year ended 31 December 1982 as it would appear in his private ledger.

(26 marks)

(RSA I Bookkeeping, March 1983)

---

# E.  OUTLINE ANSWERS

**1** and **2** refer to trading account items. The gap for **1** is 'gross profit'. Alternative (D) describes cost of goods sold in question **2**.

**3**  This is a profit and loss question: the answer is 'net profit'.

**4**  Alternative (C) provides the definition.

**5**  (C) is correct (the 'Accounting equation', $C = A - L$).

**6**

(a)  Journal records the purchase of fixed asset on credit (May 1)
Purchases Book for credit purchases (May 2, 9, 17)
Sales Book for credit sales (May 4, 11, 18)
Cash Book: opening Dr balance; Dr May 13, 16 (£700), 24; Cr May 19 (£650), 20, 21, 30, 31 (Green £300, Store Fitments Ltd £2 000).

(b)  Journal: Dr Fittings a/c, Cr Store Fitments Ltd a/c
Purchases Book: Cr individual supplier a/cs; Dr the total (£1 750) to purchases a/c.
Sales Book: Dr individual customer a/cs; Cr the total (£1 640) to the sales a/c.
Cash Book: post cash and cheque receipts to relevant customer a/cs (Cr) and record value of cash sales on Cr of sales a/c: post cash/cheque payments to the relevant supplier a/cs and open expense a/cs (Dr) for rent, delivery expenses and wages.

(c)  and (d): Balances are – Capital 5 000 Cr, Kay 800 Cr, Hill 380 Dr, Nailor 360 Dr, Drawings 200 Dr, Fittings 2 000 Dr, Rent 200 Dr,

Delivery expenses 50 Dr, Wages 320 Dr, Purchases 1 750 Dr,
Sales 1 840 Cr, Bank 2 380 Dr. Trial balance totals: £7 640.

**7**

(a) Your answer should state the 'arithmetical accuracy' function of
the trial balance. Here **are** some points your answer may include
regarding the steps to take if the trial balance totals disagree:

  check that all balances are recorded on the correct side of the
  trial balance;
  check no balance has been omitted;
  check there is no error in totalling the trial balance columns;
  check no errors of addition in the day books;
  check no errors in calculating individual account balances;
  check whether there is a transaction for the amount of the
  difference (implies only single entry for this transaction);
  check whether a transaction worth half the amount of the
  difference (implies two debit entries or two credit entries).

(b) You need to recall PEARLS: purchases, expenses and assets = Dr
balances; revenues, liabilities and sales = Cr balances. In the list of
balances, Drawings = Dr (drawings reduce capital, a credit
balance) and the two Provision a/cs = Cr (they reduce the relevant
asset, debit, balances).

Credit balances in the trial balance are: sales, creditors, discount
received (revenue), provision for depreciation, provision for
doubtful debts.

**9**

(a)

**J. Mellor**

*Balance Sheet at 31 December 1982*

| | £ | £ | | £ | £ |
|---|---|---|---|---|---|
| *Fixed Assets:* | | | *Capital:* | | |
| Premises | | 85 000 | Opening | | |
| Furniture & | | | balance | | 128 380 |
|   Equipment | | 16 000 | Net loss | | 280 |
| | | ——— | | | ——— |
| | | 101 000 | | | 128 100 |
| *Current Assets:* | | | Drawings | | 9 000 |
| Stock | 22 000 | | | | ——— |
| | | | | | 119 100 |
| Debtors | 3 400 | | *Long-term* | | |
| Prepaid | | | *Liabilities:* | | |
| expenses | 650 | | Loan | | 5 000 |
| Cash | 50 | | | | |
| | ——— | | | | |
| | | 26 100 | | | |

46

|  | Current Liabilities: |  |  |  |
|  | Trade creditors 1 120 |  |  |  |
|  | Expense creditors | 520 |  |  |
|  | Bank overdraft | 1 360 |  |  |
|  |  |  |  | 3 000 |
|  |  | 127 100 |  | 127 100 |

(b) **J. Mellor**

*Capital account*

| 1982 | | £ | 1982 | | £ |
|------|---|---|------|---|---|
| Dec 31 | Drawings | 9 000 | Jan 1 | Balance b/d | 128 380 |
|  | Net loss | 280 |  |  |  |
|  | Balance c/d | 119 100 |  |  |  |
|  |  | 128 380 |  |  | 128 380 |

---

**F. A TUTOR'S ANSWER**

Question **8** is answered below. It is a demanding question which tests your understanding of how transactions are recorded, and how the transactions affect profits and working capital.

(a)

| Book of original entry | Debit | Credit |
|------------------------|-------|--------|
| (2) Cash book | Cash £462 | Sales £462 |
| (3) Cash book | Bank £500 | Richards £500 |
| (4) Journal | Vehicles £2 350 | Ramsay Motors £2 350 |
| (5) Petty cash book | Cleaning or Sundry Expenses £5 | Petty cash £5 |

(b) (G.P. = Gross profit, N.P. = Net profit)

| Gross profit | Net profit | Working capital |
|--------------|-----------|-----------------|
| (2) Purchases + £300 | G.P. + £162: | Cash = current asset: |
| Sales + £462 | N.P. + £162 | Cash + £462 |
| G.P. + £162 |  | Working capital + £462 |

| | | |
|---|---|---|
| (3) No effect | No effect | Debtor and Bank are current assets: Debtor − £500 Bank + £500 Working capital + £500 and − £500 (no effect) |
| (4) No effect | No effect | Ramsay Motors = current liability: + £2 350. Working capital − £2 350 |
| (5) No effect | Expenses + £5: N.P. − £5 | Cash (current asset) − £5 Working capital − £5 |

**Workings**

(i) *Gross profit:* are trading a/c items affected? Item (2) involves purchases and sales – both trading a/c items – where both increase in value. Sales increase is £162 greater than purchases, so G.P. must increase by £162.

(ii) *Net profit:* if G.P. alters, then N.P. also alters, as in (2). We need to identify any profit and loss a/c items, such as cleaning expenses (5): expenses will reduce net profit, just as revenues would increase it.

(iii) *Working capital:* calculated by current assets (C.A.) minus current liabilities (C.L.). If either C.A. or C.L. are affected, working capital will be affected.

In (2), a current asset increases: no change in current liabilities: so working capital must increase.
In (3), both items are current assets, cancelling each other out as far as working capital is concerned.
In (4), no current assets (vehicles a fixed asset), but current liabilities have increased, thereby reducing working capital.
In (5), no current liabilities, but current assets (cash) reduced, thereby reducing working capital.

(c) We use the working capital calculation to assess a firm's ability to meet short-term debts (current liabilities) from its cash or 'near-cash' resources (current assets). This establishes its liquidity: any shortage of working capital may cause difficulties to the firm, should its creditors demand payment of their debts in the near future.

## G. A STEP FURTHER

Many textbooks now refer to the recent developments which have taken place in the area of 'Inflation Accounting'. I would recommend that you find a book containing a chapter on this subject, such as

*Advanced Financial Accounting* by Lewis, Pendrill and Simon (Pitman), because it will give you further insights into just how arbitrary the calculation of profit can be.

There are many books which explain the trial balance and the nature of final accounts, together with worked examples or illustrations of final account layouts. Listed below is a selection of books which contain relevant chapters. 'TB' refers to a chapter on the trial balance, 'TPL' refers to a trading and profit and loss chapter, and 'BS' to a chapter on the balance sheet.

Garbutt, *Carter's Advanced Accounts* (7th edn) (Pitman). Ch. 02 (TPL, BS).

Piper, *Teach Yourself Bookkeeping* ('Teach Yourself' Series). Ch. 9 (TB); Ch. 12 (TPL); Ch. 13 (BS).

Whitehead, *Bookkeeping Made Simple* ('Made Simple' Series). Chs 8 and 16 (TB); Chs 17 and 18 (TPL); Ch. 19 (BS).

Whitehead, *Success in Principles of Accounting* (John Murray). Unit 4 (TB); Units 5 and 6 (TPL); Unit 7 (BS).

Wood, *Business Accounting 1* (4th edn) (Longman). Ch. 6 (TB); Chs 7 and 9 (TPL); Ch. 8 (BS).

Wood, *Bookkeeping and Accounts* (Longman). Ch. 7 (TB); Chs 8 and 10 (TPL); Ch. 9 (BS).

# Chapter 6

# Cash and bank records

## A. GETTING STARTED

Under the heading 'Cash and bank records' we include three topics which are quite commonly examined. These are the Petty Cash Book, the Cash Book, and Bank Reconciliation.

Questions on the *Petty Cash Book* tend to be computational. However, you may be asked an essay style question which requires an explanation of its purpose or operation, or, alternatively, you may have to describe the paperwork associated with it.

The *three-column Cash Book* forms one of the separate ledgers, following the division of the ledger. Questions asked on this topic usually require you to make entries in the cash book, to use the discount columns correctly, and to balance the cash book at the end of the period.

The final area covered by the chapter involves *bank reconciliation*. A question on bank reconciliation will give you information about a firm's bank account and the statement the firm has received from its bank. You are then given further information about entries which have been made in one of these records, but not in the other. Your task will be to reconcile the two balances from these records.

What background knowledge do you need in order to study the chapter effectively? An understanding of basic double entry is required, as well as a knowledge of the division of the ledger. The best preparation is to revise methods for working out whether an account is to be debited or credited, and to concentrate on the nature of the debtor–creditor relationship (which is important in bank reconciliation).

## B. ESSENTIAL PRINCIPLES

This particular accounting topic is usually quite straightforward. However, even though it is one of the easier parts of the syllabus to study, it contains some important concepts and principles.

### THE PETTY CASH BOOK

## Reasons for having a petty cash book

You may be required to state the purpose of keeping a petty cash book.

1.  One reason that a business keeps a petty cash book is to help keep detail out of the cash book. The petty cash book handles small cash transactions (payments), which would otherwise have to be recorded in the cash book.
2.  The analysis section of the petty cash book collects the individual expense payments, and at the end of the period the analysis columns are totalled. This results in one large total being entered in the relevant expense account in the general ledger, instead of a series of smaller entries being made. Again, this will help keep detail out of the general ledger.
3.  The use of analysis columns will help the accountant to analyse where the money is being spent: this will lead to greater control of expenditure.

## The imprest system

To illustrate the imprest system, let us assume that the petty cash float is £50. If, at the end of the first period, a total of £35.50 has been spent, how much does the Petty Cashier receive to operate the petty cash book in the next period? The answer is £35.50: this is the amount required to bring the float back up to its agreed total of £50. Thus, *whatever is spent is received back* by the Petty Cashier.

## The voucher

If you are asked about the purpose of the petty cash voucher you could include the following points:

(a) It is like a cheque, an invoice or a credit note: it is a source document.
(b) Its purpose is to authorize petty cash expenditure. It must therefore be signed by an authorized official.
(c) It acts as a check on petty cash operations by recording details and amounts spent.
(d) A business will file the vouchers for a period of time, for audit purposes.

## Constructing a petty cash book

The typical steps in the construction of the account are:

1.  Enter opening balance in the 'Receipts' column.
2.  Enter items of expenditure in the 'Total' column and in the appropriate analysis column.
3.  Rule off and total the analysis section.
4.  Add up the 'Total' column (note: you can check the accuracy of your addition because the individual analysis column totals, when added together, should agree with the total shown in the 'Total' column).
5.  Balance the account: you will probably need to use the imprest principle of 'whatever is spent is received' to calculate the amount of petty cash to debit in the 'Receipts' column in order to make up the float.

The answer to question 5, in section E, provides an illustration of a petty cash book.

## THE CASH BOOK

The design and layout of cash books varies in practice. Examinations concentrate on the '2-column' and '3-column' cash books, often asking you to enter a series of transactions in the cash book and then balance it.

We have two questions to answer:
1. Does the transaction involve *cash* or *cheques*? (the cash account or the bank account?).
2. Is it *money received* (Dr) or *money given* (Cr)?

Answering these two questions will identify which account and which side of the account is used.

## Contra items

One complication which is often included in a cash book question involves those transactions which affect both the bank account and the cash account. These *contra entries* affect the cash book twice, unlike the other entries, because both cash and bank are affected.

If the transaction involves surplus cash being paid into the bank,

| | |
|---|---|
| The *bank* receives | *Cash* is given |
| Dr the bank account | Cr the cash account |

Where cash is withdrawn from the bank (a cheque is cashed for business use),

| | |
|---|---|
| *Cash* is received | The *bank* gives |
| Dr the cash account | Cr the bank account |

## The discount columns

In summary,

| The debit discount column | The credit discount column |
|---|---|
| ↓ | ↓ |
| discount ALLOWED from debtors | discount RECEIVED from creditors |
| ↓ | ↓ |
| an *Expense* | a *Revenue* |
| ↓ | ↓ |
| total shown in Discount Allowed account (Dr) | total shown in Discount Received account (Cr) |

Question 6 in section D is based on a three-column cash book: it includes contra items and discounts, and its layout is illustrated in the answer given in section E.

## BANK RECONCILIATION STATEMENTS

The debtor–creditor relationship between a business and its bank can be seen from the two business records; the *bank account* in the books of the business, and the *bank statement* prepared by the bank from its own records. For the business, any value (cheques or cash) paid into the bank will be debited in its bank account; the bank has received the value. From the bank's viewpoint, any cash or cheques paid into the business bank account will be credited by the bank in its accounts: the business has given value. This explains why a debit entry in the bank account of the business is shown as a credit entry in the bank statement. Similarly, a credit entry in the business bank account will be debited in the bank statement.

| | |
|---|---|
| **Reasons for reconciliation** | Sometimes, part of a question on bank reconciliation will ask you to explain why there is a need to reconcile the two sets of records. Your answer should stress that the need to reconcile arises from the fact that both records are typically incomplete, because each contains information which is missing from the other. |
| | There will be items shown on the bank statement which are not recorded in the firm's cash book (bank account). Credit transfers, or dividends received by the bank on behalf of the firm, are items which, while appearing in the *credit* column of the bank statement, may not be recorded in the firms bank account. There may also be items *debited* on the statement which are not recorded in the firm's bank account, such as bank charges. Items recorded in the firm's bank account which are not shown on the bank statement received from the bank might include cheques received and debited in the bank account but not paid into the bank (or paid in but not yet credited by the bank); or cheques paid out by the firm and credited in the bank account, but not recorded by the bank on the statement ('unpresented cheques'). |
| | Another important reason for reconciliation is that by examining both records, any errors should be identified and can then be corrected. |
| **Procedure for reconciliation** | The procedure for carrying out reconciliation generally involves first, updating the firm's bank account, and, second, updating the bank statement (i.e. preparing a *Bank Reconciliation Statement*). Although quite a difficult topic, it becomes easier if we remember that we have two incomplete records to consider, and that both require completing. |
| Updating the firm's bank account | Here is the normal procedure: |
| | (i)  Identify those items on the statement which are not as yet recorded in the bank account. |
| | (ii) Work out whether the item will increase or reduce the balance at the bank. If the item *increases* the firm's bank balance it is a credit on the bank's statement and must therefore be debited in the bank account (because it increases the asset of 'Bank' in the firm's books). If the item *reduces* the firm's bank balance, it is a debit on the bank's statement, and must therefore be credited in the bank account. |
| Updating the bank statement | Having updated the firm's record – its bank account – and having calculated the updated bank account balance, we then have to construct a bank reconciliation statement. There are two possible approaches to constructing this statement. With either approach, we will have to identify those items which are in the firm's bank account but which are *not yet recorded on the bank statement*. |
| | (a) Start with the given statement balance, and work to the updated bank account balance. To do this we consider whether, when the bank updates its own records, the item not yet on the statement will increase or reduce the amount owed by the bank to the firm. |
| | (i)  If the item will *increase* the amount owed by the bank, then we add it to the opening balance. |

(ii) If the item will *reduce* the amount owed by the bank, then we deduct it from the opening balance.

We are updating the statement, starting with the incomplete balance and inserting all the missing information.

(b) The alternative approach, which may be required by the question, is where we start (rather than finish) with the updated bank account balance. Here we again have to identify those items in the bank account which are not yet recorded on the statement. We are, in effect, working 'backwards'.

(i) Those items which have *increased* the bank account balance will need to be deducted on the reconciliation statement.

(ii) Those items which have *reduced* the bank account balance will have to be added on the statement.

The reason here is that we are working backwards from a complete picture (the bank account balance, updated earlier) to an incomplete one (the bank statement balance).

## C. USEFUL APPLIED MATERIALS

**Figure 6.1** is an illustration of the layout for a bank statement used by a major commercial bank.

| DETAILS | | PAYMENTS | RECEIPTS | DATE | BALANCE |
|---|---|---|---|---|---|
| BALANCE FORWARD | | | | 26APR | 1608.00 |
| | 100428 | 3.50 | | 29APR | |
| | 100435 | 123.97 | | 29APR | |
| N /29/PS711616 | DDR | 3.29 | | 29APR | |
| REMITTANCE | | | 15.54 | 29APR | 1492.78 |
| | 100433 | 8.40 | | 30APR | |
| 9011245 | BGC | | 770.58 | 30APR | 2254.96 |
| 851871500010002 | DDR | 48.18 | | 1MAY | |
| | 100436 | 86.50 | | 1MAY | 2120.28 |
| | 100438 | 45.00 | | 3MAY | 2075.28 |
| 332BB424 | DDR | 10.20 | | 7MAY | 2065.08 |
| | 100440 | 10.00 | | 9MAY | |
| | 100441 | 45.00 | | 9MAY | 2010.08 |
| | 100437 | 100.00 | | 10MAY | 1910.08 |
| | 100443 | 44.41 | | 13MAY | |
| REMITTANCE | | | 400.22 | 13MAY | 2265.89 |
| N /14/00022408 | DDR | 19.29 | | 14MAY | |
| 1597027LL | DDR | 3.95 | | 14MAY | 2242.65 |
| | 100439 | 29.00 | | 16MAY | 2213.65 |
| | 100448 | 76.27 | | 17MAY | |
| | 100449 | 45.00 | | 17MAY | 2092.38 |
| | 100442 | 93.00 | | 20MAY | |
| 6276430202357 | DDR | 181.67 | | 20MAY | 1817.71 |
| BTEC | BGC | | 24.68 | 21MAY | 1842.39 |
| | 100450 | 45.00 | | 22MAY | |
| 8104295496 | DDR | 40.50 | | 22MAY | 1756.89 |
| | 100451 | 122.32 | | 28MAY | 1634.57 |

87L

CHEQUE
STATEMENT OF ACCOUNT

DIARY

28MAY

POST

BARCLAYS BANK PLC. Registered in London, England. Reg. No. 1026167. Reg. Office. 54 Lombard Street, London, EC3P 3AH

ABBREVIATIONS   DIV Dividend   STO Standing Order   BGC Bank Giro Credit   DDR Direct Debit   DR Overdrawn Balances

*Fig. 6.1   Bank statement*
Courtesy: Barclays Bank PLC

## D. RECENT EXAMINATION QUESTIONS

Questions **1–4** are either multiple choice or sentence completion questions on the three topics covered in the chapter. They should take approximately five minutes to complete.

Question **5** tests your ability to construct a petty cash book. Question **6** involves the construction of a three-column cash book, together with the construction of personal accounts.

Questions **7, 8** and **9** are on bank reconciliation. They represent the different approaches which can be found in questions on this topic. *Question 9 is answered in full in section F, 'A tutor's answer'.*

### Objective questions

**1** A petty cash account has an imprest of £25. Currently the account has a debit balance of £3. How much cash is needed to restore the imprest?

A £3     B £22     C £25     D £28

(AEB Specimen Accounting O level Paper, 1980)

**2** The cash balance in the cash book is always brought down as a
. . . . . . balance.

(JMB Bookkeeping and Accounting O level, June 1984)

**3** Discount Received is entered on the . . . . . . side of the Cash Book and the total for the period is posted to the . . . . . . of the Discount Received account.

(Cambridge Board Principles of Accounts O level, Summer 1983)

**4** The bank statement shows an overdraft of £300. A creditor has not presented a cheque for £75. When this is presented for payment, the bank balance will be:

A £375     B £225     C £225 overdrawn     D £375 overdrawn

(AEB Specimen Accounting O level, 1980)

### Essay and computational questions

**5** Walter Holmes is a sole trader who keeps his Petty Cash on the Imprest system – the Imprest amount being £40. For the month of December 1983 his petty cash transactions were as follows:

1983

| | |
|---|---|
| 1 December | Petty cash in hand £3.47 |
| 1 December | Petty cash restored to the Imprest amount |
| 4 December | Stamps purchased £3.96 |
| 8 December | Envelopes purchased £4.15 |
| 10 December | Paid wages £6.30 |
| 14 December | Paid to Alfred Jackson, a creditor, £5.60 |
| 19 December | Stamps purchased £4.29 |
| 21 December | Typing paper purchased £3.70 |
| 24 December | Paid wages £7.10 |
| 31 December | Stamps purchased £2.00 |

*REQUIRED:*

(i) Draw up the Petty Cash Book of Walter Holmes and enter the above transactions in it.

(ii) Balance the Petty Cash Book as at the close of business on 31 December 1983 and carry down the balance.

(iii) Give the entry necessary on 1 January 1984 to restore the Petty Cash to the Imprest amount.

*Note:* Your analysis columns should be postages, stationery, wages and ledger. (25 marks)

(LCCI Elementary Bookkeeping, Winter 1984)

**6** Jean Jones opened a greengrocer's shop on 1 April 1984. She had £1 000 cash, of which she placed £900 into a bank account. The transactions for the shop during the month of April were:

| | | | £ |
|---|---|---|---:|
| April | 3 | Purchased goods from T. Duke on credit | 150.00 |
| | 4 | Paid half year's rent by cheque | 600.00 |
| | 7 | Cash sales for week | 685.40 |
| | | Cash drawings by J. Jones | 100.00 |
| | | Paid cash into bank | 500.00 |
| | 8 | Purchased goods from B. Prince on credit | 75.50 |
| | | Purchased goods from R. Knight on credit | 115.00 |
| | 11 | Paid T. Dukes a/c by cheque in full settlement | 135.00 |
| | 14 | Cash sales for week | 732.80 |
| | | Paid cash into bank | 600.00 |
| | | Cash drawings by J. Jones | 100.00 |
| | | Purchases from B. Prince on credit | 125.00 |
| | 18 | Paid B. Prince by cheque | 75.50 |
| | | Paid R. Knight by cheque, on account | 50.00 |
| | 19 | Sales to J. Lord on credit | 30.00 |
| | 21 | Cash sales for week | 483.70 |
| | | Paid cash into bank | 500.00 |
| | 23 | Purchases from R. Knight on credit | 176.30 |
| | 24 | Bought cash register from ABC Ltd. for credit | 172.00 |
| | 25 | J. Lord settled his account by cheque (less 10% discount) | |
| | 28 | Cash sales for week | 572.50 |
| | | Paid into bank | 700.00 |
| | | Drawings by cheque – J. Jones | 200.00 |

*Note:*

Candidates should calculate the amount of the cheque paid by J. Lord on 25 April.

From this information you are required to:

(a) record the appropriate transactions in a three-column cash book, and bring down the balances as at 30 April 1984,

(b) write up the ledger accounts of T. Duke, B. Prince, R. Knight and J. Lord and bring down the balances as at 30 April 1984.

(55 marks out of 200)

(JMB Bookkeeping and Accounting O level, June 1984)

**7** Jim Duddy received a statement from his bank at 30 April 1983, showing a balance of £1 420 in his favour. The differences between his cash book and bank statement balances at 30 April are given below.

1. An amount of £421, paid into bank on 29 April, has not been entered by the bank.
2. Two cheques drawn by Duddy were not presented for payment until after 30 April: C. Walker £206, P. Higgins £39.
3. The bank made standing order payments, amounting to £168, on behalf of Duddy. This had not been recorded in the cash book.
4. On 23 April 1983, Duddy received from V. Bennett a cheque for £306, which he paid to bank on the same day. The bank statement showed that this cheque was dishonoured on 28 April 1983.
5. On 24 April, Duddy paid into bank a cheque for £360, which was received from a customer in full settlement of a debt of £375. This item was shown correctly in the bank statement but Duddy had entered the full £375 in the bank column of his cash book.
6. J. Elliss, a debtor, had made a payment of £292 direct to the bank but this entry had not been entered in Duddy's cash book.

*REQUIRED:*
(a) A statement showing the corrected bank statement balance.
(4 marks)
(b) The cash book (bank columns only) showing the opening balance at 30 April, the additional entries now made necessary and closing with the corrected balance. (7 marks)
(c) An explanation of why a credit balance on a bank statement represents an asset to the firm concerned. (4 marks)
(AEB Accounting O level, November 1983)

**8** The bank columns of your cash book for the month of January 1983 are shown below:

| 1983 | | £ | 1983 | | ChequeNo. | £ |
|---|---|---|---|---|---|---|
| Jan | 1 Balance b/fwd | 482.30 | Jan | 1 Z A Insurance Co | 405 | 43.00 |
| | 6 Cash sales | 100.50 | | 2 D. McIntosh | 406 | 17.50 |
| | 9 S. Attwood | 62.70 | | 15 M. Jibb | 407 | 4.80 |
| | 14 Cash sales | 75.00 | | 20 Gas Board | 408 | 19.20 |
| | 23 E. Sheppard | 37.18 | | 24 Blackwood & Co | 409 | 39.35 |
| | 31 Cash sales | 92.60 | | 28 L. Henning | 410 | 15.30 |
| | | | | 30 UZ Garages | 411 | 400.00 |
| | | | | 30 British Telecom | 412 | 7.75 |
| | | | | 31 Balance c/fwd | | 303.38 |
| | | 850.28 | | | | 850.28 |

Feb 1 Balance b/fwd 303.38

The following bank statement was received for the month of January:

| | | *Dr* | *Cr* | *Balance* |
|---|---|---|---|---|
| Jan | 1 Balance | | | 482.30 |
| | 5 Cheque No. 405 | 43.00 | | 439.30 |
| | 6 Cash | | 100.50 | 539.80 |
| | 8 Cheque No. 406 | 17.50 | | 522.30 |
| | 10 S. Attwood | | 62.70 | 585.00 |
| | 14 Cash | | 75.00 | 660.00 |
| | 24 Cheque No. 408 | 19.20 | | 640.80 |
| | 24 Cheque No. 407 | 4.80 | | 636.00 |
| | 24 E. Sheppard | | 37.18 | 673.18 |
| | 28 Cheque No. 409 | 39.35 | | 633.83 |
| | 28 Bank Giro Credit: C. Brown | | 60.40 | 694.23 |
| | 28 Standing order:subscription | 49.80 | | 644.43 |
| | 30 Bank charges | 14.10 | | 630.33 |

*REQUIRED:*

(a) Make the necessary entries in the cash book to ascertain a corrected balance as on 31 January 1983, and

(b) Reconcile your revised cash book balance with the balance shown in the bank statement.

(12 marks)

(RSA I Bookkeeping, February 1984)

**9** Hay has received his bank pass sheets for the year to 31 October 1983. At that date, his balance at the bank amounted to £14 130 whereas his own cash book showed a balance of £47 330. His accountant investigated the matter, and discovered the following discrepancies:

1. Bank charges of £60 had not been entered in the cash book.
2. Cheques drawn by Hay and totalling £450 had not yet been presented to the bank.
3. Hay had not entered receipts of £530 in his cash book.
4. The bank had not credited Hay with receipts of £1 970 paid in to the bank on 31 October 1983.
5. Standing order payments amounting to £1 240 had not been entered in the cash book.
6. Hay had entered a payment of £560 in his cash book as £650.
7. A cheque received for £300 from a debtor had been returned by the bank marked 'refer to drawer', but this had not been written back in the cash book.
8. Hay had brought down his opening cash book balance of £6 585 as a debit balance instead of as a credit balance.
9. An old cheque payment amounting to £880 had been written back in the cash book, but the bank had already honoured it.

10. Some of Hay's customers had agreed to settle their debts by direct debit. Unfortunately, the bank had credited some direct debits amounting to £16 650 to another customer's account.

*REQUIRED:*

(a) Prepare a statement showing Hay's adjusted cash book balance as at 31 October 1983. (12 marks)

(b) Prepare a bank reconciliation statement as at 31 October 1983. (4 marks)

(c) State briefly the main reasons for preparing a bank reconciliation statement.

(4 marks)

(Total 20 marks)

(AAT Accounting 2, December 1983)

---

# E. OUTLINE ANSWERS

Question **1** involves the imprest system: alternative (B) is correct (£3 + £22 to give the float of £25). For questions **2** and **3**, the missing words are 'debit' (**2**) and 'credit' (both gaps in question **3**).

**4** The £75 unpresented cheque will increase the overdraft, so (D) is correct.

**5**

| Receipts £ | Date | Details | Total £ | Postage £ | Stationery £ | Wages £ | Ledger £ |
|---|---|---|---|---|---|---|---|
| 3.47 | Dec. 1 | Balance b/d | | | | | |
| 36.53 | 1 | Cash | | | | | |
| | 4 | Stamps | 3.96 | 3.96 | | | |
| | 8 | Envelopes | 4.15 | | 4.15 | | |
| | 10 | Wages | 6.30 | | | 6.30 | |
| | 14 | Jackson | 5.60 | | | | 5.60 |
| | 19 | Stamps | 4.29 | 4.29 | | | |
| | 21 | Paper | 3.70 | | 3.70 | | |
| | 24 | Wages | 7.10 | | | 7.10 | |
| | 31 | Stamps | 2.00 | 2.00 | | | |
| | | | 37.10 | 10.25 | 7.85 | 13.40 | 5.60 |
| | 31 | Balance c/d | 2.90 | GL | GL | GL | PL |
| 40.00 | | | 40.00 | | | | |
| 2.90 | Jan. 1 | Balance b/d | | | | | |
| 37.10 | 1 | Cash | | | | | |

**6**

(a)

**Cash Book**

| Date | Details | Disc. £ | Cash £ | Bank £ | Date | Details | Disc. £ | Cash £ | Bank £ |
|------|---------|---------|--------|--------|------|---------|---------|--------|--------|
| Apr. 1 | Balances | | 100.00 | 900.00 | Apr. 4 | Rent | | | 600.00 |
| 7 | Sales | | 685.40 | | 7 | Drawings | | 100.00 | |
| | Contra | | | 500.00 | | Contra | | 500.00 | |
| 14 | Sales | | 732.80 | | 11 | Duke | 15.00 | | 135.00 |
| | Contra | | | 600.00 | 14 | Contra | | 600.00 | |
| 21 | Sales | | 483.70 | | | Drawings | | 100.00 | |
| | Contra | | | 500.00 | 18 | Prince | | | 75.50 |
| 25 | Lord | 3.00 | | 27.00 | | Knight | | | 50.00 |
| 28 | Sales | | 572.50 | | 21 | Contra | | 500.00 | |
| | Contra | | | 700.00 | 28 | Contra | | 700.00 | |
| | | | | | | Drawings | | | 200.00 |
| | | | | | 30 | Balances | | 74.40 | 2 166.50 |
| | | 3.00 | 2 574.40 | 3 227.00 | | | 15.00 | 2 574.40 | 3 227.00 |
| May 1 | Balances | | 74.40 | 2 166.50 | | | | | |

Note that the credit transactions are not entered in the cash book. On the 11th, Dukes is paid £135 in full settlement of £150 owed (thus £15 discount). On the 25th, Lord pays £27 (£30 less 10%).

(b) Duke: Dr bank £135 and discount £15; Cr purchases £150 (no balance).
Prince: Dr bank £75.50; Cr purchases £75.50 and £125; Cr bal. £125.
Knight: Dr bank £50; Cr purchases £115 and £176.30; Cr bal. £241.30.
Lord: Dr sales £30; Cr bank £27 and discount £3 (no balance).

**7**

(a) Statement balance is £1 420. You need to identify items not yet recorded on the statement, and enter them: if they increase the statement balance add them; if they reduce the balance, subtract them. Thus:

| | £ |
|---|---|
| given balance | 1 420 |
| add amount paid in (1) | 421 |
| less unpresented cheques (2) | (206) |
| | (39) |
| updated statement balance | 1 596 |

(b) Update cash book, entering missing items:

*Cash Book*

| | £ | | £ |
|---|---|---|---|
| Elliss (6) | 292 | Standing order (3) | 168 |
| | | Dishonoured cheque (4) | 306 |
| | | Adjustment (375–360) (5) | 15 |

Dishonoured cheque originally debited, so must be credited in the cash book to cancel the debit entry. The £375 was debited; this should have been £360, so credit the cash book £15 to obtain a 'net debit' of £360.

We know the closing (updated) cash book balance: it is the same as the updated statement balance, i.e. £1 596. Including this in the cash book (initially on the Cr side), we can calculate the opening balance (the difference between the two sides). The opening balance is £1 793.

(c) Your answer should concentrate on the debtor–creditor relationship: a credit balance on the statement (the bank's records) signifies that the business has given more to the bank than it has received from the bank. The business is a liability to the bank. To the business, the bank is holding some of its money; the bank is an asset (= Dr balance).

**8**

(a)

*Cash Book*

|  | £ |  | £ |
|---|---|---|---|
| Balance | 303.38 | Standing order | 49.80 |
| Giro credit | 60.40 | Charges | 14.10 |
|  |  | Updated balance c/d | 299.88 |
|  | 363.78 |  | 363.78 |

An opening Dr balance; this is increased by the bank giro credit, and reduced by charges and the standing order.

(b) *Bank reconciliation statement as at 31 January 1983*

|  | £ | £ |
|---|---|---|
| Balance as per Cash Book |  | 299.88 |
| Add: unpresented cheques | 15.30 |  |
|  | 400.00 |  |
|  | 7.75 | 423.05 |
|  |  | 722.93 |
| Less: unrecorded cash sales |  | 92.60 |
| Balance as per Bank Statement |  | 630.33 |

The above reconciliation statement starts with the cash book (updated) balance, and works to (reconcile with) the bank statement balance. Compare this approach with the approach in question 9 (in the next section); here, the bank statement balance was entered first, and reconciled with the updated cash book balance. Either approach is acceptable, unless a question specifically requests one approach to be used.

Question **9** is a comprehensive test of knowledge of bank reconciliation, and is answered below.

(a) **Hay**

*Statement of adjusted cash book balance as at 31 October 1983*

| | £ | £ |
|---|---|---|
| Original balance at bank | | 47 330 |
| Add: receipts (3) | 530 | |
| transposition error (6) | 90 | |
| | | 620 |
| | | 47 950 |
| Less: bank charges (1) | 60 | |
| standing order (5) | 1 240 | |
| 'R/d' cheque (7) | 300 | |
| incorrect recording of balance (8) | 13 170 | |
| honoured cheque (9) | 880 | 15 650 |
| Corrected cash book balance as at 31 October | | 32 300 |

**Workings**

Note that the question asks for 'statement' showing adjustments, so the account is laid out in statement form, debit section at top, credit section at bottom.
Items (1) and (5) will reduce balance, so subtract.
Item (3) will increase balance, so add.
Item (6) payment (Cr) side £90 too much: add back to Dr side.
Item (7) originally debited, so must be credited.
Item (8) credit (subtract) twice the amount: once to cancel the incorrect debit, once to record as the correct credit.
Item (9) has been debited in the account, so now needs crediting.

(b) **Hay**

*Bank reconciliation statement at 31 October 1983*

| | £ | £ |
|---|---|---|
| Balance at bank as per pass sheets | | 14 130 |
| Add: receipts not credited (4) | 1 970 | |
| direct debits not credited (10) | 16 650 | |
| | | 18 620 |
| | | 32 750 |
| Less: unpresented cheques (2) | | 450 |
| Balance as per cash book, 31 October | | 32 300 |

**Workings**

Note that you could have started with cash book corrected balance and worked back to statement (pass sheets) balance.
Item (2) will reduce bank statement balance, so subtract.
Items (4) and (10) will increase bank balance, so add.

(c) The main reasons include:
  (i) a check for errors or omissions which may exist in either the bank statement or in the firm's bank account;
  (ii) it provides a further check on the work of the official responsible for the firm's bank account;
  (iii) it allows an updating of the firm's bank account at regular intervals.

## G. A STEP FURTHER

Here is a selection of books containing chapters on the three accounting topics covered in the chapter. The abbreviations 'PCB', 'CB' and 'BR' refer respectively to the petty cash book, the cash book and bank reconciliation.

Castle and Owens, *Principles of Accounts* (7th edn) (M&E Handbooks). Ch. 7 (PCB); Ch. 8 (BR).

Etor and Muspratt, *Keep Account* (Pan 'Breakthrough' series). Ch. 10 (PCB and BR).

Harrison, *Stage One Financial Accounting* (Northwick). Ch. 13 (CB and BR).

Piper, *Teach Yourself Bookkeeping* ('Teach Yourself' Series). Ch. 6 (PCB); Ch. 5 (BR)

Whitehead, *Bookkeeping Made Simple* ('Made Simple' Series). Ch. 7 (PCB); Ch. 5 (CB); Ch. 11 (BR).

Wood, *Business Accounting 1* (4th edn) (Longman). Ch. 28 (PCB); Chs 13 and 14 (CB); Ch. 26 (BR).

Wood, *Bookkeeping and Accounts* (Longman). Ch. 24 (PCB); Chs 13 and 14 (CB); Ch. 22 (BR).

| Chapter 7 | # Adjustments in accounts (1): Provisions |
|---|---|

## A. GETTING STARTED

To record the loss in value of fixed assets or the expected true value of year-end debtors, the accountant will create a *provision*. Questions are often set on the topic of provisions: in particular, on *Provision for Depreciation* or *Provision for Bad (Doubtful) Debts*. The questions tend to fall into three categories:

1.  Essay-type questions which ask you to describe the nature, importance or limitations of providing for depreciation. Alternatively, you may be asked to explain the nature of bad debts and the provision for bad debts.

2.  Computational questions which are set on the bookkeeping entries made in the relevant ledger accounts. Such questions may involve the disposal of a fixed asset, or an adjustment on the provision for bad debts.

3.  Computational questions set on the trial balance, which is given in the question together with supporting notes. The notes will usually include details on the provisions, the provision balances being included in the trial balance. The type of question which involves constructing final accounts from a trial balance and a series of notes will be considered in the next chapter, when we examine the nature of the other main adjustments, i.e. prepayments and accruals.

What background knowledge do you require to answer questions on provisions? A good understanding of the way transactions are recorded in ledger accounts is needed, as well as a basic knowledge of the layout and purpose of final accounts.

## B. ESSENTIAL PRINCIPLES

## THE NATURE AND EFFECT OF DEPRECIATION

You may be given an essay question which asks you to define 'depreciation', or to state how it arises in practice. The main point to make is that depreciation refers to the cost of a fixed asset consumed through its use by a business.

Depreciation is therefore an expense, which must be shown in the profit and loss account as a deduction from gross profit. Because depreciation is based on a fixed asset (and tries to indicate a fairly accurate value for that fixed asset), it will also be shown in the balance sheet, as a deduction from the cost value of the asset.

### How depreciation arises

Depreciation can arise in various ways, depending on the nature of the fixed asset. In an answer, you could provide examples of how different fixed assets depreciate in practice:

- mines are *depleted* (as reserves of coal, ores, etc. are reduced through extraction);
- machinery may become technologically *obsolete* (as new, more automated machines are developed);
- vehicles may physically *deteriorate*;
- computers may become *inadequate* for the needs of the firm (e.g. through their lack of memory size);
- leases or patents are *amortized* (written off over their lifespan).

It may be appropriate to recognize in your answer that asset values may rise as well as fall: assets such as land and buildings may *appreciate*.

### Calculating depreciation

There are three main methods used to calculate depreciation amounts that you are normally expected to know:

1. The *Straight Line* (or *Equal Instalment*) method requires you to memorize a formula:

$$\frac{\text{Cost of asset less estimated scrap value}}{\text{Estimated life of asset}}$$

The calculation will provide you with the depreciation per annum. The same amount of depreciation – 'equal instalment' – is provided each year of the asset's life.

An asset costing £1 000 and having an estimated life of 4 years and an estimated scrap value of £100 will be depreciated at £225 each year for the 4 years under this method:

$$\frac{£1\,000 - £100}{4} = £225 \text{ p.a.}$$

2. The *Reducing Balance* method applies a fixed percentage to the written-down value of the asset. This gives a different, reducing figure for each year.

To calculate the value of depreciation in the example above, using the reducing balance method, we need to apply the given percentage figure. We shall use the figure of 20%.

| | | | |
|---|---|---|---|
| Depreciation year 1 | = | 20% of £1 000 | = £200 |
| Written-down value of asset | = | £1 000 − £200 | = £800 |
| Depreciation year 2 | = | 20% of £800 | = £160 |
| Written-down value, end of year 2 | = | £800 − £160 | = £640 |

The depreciation charge in the third year will therefore be based on calculating 20% of £640 (i.e. £128), and the new written-down value will be £512; and so on, with the value of depreciation falling in each successive year.

3. The *Revaluation* method compares the opening value of the relevant fixed asset to the closing, revalued figure. The difference (the loss in value) is the depreciation to be charged.

**Depreciation in the ledger**

To record depreciation in a provision account, we need to remember that the relevant fixed assets are recorded in their accounts at cost value, and remain in the account at cost. Other assets bought, and existing assets sold, are debited and credited respectively at cost price.

One of the purposes of depreciation is to reduce the cost value of the asset to a more accurate value. If we reduce the value of an asset (which has a debit balance), we must make a credit entry. This credit entry is recorded in the provision account, with its matching debit entry being made in the profit and loss account.

After these entries have been made in the accounts, we are left with a debit balance on the asset account and a credit balance on the provision account. These balances are brought down at the year-end in the normal way. Further years' depreciation will again involve crediting the account and debiting the profit and loss account with the appropriate amounts.

**Fixed asset account**

| | £ | | £ |
|---|---|---|---|
| Assets bought (at cost) | | Assets sold (at cost) Balance c/d | |
| Balance b/d | | | |

**Depreciation provision account**

| | £ | | £ |
|---|---|---|---|
| Balance c/d | | Annual depreciation (to profit and loss) | |
| | | Balance b/d Annual depreciation | |

## DISPOSAL OF ASSETS

Here is the procedure involved in disposal.

(a) Fixed assets are recorded in their accounts at their original cost price. When a fixed asset is sold, we transfer it out of its account (credit entry since it is 'given'; or since the asset value is reduced) at its cost price. It is transferred to the debit of the asset disposal account.

(b) Because the asset no longer exists in the business, the total depreciation charged on the asset must also be removed from the depreciation provision account. It is transferred (debited) from this account and credited in the asset disposal account.

(c) What the business receives from the asset sale is debited to the relevant account (cash, bank or debtor) and credited to the asset disposal account.

### Asset disposal account

| | £ | | £ |
|---|---|---|---|
| (a) Asset (at cost) | | (b) Depreciation on asset | |
| | | (c) Value received for asset | |

(d) A debit balance on the account, where the cost price of the asset exceeds the depreciation charged on it plus the cash (or value) received from its sale, means that the business has *under-depreciated* the asset and has therefore made a loss on its sale. A credit balance will therefore mean a profit to the business as a result of selling the asset.

A loss on sale is debited to the profit and loss account (as a debit balance, it is in fact recorded in the disposal account on the credit side so that the account totals agree). A profit on sale will be added to gross profit on the credit side of profit and loss (again, double entry is completed by debiting the disposal account.)

Questions 6 and 7 in section D involve disposal of assets: answers and workings are given.

## PROVISION FOR BAD DEBTS

We need to know the difference between *Bad Debts* and *Provision for Bad Debts*.

If a debtor cannot pay, the account can no longer be regarded as an asset to the business. The asset of debtor needs writing off, and the expense of the bad debt needs recording, so that it can be set against the period's profits in the profit and loss account: for example,

| Debtor X a/c | | | | Bad Debts a/c | | | |
|---|---|---|---|---|---|---|---|
| | £ | | £ | | £ | | £ |
| | | Transfer to Bad | | Debtor X | 100 | (P&L | 100) |
| Balance | 100 | Debits a/c | 100 | | | | |

The bad debt is therefore a known cost to the business.

| The provision | Should you be set a question on the nature of the Provision for Bad Debts, you will need to explain that this is an adjustment made on the closing value of debtors, typically on a percentage basis (the actual percentage used being based on past experience). The provision reduces the value of total debtors in an attempt to give a 'true and fair view' of their real worth to the business. The provision is also charged against profits, in the same way that the provision for depreciation is set against profits. |
|---|---|

**Creating the account**

To create a new provision account, we need to remember that its purpose is to reduce the total value of debtors. To reduce a series of debit balances requires a credit entry, and so the provision account is credited with the appropriate amount. The corresponding debit entry is made in the profit and loss account as a charge against the profits. The credit balance in the provision account is brought down in the normal way.

| *Debtor accounts* | | | | *Provision for bad debts account* | | |
|---|---|---|---|---|---|---|
| | £ | | £ | | £ | £ |
| Balances (Dr = asset) | | | Balance c/d | Transfer to P&L | | |
| | | | | | ——— | ——— |
| | | | | | ═══ | ═══ |
| | | | | Balance b/d | | |

**Adjusting the existing account**

Once the provision account is created, it will therefore contain a credit balance. Any increase in the new provision must be added (i.e. credited) to this existing balance, the debit entry for the increase again being shown in profit and loss.

Should the amount required for the provision have to be reduced (where, for instance, the total value of year-end debtors has fallen), the provision account must be debited to reduce its credit balance. The corresponding credit entry will be made in the profit and loss account, being added to gross profit.

**Provision account**

| | (Balance b/d) |
|---|---|
| Dr = DECREASE | Cr = INCREASE |
| provision | provision |

## C. USEFUL APPLIED MATERIALS

We have seen that a risk of trading on credit is that a business may not be paid by some of its debtors. In an attempt to highlight problem areas, a business may undertake an analysis of its outstanding debts on the basis of their age.

**Figure 7.1** illustrates an approach that a business could take, identifying the value of outstanding debts according to the age of those debts.

| | Outstanding | | | | | | | Remarks |
|---|---|---|---|---|---|---|---|---|
| | AUG Current | JULY 1 | JUNE 2 | MAY 3 | APRIL 4 | MARCH 5 | 6 | |
| | 2310.30 | 1460.93 | 602.04 | 120.80 | 146.25 | 180.20 | | |
| 1 | 392.96 | | | | | | | |
| 2 | 120.15 | 120.78 | | | | | | |
| 3 | 82.10 | 136.15 | 100.90 | 107.00 | | | | Final letter sent 1/8/81 |
| 4 | | | | | 23.10 | | | Solicitors letter 1/8/81 |
| 5 | | 533.00 | | | | | | |
| 6 | 111.37 | | | | | | | |
| 7 | 206.10 | 186.47 | | | | | | |
| 8 | | | 850.90 | | | | | |
| 9 | 125.00 | | | | | | | |
| 10 | 43.20 | | | | | | | |
| 11 | 225.27 | 220.00 | | | | | | |
| 12 | 82.12 | | | | | | | |
| 13 | 86.00 | | | 208.00 | | | | Final letter sent 1/8/81 |
| 14 | 94.80 | | | | | | | |
| 15 | 357.22 | | | | | | | |
| 16 | 4236.59 | 2657.33 | 1553.84 | 485.80 | 146.25 | 203.30 | | |
| 17 | | | | | | | | |
| 18 | | | | | | | | |
| 19 | | | | | | | | |
| 20 | | | | | | | | |

*Fig. 7.1   Debtor Age Analysis*
Courtesy: Kalamazoo Business Systems

**Figure 7.2** shows how a business (in this example, a building society) analyses its fixed assets in the annual report and accounts.

| FIXED ASSETS | Freehold Premises £'000s | Leasehold Premises 50 or more years unexpired £'000s | Leasehold Premises less than 50 years unexpired £'000s | Office & Computer Equipment £'000s | Other Fixed Assets £'000s |
|---|---|---|---|---|---|
| **Cost or Valuation** | | | | | |
| 1 January 1984 | 6,945 | 398 | 464 | 7,284 | 650 |
| Additions | 255 | — | 49 | 726 | 316 |
| Disposals | (30) | — | (3) | (5) | (264) |
| Introduced by merger | 286 | — | — | 31 | 12 |
| at 31 December 1984 | 7,456 | 398 | 510 | 8,036 | 714 |
| | | | | | |
| **Depreciation** | | | | | |
| 1 January 1984 | — | — | 189 | 3,864 | 248 |
| Charge for year | — | — | 56 | 1,175 | 170 |
| Disposals | — | — | (3) | (1) | (115) |
| Introduced by merger | — | — | — | 20 | 4 |
| at 31 December 1984 | — | — | 242 | 5,058 | 307 |
| | | | | | |
| **Net Book Values** | | | | | |
| at 31 December 1984 | 7,456 | 398 | 268 | 2,978 | 407 |
| (Total £11,507,000) | | | | | |
| | | | | | |
| **Net Book Values** | | | | | |
| at 31 December 1983 | 6,945 | 398 | 275 | 3,420 | 402 |
| (Total £11,440,000) | | | | | |
| Cost or Valuation at 31 December 1984 comprises: | | | | | |
| Valuation | | | | | |
| 1973 and earlier years | 1,045 | — | — | — | — |
| 1976 | 1,212 | — | 71 | — | — |
| 1977 | 522 | — | 32 | — | — |
| 1981 | 286 | — | — | — | — |
| 1982 | — | 315 | — | — | — |
| Cost | 4,391 | 83 | 407 | 8,036 | 714 |
| | 7,456 | 398 | 510 | 8,036 | 714 |

*Fig. 7.2    Analysis of fixed assets*
Courtesy: Midshires Building Society

Questions **1–4** are short-answer or multi-choice, and should take you about five minutes to complete.

Questions **5**, **6** and **7** test your knowledge of depreciation. Question **5** is an essay question on depreciation; questions **6** and **7** involve ledger accounts for depreciation and the disposal of assets. *Question 6 is fully answered in section F.*

Question **8** is on bad debts provision; it also involves ledger and final accounts work.

## Objective questions

**1** The current book value of an asset is its cost less . . . . . . to date.
(London Board Principles of Accounts O level, January 1983)

**2** Using the straight line method, the annual depreciation at 20% for a motor car which cost £2 000 now valued at £1 200 would be
A   £160
B   £240
C   £400
D   £800
(AEB Specimen Accounting O level Paper, 1980)

**3** Which one of the following would result from a decrease in the provision for bad and doubtful debts?
A   An increase in gross profit
B   A reduction in gross profit
C   An increase in net profit
D   A reduction in net profit
(AEB Specimen Accounting O level Paper, 1980)

**4** Given the following details:

| | |
|---|---:|
| Trade debtors, per trial balance | £10 000 |
| Provision for bad debts | £1 000 |
| Provision for discount allowed to debtors | 5% |

the amount shown as a current asset in the balance sheet is
A   £8 500
B   £8 550
C   £8 950
D   £9 000
(AEB Specimen Accounting O level Paper, 1980)

## Essay and computational questions

**5**
(a) 'Depreciation is a process of allocation, not of valuation'. Explain.
(10 marks)
(b) 'The diminishing balance method of depreciation reflects the cost of using an asset more accurately than does the straight line method'. Explain.

(10 marks)
(Total 20 marks)
(AAT Numeracy and Accounting, June 1984)

**6** Plant Ltd was established and started trading on 1 January 1980, and its purchases and disposals of fixed assets over the subsequent three years were as follows:

| Asset | Date of Purchase | Cost £ | Date of Disposal | Proceeds on Disposal £ |
|---|---|---|---|---|
| A | 1 January 1980 | 2 500 | — | — |
| B | 1 January 1980 | 1 250 | 1 January 1982 | 450 |
| C | 1 January 1982 | 3 500 | — | — |

*REQUIRED:*
(a) Prepare the following accounts as they would appear in the books of Plant Ltd for the years 1980, 1981 and 1982 on the assumption that the company charges depreciation of *20% per annum calculated on the straight-line basis*:
  (i) Fixed Assets at Cost Account
  (ii) Provision for Depreciation Account
  (iii) Disposal of Fixed Assets Account
(b) Show your calculation of the depreciation charge for the years 1980, 1981 and 1982 and the profit or loss on the disposal of asset B which would result from calculating depreciation at the rate of *30% per annum on the reducing balance basis.*
(c) Discuss the purpose of charging depreciation when preparing a set of accounts and indicate on what basis the choice of method should be made.

(30 marks)
(RSA II Accounting, June 1983)

**7** Brown is in business as a building contractor. At 1 May 1982 he had three lorries, details of which are as follows:

| Lorry registration number | Date purchased | Cost | Accumulated depreciation to date |
|---|---|---|---|
| | | £ | £ |
| BAB 1 | 1 July 1979 | 16 000 | 9 000 |
| CAB 2 | 1 January 1981 | 21 000 | 8 000 |
| DAB 3 | 1 April 1982 | 31 000 | 6 000 |

During the year to 30 April 1983, the following lorry transactions took place:
1. BAB 1 was sold on 31 July 1982 for £3 000 on cash terms. On 1 August 1982 Brown replaced it with a new lorry, registration number FAB 4 for which he paid £35 000 in cash.
2. On 15 December 1982, the new lorry (FAB 4) was involved in a major accident, and as a result was completely written off. Brown was able to agree a claim with his insurance company, and on 31 December 1982 he received £30 000 from the company. On 1 January 1983 he bought another new lorry (registration number HAB 6) for £41 000.

3    During March 1983, Brown decided to replace the lorry bought
      on 1 April 1982 (registration number DAB 3) with a new lorry. It
      was delivered on 1 April 1983 (registration number JAB 6). He
      agreed a purchase price of £26 000 for the new lorry, the terms of
      which were £20 000 in part exchange for the old lorry and the
      balance to be paid immediately in cash.

Notes:
(i)   Brown uses the straight-line method of depreciation based on
      year-end figures.
(ii)  The lorries are depreciated over a five-year period by which time
      they are assumed to have an exchange value of £1 000 each.
(iii  A full year's depreciation is charged in the year of acquisition, but
      no depreciation is charged if a lorry is bought and sold or
      otherwise disposed of within the same financial year.
(iv)  No depreciation is charged in the year of disposal.
(v)   Brown does not keep separate accounts for each lorry.

*REQUIRED:*
(a)   Write up the following accounts for the year to 30 April 1983:
      (i)   Lorries Account
      (ii)  Lorries Disposal Account
      (iii) Provision for Depreciation on Lorries Account.

                                                        (18 marks)
(b)   Show how the Lorries Account and the Provision for Depreci-
      ation Account would be presented in Brown's Balance Sheet as at
      30 April 1983.

                                                        (2 marks)
                                                  (Total 20 marks)
                                       (AAT Accounting, 2 June 1983)


**8**   On 31 December 1981 J. Brodie balanced his accounts at the end
of the financial year and found that his total debtors were £24 000.
Included in this amount were irrecoverable debts of £120 owing by
U. Wate, and £160 owing by V. Slow which J. Brodie wrote off.
     In addition he decided to make a provision for doubtful debts of
15% of the remaining debtors.
     In the following year ending 31 December 1982 debtors totalled
£20 000 and there were no bad debts, but J. Brodie decided to maintain
the provision for doubtful debts at 15% of current debtors.

*REQUIRED:*
To show for each of the years ended 31 December 1981 and 1982:
(a)   the provision for doubtful debts account;              (5)
(b)   the appropriate entries in the Profit and Loss Accounts   (3)
(c)   the Balance Sheet entries on each of the above dates      (5)
                                                        (13 marks)
      (Cambridge Board Principles of Accounts O level, Summer 1983)

Questions **1** and **2** are based on depreciation. The gap for question 1 is 'depreciation': alternative (C) is correct in question 2 (20% of £2 000: the straight-line method).

Questions **3** and **4** involve bad debts provision. The correct alternative in question 3 is (C); a decrease in the provision is added to gross profit and increases net profit. For question 4, the £1 000 provision is deducted, and the 5% is deducted from the net figure; (B) is therefore the correct alternative.

**5**

(a)  Your answer should refer to the nature of fixed assets; because they last in the business for more than one accounting period and because they lose value (for a variety of reasons), the business has to spread this cost fairly over the expected life of the assets. This relates to the accruals (matching) concept, where a business attempts to *allocate* costs to the period to which they refer.

To comment on the 'valuation' reference in the question, you could mention that, since fixed assets are not bought with the object of resale, we are not primarily concerned with their market value (although a true and fair view should be borne in mind, e.g. in the balance sheet valuation of the fixed assets).

(b)  Your answer should describe briefly the diminishing (i.e. reducing) balance and straight-line methods. You need to explain – and illustrate, with a simple numerical example – that, with the reducing balance method, the amount of depreciation reduces each year, which gives a closer approximation to the true position (heavier depreciation in the earlier years when the asset is new). Also, as the depreciation cost reduces, maintenance/repair cost increases (as the asset ages); thus, with reducing balance, a more even *total* cost may result.

**7**

(a)  (i)

*Lorries account*

| | | £ | | | £ |
|---|---|---|---|---|---|
| 1/5/82 | Balance b/d | 68 000 | 31/7/82 | Disposal a/c (BAB) | 16 000 |
| 1/8/82 | Bank (FAB) | 35 000 | 15/12/82 | Disposal a/c (FAB) | 35 000 |
| 1/1/83 | Bank (HAB) | 41 000 | 1/4/83 | Disposal a/c (DAB) | 31 000 |
| 1/4/83 | Bank (JAB) | 6 000 | 30/4/83 | Balance c/d | 88 000 |
| | Disposal a/c (JAB) | 20 000 | | | |
| | | 170 000 | | | 170 000 |

| | | £ |
|---|---|---|
| 1/5/83 | Balance b/d | 88 000 |

Balance represents CAB £21 000 + HAB £41 000 + JAB £26 000

(ii)

*Disposal (Lorries) account*

|  |  | £ |  |  | £ |
|---|---|---|---|---|---|
| 31/7/82 | Lorries a/c (BAB) | 16 000 | 31/7/82 | Depreciation (BAB) | 9 000 |
| 15/12/82 | Lorries a/c (FAB) | 35 000 |  | Bank (BAB) | 3 000 |
| 1/4/83 | Lorries a/c (DAB) | 31 000 | 31/12/82 | Bank (FAB) | 30 000 |
|  |  |  | 1/4/83 | Depreciation (DAB) | 6 000 |
|  |  |  |  | Lorries a/c (DAB) | 20 000 |
|  |  |  | 30/4/83 | Profit & Loss a/c | 14 000 |
|  |  | 82 000 |  |  | 82 000 |

Depreciation on BAB = £3 000 per annum × 3 years; on FAB = nil (note (iii)); on DAB = 1 year at £6 000.
Loss on sale (Dr balance) £14 000 to profit & loss.

(iii)

*Depreciation Provision (Lorries) account*

|  |  | £ |  |  | £ |
|---|---|---|---|---|---|
| 31/7/82 | Disposal a/c (BAB) | 9 000 | 1/5/82 | Balance b/d | 23 000 |
| 1/4/83 | Disposal a/c (DAB) | 6 000 | 30/4/83 | P & L a/c | 17 000 |
| 30/4/83 | Balance c/d | 25 000 |  |  |  |
|  |  | 40 000 |  |  | 40 000 |
|  |  |  | 1/5/83 | Balance b/d | 25 000 |

Opening balance = £9 000 BAB (3 years × £3 000) + £8 000 CAB (2 × £4 000) + £6 000 DAB (1 year).
Depreciation to profit & loss = £4 000 CAB + £8 000 HAB + £5 000 JAB.
Closing balance = £12 000 CAB (3 years × £4 000) + £8 000 HAB (1 year) + £5 000 JAB (1 year).

(b)   Balance Sheet: Fixed assets = £88 000 lorries (cost)
                        − £25 000 depreciation

                        £63 000 net

**8**

(a)

*Provision for Doubtful Debts account*

| 1982 | | £ | 1982 | | £ |
|---|---|---|---|---|---|
| 31 Dec | Balance c/d | 3 558 | 31 Dec | Profit & Loss | 3 558 |
| | | | | | |
| 1982 | | | 1982 | | |
| 31 Dec | Profit & Loss | 558 | 1 Jan | Balance b/d | 3 558 |
| | Balance c/d | 3 000 | | | |
| | | 3 558 | | | 3 558 |

1981 provision based on £23 720 (£24 000 less the two bad debts).
1982 provision is £3 000; reduced by £558.

(b) Profit & Loss 1981 shows Provision for Doubtful Debts £3 558 Dr.
Profit & Loss 1982 shows Reduction in Provision £558 Cr.

(c) Balance Sheets:

| | 1981 | 1982 |
|---|---|---|
| Debtors | 23 720 | 20 000 |
| less Provision | 3 558 | 3 000 |
| | 20 162 | 17 000 |

---

**F. A TUTOR'S ANSWER**

Question **6** is a good example of a typical examination question involving the disposal of assets. Here is the suggested answer:

(a)

*Fixed Assets account*

| 1980 | | £ | 1980 | | £ |
|---|---|---|---|---|---|
| 1 Jan | Bank (A) | 2 500 | 31 Dec | Balance c/d | 3 750 |
| | Bank (B) | 1 250 | | | |
| | | 3 750 | | | 3 750 |
| | | | | | |
| 1981 | | | 1981 | | |
| 1 Jan | Balance b/d | 3 750 | 31 Dec | Balance c/d | 3 750 |
| | | 3 750 | | | 3 750 |
| | | | | | |
| 1982 | | | 1982 | | |
| 1 Jan | Balance b/d | 3 750 | 1 Jan | Assets disposal (B) | 1 250 |
| | Bank (C) | 3 500 | 31 Dec. | Balance c/d | 6 000 |
| | | 7 250 | | | 7 250 |
| | | | | | |
| 1983 | | | | | |
| 1 Jan | Balance b/d | 6 000 | | | |

## Provision for Depreciation account

| 1980 | | £ | 1980 | | £ |
|---|---|---|---|---|---|
| 31 Dec | Balance c/d | 750 | 31 Dec | Profit and loss | 750 |
| 1981 | | | 1981 | | |
| 31 Dec | Balance c/d | 1 500 | 1 Jan | Balance b/d | 750 |
| | | | 31 Dec | Profit and loss | 750 |
| | | 1 500 | | | 1 500 |
| 1982 | | | 1982 | | |
| 1 Jan | Assets disposal (B) | 500 | 1 Jan | Balance b/d | 1 500 |
| 31 Dec | Balance c/d | 2 200 | 31 Dec | Profit and Loss | 1 200 |
| | | 2 700 | | | 2 700 |
| | | | 1983 | | |
| | | | 1 Jan | Balance b/d | 2 200 |

## Assets Disposal account

| 1982 | | £ | | | £ |
|---|---|---|---|---|---|
| 1 Jan | Fixed assets | 1 250 | 1 Jan | Depreciation | 500 |
| | | | | Bank | 450 |
| | | | 31 Dec | Profit and loss | 300 |
| | | 1 250 | | | 1 250 |

**Workings**

(1) Fixed assets debited at cost, and credited at cost.
Closing balance = asset A (£2 500) plus asset C (£3 500).

(2) Depreciation:
  1980: 20% A + 20% B: £500 + £250 = £750
  1981: same as 1980 (straight-line method, fixed amount charged).
  1982: B disposed of, so remove (Dr) the depreciation to date (£250 + £250).
  Depreciation for year = 20% A (£500) plus 20% C (£700).
  Balance: A = 3 years at 20% = £1 500
  C = 1 year at 20% = £  700

  £2 200

(3) In the disposal account, the asset is debited at cost and depreciation credited. Bank receipt credited (a debit in the bank account). There is a balance of £300; amount received on sale is £300 less than book value, so a loss on sale made. This is transferred to the debit side of profit and loss.

(b) *Depreciation charge*:

|  |  | £ |
|---|---|---:|
| 1980: 30% of £3 750 | | = 1 125.00 |
| 1981: 30% of £2 625 (£3 750 − £1 125) | | = 787.50 |

1982: 30% of asset A:

|  | £ |
|---|---:|
| | 2 500 |
| − | 750 (1980 charge) |
| | 1 750 |
| − | 525 (1981 charge) |
| | 1 225 net book value |

| | |
|---|---:|
| 30% of net book value | = £367.50 |
| 30% of asset C £3 500 | = £1 050.00 |
| | = 1 417.50 |

*Disposal of asset B:*

|  |  | £ |
|---|---|---:|
| 1980 = 30% of £1 250 | | = 375.00 |
| 1981 = 30% of £875 (£1 250–£375) | | = 262.50 |
| | | 637.50 |

Net book value of B = £1 250–£637.50 = £612.50
Received on sale of B: £450

Loss on sale:  £612.50 net book value
− £450.00 proceeds of sale

£162.50 LOSS ON SALE

(c) The purpose of providing for depreciation is to ensure that the cost of owning fixed assets is spread over the useful life of the assets. It would be unfair to charge against one year's profits the total cost associated with the purchase of a fixed asset in that year; this cost (arising from, for example, physical deterioration) should be apportioned over the expected life of the asset. The choice of method may be made on the basis of current policy (following the Consistency concept). The chosen method should be one which provides a fair estimate of the assets' value.

---

**G.  A STEP FURTHER**

All the major accountancy textbooks will contain chapters which explain and illustrate depreciation and bad debt provisions. Here is a selection:

---

**Depreciation provision and disposal of assets**

Garbutt, *Carter's Advanced Accounts* (7th edn) (Pitman). Ch. 06.

Whitehead, *Bookkeeping Made Simple* ('Made Simple' series). Ch. 14.

Whitehead, *Success in Principles of Accounting* (John Murray). Units 12 and 22.

**Provision for bad debts**

Castle and Owens, *Principles of Accounts* (7th edn) (M & E). Ch. 12.

Wood, *Business Accounting 1* (4th edn) (Longman). Ch 21.

Wood, *Bookkeeping and Accounts* (Longman). Ch. 20.

**Chapter 8**

# Adjustments in accounts (2): Prepayments and Accruals

**A. GETTING STARTED**

Expenses and revenues may be *prepaid*: at the end of its financial period, a business may have paid for something (or received in connection with a revenue) in advance of 'using up' that item. Alternatively, expenses and revenues may be *accrued*: at the end of its financial year, the business could have outstanding debts, either owed to it (accrued revenue) or owed by it (accrued expense).

Questions are often set on prepayments or accruals. They are mainly computational; essay type questions are not commonly found, although you may be asked to explain the nature of the accruals concept (as in the sample questions of Chapter 3) or to give an example of how it operates.

The computational questions usually fall into one of two categories:

1. First, you are given details of ledger accounts, and from these details you are expected to construct the accounts and transfer the correct amounts to the profit and loss account.

2. Second, you may be given a trial balance with a supporting series of notes. From this information, you have to construct final accounts, using the notes to adjust the relevant figures.

What basic knowledge do you need? A good understanding of double entry procedures is required, including balancing ledger accounts, as well as an appreciation of the nature of the accruals concept. In addition, you should be familiar with the basic layout and structure of simple (sole trader) final accounts.

## B. ESSENTIAL PRINCIPLES

### LEDGER ACCOUNTS: ACCRUED ITEMS

Where a question mentions *accrued* or *in arrears*, it is referring to something owed: this something may be *owed to* the business (accrued revenue) or *owed by* the business (accrued expense).

Here are examples of how the ledger accounts are constructed. These examples are similar to the type of ledger account questions that are often set on this topic.

A firm's financial year runs from January 1 to December 31. It pays rates on its premises at £500 per quarter, and sublets part of its premises for £100 per quarter. Rates during the year were paid on March 29, July 2 and September 30.

Rent from subletting was received on April 2, July 3 and September 28.

The rates account is a typical expense account: entries are debited (credit the cash book). The rent receivable account is a revenue account, where the entries will be credited (and the cash book debited). As things stand at the end of December – the end of the firm's financial year – we have:

| Rates account | | | | Rent receivable account | | |
|---|---|---|---|---|---|---|
| | £ | £ | | £ | | £ |
| Mar 29 Bank | 500 | | | | Apr 2 Bank | 100 |
| July 2 Bank | 500 | | | | July 3 Bank | 100 |
| Sep 30 Bank | 500 | | | | Sep 28 Bank | 100 |

STEP 1: Record what *has* been paid or received.

A question may require the appropriate amounts to be transferred to the profit and loss account. The accruals concept helps us here: we have to show the true value or cost, rather than show only the amount of money received or paid. We transfer to the profit and loss account the full yearly cost of rates and the full yearly value of rent receivable; that is, we transfer those amounts that should have been paid or received in the year.

| Rates account | | | | | Rent receivable account | | | |
|---|---|---|---|---|---|---|---|---|
| | £ | | £ | | | £ | | £ |
| Mar 29 | | Dec 31 | | | Dec 31 | | April 2 | |
| Bank | 500 | P&L | 2000 | | P&L | 400 | Bank | 100 |
| July 2 | | | | | | | July 3 | |
| Bank | 500 | | | | | | Bank | 100 |
| Sept 30 | | | | | | | Sept 28 | |
| Bank | 500 | | | | | | Bank | 100 |

81

STEP 2: Transfer to P & L what *should* have been paid or received.

Both accounts contain a balance which has to be brought down to the next accounting period. Closing the accounts, we have:

*Rates account*

| | | £ | | | £ |
|---|---|---|---|---|---|
| 29 March | Bank | 500 | 31 Dec. P & L | | 2 000 |
| 2 July | Bank | 500 | | | |
| 30 Sept | Bank | 500 | | | |
| 31 Dec | Balance c/d | 500 | | | |
| | | 2 000 | | | 2 000 |
| | | | 1 Jan Balance b/d | | 500 |

*Rent receivable account*

| | | £ | | | £ |
|---|---|---|---|---|---|
| 31 Dec P & L | | 400 | 2 April | Bank | 100 |
| | | | 3 July | Bank | 100 |
| | | | 28 Sept | Bank | 100 |
| | | | 31 Dec | Balance c/d | 100 |
| | | 400 | | | 400 |
| 1 Jan Balance b/d | | 100 | | | |

STEP 3: Calculating and displaying the balances.

On checking the balances, we see that the rates account is a credit balance: credit balances are either revenues or liabilities. This balance represents the value of the unpaid expense, and is therefore treated as a current liability. The rent receivable account has a debit balance; this represents an amount owed to the business, an accrued revenue, and is treated as a current asset.

In the balance sheet, current liabilities will contain 'Accrued Expenses £500' and current assets will contain 'Accrued Revenue £100'. The profit and loss acount will contain 'Rates £2 000' in its list of expenses, and 'Rent receivable £400' as a revenue which is added to gross profit on its credit side.

---

**LEDGER ACCOUNTS: PREPAID ITEMS**

Questions may also require you to account for *prepayments*, or *payments made in advance*. The question will usually involve a prepaid expense, as shown below:

A business whose financial year runs from 1 January to 31 December takes out an insurance policy on 1 March. The yearly premium, paid on 1 March, is £180.

The insurance account will be debited, and the cash book credited, with the payment of the premium in March. When the business comes to balance its accounts at the end of December, that payment of £180 represents the value of insurance cover through to the end of the following February. There is a prepayment represented here.

At the end of December, the business is still owed two months' value of insurance. It has paid for something which it has not fully received. The cost of insurance for the business to record in this financial year's profit and loss account is therefore, not the full £180, but ten months' 'worth'.

**Constructing the account**

If the annual cost of the premium is £180, the monthly cost will be £15 (£180 ÷ 12). By the end of December, the business has used up ten months of cover at £15 per month. The cost this year is £150, and £30 (two months at £15 per month) has been paid in advance for the coming year. The account is constructed to show this prepayment in the same way that the rates and rent receivable accounts were constructed earlier.

STEP 1:    record what has been paid (Dr £180 payment on 1 March).
STEP 2:    transfer to P&L what should have been paid, i.e. the true cost (Cr £150, ten months' cost of insurance).
STEP 3:    calculate and display the balance (Dr balance of £30, initially recorded on the Cr side).

The completed insurance account looks like this:

*Insurance account*

|  |  | £ |  |  | £ |
|---|---|---|---|---|---|
| 1 March | Bank | 180 | 31 Dec | Profit and Loss | 150 |
|  |  |  | 31 Dec | Balance c/d | 30 |
|  |  | 180 |  |  | 180 |
| 1 Jan | Balance b/d | 30 |  |  |  |

A debit balance is shown; prepaid expenses are an asset to the business, because the business is owed the value of the prepayment.

Prepaid revenue, however, would be treated as a liability. The business has received value (income) in advance. The entries to record prepaid revenue would again follow the same logic: the revenue account is credited with the amounts received, the true value for the year is transferred out (debited) to the profit and loss account, and the balance (a credit balance) is calculated and brought down.

In the balance sheet, prepaid expenses are shown alongside accrued revenues as current assets; the example above would show 'Prepaid Expenses £30'. Prepaid revenues will be shown as current liabilities, together with any accrued expenses.

## FINAL ACCOUNTS

As far as prepayments or accruals are concerned, the accruals (or matching) concept will again enable us to make correct adjustments. A series of year-end notes is given in the question, and these notes will include a list of prepaid or accrued items. The task is to show the true amounts for the year in question in the profit and loss account, and also to record the prepayments or accruals in the balance sheet.

## The balance sheet

This chapter has already outlined how prepaid and accrued items are shown in the balance sheet. Here is a summary:

| Current Assets | Current Liabilities |
|---|---|
| Prepaid expenses | Accrued expenses |
| Accrued revenues | Prepaid revenues |

## The profit and loss account

The profit and loss items need adjusting on the basis of the information given in the notes. If a prepaid item exists at the end of the year and is included in the total for the expense or revenue, it must be deducted from that total because it applies to next year's final accounts. If there is an accrued item, this refers to income or expenditure relating to this period, but which has not involved cash receipts or payments. Because the accrual applies to this year, it must be added to the expense or revenue.

For closing prepaid and accrued items, the rule is:

LESS PREPAID

ADD ACCRUED

## Opening prepayments and accruals

An examiner may set a question which tests your knowledge of how to deal with opening prepayments or accruals.

1. An opening prepaid balance refers to this accounting period: it was paid last period 'in advance' for this period. It must therefore be included in this period's figures.
2. An opening accrued balance refers to the last accounting period. At the end of the last period, it was owed for that period and therefore must not be included in this period's calculations.

## C. USEFUL APPLIED MATERIALS

Although we have not yet studied the accounts of limited companies, their published accounts serve to illustrate the range and the importance of accrued and prepaid items. These accounts, which certain large companies have to publish, are available from the companies themselves; back copies of the accounts are often kept in college or other libraries.

Although most companies attempt to keep these accounts as simple and straightforward as possible, by their very nature the accounts remain rather complex. For the moment, we shall select part of the 'Notes to the Accounts' from a set of published accounts. This extract illustrates the various prepayments which are included under the heading 'Debtors'. Although **Figure 8.1** shows debtors as the major item, it is interesting to note the value of 'Prepayments and accrued income'.

### 13 Debtors

|  | 1984 £m | 1983 £m |
|---|---|---|
| Falling due within one year: |  |  |
| Trade debtors | **87·8** | 76·4 |
| Amounts owed by group companies | — | — |
| Amounts owed by related companies | **1·7** | 2·5 |
| Other debtors | **8·4** | 6·6 |
| Prepayments and accrued income | **11·9** | 8·8 |
|  | **109·8** | 94·3 |
| Debtors falling due after more than one year: |  |  |
| Deferred taxation recoverable: |  |  |
| Advance corporation tax | — | 9·3 |
| Short term timing differences | — | 1·9 |
| Other debtors | **2·4** | 2·0 |
|  | **2·4** | 13·2 |
|  | **112·2** | 107·5 |

*Fig. 8.1   Analysis of balance sheet 'Debtors'*
Courtesy: The Boots Company PLC

## D.   RECENT EXAMINATION QUESTIONS

There are five questions in this section. Question **1** is descriptive, testing your ability to explain about prepayments and accruals. Questions **2–5** are computational.

Questions **2** and **3** concentrate on the construction of ledger accounts and require a series of adjustments to be made for prepayments and accruals.

Questions **4** and **5** are final accounts questions. Question **4** is relatively straightforward, although you are required to make a number of adjustments for prepayments or accruals. *Question 5 is more difficult, and the answer is provided in detail in section F, 'A tutor's answer'.*

**Essay and computational questions**

**1**

(a)   Explain, using figures, what is meant by the terms
   (i)   accrued expense:
   (ii)   prepaid expense.

(4 marks)

(b) Using your figures from part (a), say how the relevant ledger accounts would be adjusted at period end for accrued and prepaid expenses.

(4 marks)

(c) Explain the effect and the significance on the balance sheet of accounting for
(i) accrued expenses;
(ii) prepaid expenses.

(7 marks)
(AEB Accounting O level, June 1984)

**2**

(i) L. George rents his premises at an annual rental of £1 200. On 1 June 1983 George had paid his rent up to the end of July, and during the year ended 31 May 1984 he made the following payments for rent, by cheque:

| | |
|---|---|
| 1 Aug | £300 |
| 5 Nov. | £300 |
| 1 Feb | £300 |
| 1 June | £400 |

(ii) George sublets part of these premises to S. Broke at a rent of £480 per annum, and on 1 June 1983 Broke's rent was one month in arrears. During the year ended 31 May 1984 George received the following amounts in cash from Broke:

| | |
|---|---|
| 25 July | £40 |
| 8 Aug | £120 |
| 4 Dec | £150 |
| 9 April | £60 |

(iii) On 1 June 1983 George owed the Electricity Board £74 for electricity supplies up to that date; during the year he made the following payments by cheque:

| | |
|---|---|
| 1 June | £74 |
| 10 Sept | £82 |
| 5 Dec | £104 |
| 7 April | £81 |

On 31 May 1984 there was a balance outstanding on the electricity account of £96.

*REQUIRED:*
(a) To write up George's rent payable account, rent receivable account, and electricity account for the year ended 31 May 1984 showing clearly the amounts to be transferred to the Profit and Loss Account in each case.

(b) To show how the balances brought down would appear in the Balance Sheet on 31 May 1984.

(24 marks)<br>(RSA I Bookkeeping, June 1984)

**3**

(a) Mr A. Breviate has the following account in his ledger:

*Rent and Rates*

| 1983 | | £ | 1982 | | £ |
|---|---|---|---|---|---|
| 31 Mar | Cash – Rent | 9 600 | 1 Apr | Balance b/f | 2 200 |
| | Rates | 2 400 | 1983 | | |
| | | | 31 Mar | Cash from sub-tenant | 800 |
| | Balance c/f | 1 200 | | P&L a/c | 10 200 |
| | | 13 200 | | | 13 200 |

Upon enquiry you find that at the beginning of the year Breviate owed £2 400 rent in respect of the previous quarter, had prepaid rates to the extent of £600 and had received £400 in advance from a sub-tenant.

At the end of his financial year Breviate owed £2 400 for rent and had paid rates in advance amounting to £800. The sub-tenant owed £400 in respect of the previous quarter.

During the year Breviate paid £9 600 in respect of rent and £2 400 in respect of rates.

*REQUIRED:*
Prepare separate accounts for rent payable, rent receivable and rates showing clearly the opening and closing balances and the transfers to Profit and Loss Account.

(15 marks)

(b) At the beginning of his financial year Mr Breviate had a stock of stationery valued at £2 200, and at the end of the year £1 670. At the beginning of the year he owed £600 for stationery, paid £6 100 to suppliers of stationery during the year, and owed £520 at the end of the year.

*REQUIRED:*
Prepare Mr Breviate's Stationery Account for the year.

(5 marks)<br>(Total 20 marks)<br>(AAT Numeracy and Accounting, December 1983)

**4** The following trial balance was extracted from the books of Brian Williams at the close of business on 31 December 1983.

|  | Dr £ | Cr £ |
|---|---|---|
| Capital (1 January 1983) | | 183 296 |
| Purchases | 46 180 | |
| Sales | | 98 408 |
| Purchase returns | | 280 |
| Sales returns | 808 | |
| Discount allowed | 910 | |
| Discount received | | 704 |
| Wages and salaries | 31 100 | |
| Rates | 2 450 | |
| Insurance | 1 780 | |
| General expenses | 4 060 | |
| Trade debtors | 18 400 | |
| Trade creditors | | 16 120 |
| Bank balance | 4 020 | |
| Stock in trade (1 January 1983) | 6 100 | |
| Land and buildings | 85 000 | |
| Plant and machinery | 61 500 | |
| Motor vehicles | 28 100 | |
| Drawings | 8 400 | |
| | 298 808 | 298 808 |

Notes:
(a)  Stock in trade on 31 December 1983 was valued at £7 420.
(b)  Rates paid in advance on 31 December 1983 amounted to £350.
(c)  An electricity bill of £124 was outstanding on 31 December 1983 (analysed under General Expenses).

*REQUIRED:*
From the information given you are to prepare the Trading and Profit and Loss Account for Brian Williams for the year ended 31 December 1983, together with a Balance Sheet as at that date.

(26 marks)
(RSA I Bookkeeping, February 1984)

5   Balances appearing in Alan Trader's ledger at 31 May 1983 were:

|  | £ |
|---|---|
| Drawings | 10 400 |
| Bank overdraft | 8 320 |
| Cash in hand | 351 |
| Fixtures and fittings, cost | 8 400 |
| Warehouse and office equipment, cost | 13 200 |
| Depreciation provisions: | |
|     Fixtures and fittings | 1 680 |
|     Warehouse and office equipment | 3 300 |
| Bad debts | 260 |
| Advertising | 3 718 |
| Loan from finance company | 10 000 |

| | |
|---|---:|
| Purchases | 100 952 |
| Sales | 195 610 |
| Loan interest | 1 125 |
| Returns inwards | 1 560 |
| Office expenses | 5 434 |
| Delivery expenses | 8 320 |
| Wages and salaries | 57 218 |
| Stock, 1 June 1982 | 26 122 |
| Debtors | 10 140 |
| Creditors | 8 290 |
| Capital | ? |

The following additional information as at 31 May 1983 is relevant:
(i)   Stock was valued at £31 148.
(ii)  Wages owing £1 794.
(iii) The Debtors figure includes an amount of £280 which is not expected to be recovered.
(iv)  The Loan from Finance Company attracts interest at 15% p.a., and one quarter's interest is owing.
(v)   Alan Trader had withdrawn goods for his personal use amounting to £1 800.
(vi)  Depreciation is to be provided using the diminishing balance rates of 20% for Fixtures and Fittings and 25% for Warehouse and Office Equipment.
(vii) Included in Wages and Salaries is an amount of £540 paid to employees for repairing the roof of Trader's private residence.

*REQUIRED:*
(a)   A Trading and Profit and Loss Account for the year.

(14 marks)

(b)   Alan Trader's Capital Account.

(6 marks)
(Total 20 marks)
(AAT Numeracy and Accounting, December 1983)

---

**E.   OUTLINE ANSWERS**

**1**

(a)   (i) and (ii): Your answer should include illustrations of expenses (and not revenues). It should state that accrued is owed by the firm (at the end of the accounting period) and that prepaid is paid in advance, for part of next accounting period. Appropriate numerical illustrations should be given.

(b)   Your answer should show (or state) that: accrued, Dr total (paid for expense) is less than Cr total (transfer to P&L), resulting in a Cr balance on the account: prepaid, Dr (payment) total is greater than Cr total (transfer to P&L), leaving a debit balance on the account. Balances b/d; accrued = current liability, prepaid = current asset.

(c) Effect on balance sheet: accrued shown as current liability (increases total current liabilities); prepaid shown as current asset (increases total current assets).

Significance: shows the accurate position (accruals concept); affects the working capital.

**2**

(a)

### Rent Payable account

| | | £ | | | £ |
|---|---|---|---|---|---|
| 1/6/83 | Balance b/d | 200 | 31/5/84 Profit and | | 1 200 |
| 1/8/83 | Bank | 300 | | Loss a/c | |
| 5/11/83 | Bank | 300 | | | |
| 1/2/84 | Bank | 300 | | | |
| 31/5/84 | Balance c/d | 100 | | | |
| | | 1 200 | | | 1 200 |
| 1/6/84 | Bank | 400 | 1/6/84 | Balance b/d | 100 |

Opening Dr balance (prepaid expense, 2 months at £100 per month). Record payments on Dr side (Cr Cash Book); transfer to P&L the *true cost* of the year's rent. Closing Cr balance represents 1 month's rent owed (check: 2 months prepaid + 9 months paid during year = 11 months; 1 month still owed). Bring down the balance; record the June 1 payment on the Dr side.

The rent receivable a/c is a revenue a/c. An opening accrued £40 balance (Dr, as an asset; it is owed to L. George). Credit the payments from S. Broke (Dr the Cash Book); transfer to profit and loss the true value of rent receivable. Closing balance (Dr) brought down.

### Rent Receivable account

| | | £ | | | £ |
|---|---|---|---|---|---|
| 1/6/83 | Balance b/d | 40 | 25/7/83 | Bank | 40 |
| 31/5/84 | Profit and Loss | 480 | 18/8/83 | Bank | 120 |
| | | | 4/12/83 | Bank | 150 |
| | | | 9/4/84 | Bank | 60 |
| | | | 31/5/84 | Balance c/d | 150 |
| | | 520 | | | 520 |
| 1/6/84 | Balance b/d | 150 | | | |

Electricity: opening Cr balance (accrued expense = liability); Dr the payments, and record the closing Cr balance initially on the Dr side. The difference between the 2 sides represents the true cost of electricity, transferred to profit and loss.

### Electricity account

| | | £ | | | £ |
|---|---|---|---|---|---|
| 1/6/83 | Bank | 74 | 1/6/83 | Balance b/d | 74 |
| 10/9/83 | Bank | 82 | 31/5/84 | Profit & Loss a/c | 363 |
| 5/12/83 | Bank | 104 | | | |
| 7/4/84 | Bank | 81 | | | |
| 31/5/84 | Balance c/d | 96 | | | |
| | | 437 | | | 437 |
| | | | 1/6/84 | Balance b/d | 96 |

(b) Balance Sheet will show accrued revenue £150 as a current asset, and accrued expenses £100 + £96 as current liabilities.

**3**

(a) Rent payable: opening Cr balance (accrued); Dr the amount paid; enter the closing accrued (Cr) balance on the Dr side. Difference is transferred to profit and loss.
Rent receivable: opening prepayment (revenue) is a liability (Cr balance); Cr cash from sub-tenant; closing accrual is an asset (owed to Breviate; a Dr balance, shown initially on the Cr side). Transfer the difference to P&L.
Rates: opening prepayment is a Dr balance; also Dr cash paid; closing balance is an asset (Dr) as prepaid expense, shown first on the Cr side. Transfer the difference to profit and loss.

*Rent payable*

| | £ | | £ |
|---|---|---|---|
| | 9 600 | b/d | 2 400 |
| c/d | 2 400 | P&L | 9 600 |
| | 12 000 | | 12 000 |
| | | b/d | 2 400 |

*Rent receivable*

| | £ | | £ |
|---|---|---|---|
| P&L | 1 600 | b/d | 400 |
| | | | 800 |
| | | c/d | 400 |
| | 1 600 | | 1 600 |
| b/d | 400 | | |

*Rates*

| | £ | | £ |
|---|---|---|---|
| b/d | 600 | P&L | 2 200 |
| | 2 400 | c/d | 800 |
| | 3 000 | | 3 000 |
| b/d | 800 | | |

(b)
### Stationery account

| | | £ | | | £ |
|---|---|---|---|---|---|
| 1/4/82 | Balance b/d | 2 200 | 1/4/82 | Accrued b/d | 600 |
| 1982/83 | Bank | 6 100 | 31/3/83 | Stock c/d | 1 670 |
| 31/3/83 | Accrued c/d | 520 | | Profit & Loss | 6 550 |
| | | 8 820 | | | 8 820 |
| 1/4/83 | Stock b/d | 1 670 | 1/4/83 | Accrued b/d | 520 |

Stock an asset balance; accrued a liability. Enter all items (closing balances on the wrong side above the totals), calculate the difference which represents the amount to be transferred to profit and loss.

**4**                                                 **Brian Williams**

*Trading and Profit and Loss accounts for the year to 31 December 1983*

|  |  | £ |  |  | £ |
|---|---|---|---|---|---|
| Opening stock | | 6 100 | Sales | | 98 408 |
| Purchases | 46 180 | | Less returns | | 808 |
| Less returns | 280 | 45 900 | | | |
| | | | | | 97 600 |
| | | 52 000 | | | |
| Less closing stock | | 7 420 | | | |
| Cost of goods sold | | 44 580 | | | |
| Gross profit c/d | | 53 020 | | | |
| | | 97 600 | | | 97 600 |
| Discount allowed | | 910 | Gross profit b/d | | 53 020 |
| Wages and salaries | | 31 100 | Discount received | | 704 |
| Rates (2 450 − 350) | | 2 100 | | | |
| Insurance | | 1 780 | | | |
| General expenses ( + 124) | | 4 184 | | | |
| Net Profit | | 13 650 | | | |
| | | 53 724 | | | 53 724 |

**Brian Williams**

*Balance Sheet at 31 December 1983*

|  | £ | £ |  | £ | £ |
|---|---|---|---|---|---|
| *Fixed Assets:* | | | *Capital:* | | |
| Land and buildings | | 85 000 | Opening balance | | 183 296 |
| Plant and machinery | | 61 500 | Net profit | | 13 650 |
| Motor vehicles | | 28 100 | | | 196 946 |
| | | 174 600 | Less drawings | | 8 400 |
| *Current Assets:* | | | | | 188 546 |
| Stock | 7 420 | | *Current Liabilities:* | | |
| Debtors | 18 400 | | Creditors | 16 120 | |
| Prepaid expense | 350 | | Accrued expense | 124 | |
| Bank | 4 020 | 30 190 | | | 16 244 |
| | | 204 790 | | | 204 790 |

**F. A TUTOR'S ANSWER**

Question **5** is a final accounts question, concentrating on the Trading and Profit and Loss accounts, while part (b) tests your knowledge of the workings of the capital account.

(a)
**A. Trader**

*Trading and Profit and Loss accounts for the year
to 31 May 1983*

| | £ | £ | | £ |
|---|---|---|---|---|
| Opening stock | | 26 122 | Sales | 195 610 |
| Purchases | 100 952 | | Less returns inwards | 1 560 |
| Less drawings | 1 800 | 99 152 | | 194 050 |
| | | 125 274 | | |
| Less closing stock | | 31 148 | | |
| Cost of sales | | 94 126 | | |
| Gross profit c/d | | 99 924 | | |
| | | 194 050 | | 194 050 |
| Depreciation: Fixtures | | 1 344 | Gross profit b/d | 99 924 |
| Equipment | | 2 475 | | |
| Bad debts (260 + 280) | | 540 | | |
| Advertising | | 3 718 | | |
| Loan interest | 1 125 | | | |
| Add accrued | 375 | 1 500 | | |
| Office expenses | | 5 434 | | |
| Delivery expenses | | 8 320 | | |
| Wages and salaries | 57 218 | | | |
| Add accrued | 1 794 | | | |
| | 59 012 | | | |
| Less drawings | 540 | 58 472 | | |
| Net profit | | 18 121 | | |
| | | 99 924 | | 99 924 |

**Workings for depreciation**

| | Fixtures | Equipment |
|---|---|---|
| Cost | 8 400 | 13 200 |
| − Depreciation to date | 1 680 | 3 300 |
| Written down value | 6 720 | 9 900 |
| Depreciation: | | |
| 20% = | 1 344 | |
| 25% = | | 2 475 |

(b) **A. Trader**

*Capital account*

| 1983 | | £ | 1982 | | £ |
|------|------|------|------|------|------|
| 31 May | Drawings | 12 740 | 1 June | Balance b/d | 20 000 |
| | Balance c/d | 25 381 | 1983 | Net profit | 18 121 |
| | | 38 121 | | | 38 121 |

**Workings**

1. Drawings = £10 400 from trial balance
   + £1 800 goods own use
   + £540 value of work

   £12 740

2. Opening balance of capital obtained from trial balance: debit balances less credit balances.

   | | | £ |
   |------|------|------|
   | Credit balances are: | Overdraft | 8 320 |
   | | Depreciation | 1 680 |
   | | Depreciation | 3 300 |
   | | Loan | 10 000 |
   | | Sales | 195 610 |
   | | Creditors | 8 290 |
   | | | 227 200 |

   Debit balances total £247 200. Difference between the totals is £20 000.

## G. A STEP FURTHER

The adjustments required for prepayments or accruals are often extremely difficult to follow, particularly in the ledger accounts. It will help if you read the appropriate chapters in textbooks which describe both the reasons behind the adjustments and the steps involved in making these adjustments.

The following list may give you some guidance:

Harrison, *Stage One Financial Accounting* (Northwick). Ch. 9.

Whitehead, *Bookkeeping Made Simple* ('Made Simple' series). Ch. 22.

Whitehead, *Success in Principles of Accounting* (John Murray). Unit 26.

Wood, *Business Accounting 1* (4th edn) (Longman). Ch. 22.

Wood, *Bookkeeping and Accounts* (Longman). Ch. 21.

# Chapter 9

# Correction of errors and the suspense account

## A. GETTING STARTED

Questions which involve the correction of errors are commonly found in examinations. These questions tend to fall into one of the three following categories:

1.  Essay questions which test your understanding of the function and purpose of the trial balance, and of the nature of errors which may or may not affect it balancing.
2.  Computational questions where a series of errors has been made in the ledger. These must be identified and corrected, using the Journal and suspense account.
3.  Computational questions involving the correction of a given profit figure, where the profit is incorrect because a number of errors have been made. Some of the errors will affect profit, and some will not.

What background knowledge should you have in order to study the topic? Correction of errors requires a detailed understanding of the mechanics of double entry. You should be familiar with the nature and purpose of the trial balance and of the Journal, and you should also understand how net profit is calculated.

## B. ESSENTIAL PRINCIPLES

### ERRORS AND THE TRIAL BALANCE

Chapter 5 introduced us to the trial balance. The trial balance has its limitations, because it only serves as an *arithmetical check* that the books are accurate. If every debit entry has an equal and opposite credit entry to match it, then of course the trial balance will balance; but it will not identify, for instance, whether each debit entry or each credit entry is recorded in the correct account.

## Errors which are not disclosed by the trial balance

The errors which are *not* disclosed by the trial balance occur in situations where the debit entry or total matches the credit entry or total. There are six types of errors found, and questions on the correction of these errors require you to study their nature. The errors, with examples, are:

| Description | Name and example |
|---|---|

1. Transaction completely omitted from the ledger: i.e. omitted from both accounts

ERROR OF OMISSION
'Cash sales, £10'

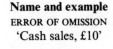
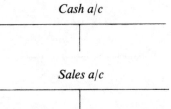

2. Wrong personal account is used: e.g. wrong debtor account.

ERROR OF COMMISSION
'Sold goods to J. Jones, £50'

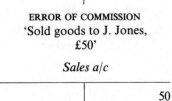

3. Wrong class of account is used: e.g. an expense debited to an asset account

ERROR OF PRINCIPLE
'Paid motor expenses, £50'

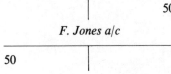

4. The account which should be debited has been credited, and vice versa

REVERSAL ERROR
'Cash sales, £50'

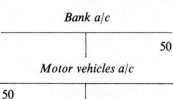
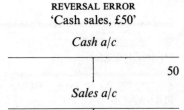

5.  Errors which cancel each other out: e.g. credit balance totalled as £10 too much, and debit balance also overcast by £10

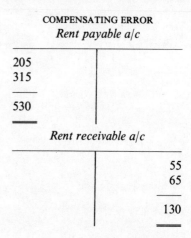

COMPENSATING ERROR
*Rent payable a/c*

| | |
|---|---|
| 205 | |
| 315 | |
| 530 | |

*Rent receivable a/c*

| | |
|---|---|
| | 55 |
| | 65 |
| | 130 |

6.  The original figure is entered incorrectly in both accounts

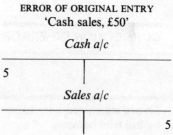

ERROR OF ORIGINAL ENTRY
'Cash sales, £50'

*Cash a/c*

| | |
|---|---|
| 5 | |

*Sales a/c*

| | |
|---|---|
| | 5 |

In each case it is still true that

### DEBIT EQUALS CREDIT

The balancing of the trial balance will therefore *not* be affected.

One way to help remember the six errors is to memorize 'COPCOR'. This is a 'word' constructed by taking the first letter from each error name:

- **C**ommission
- **O**mission
- **P**rinciple
- **C**ompensating
- **O**riginal entry
- **R**eversal

---

**Errors which are disclosed by the trial balance**

The errors identified below will stop the trial balance from balancing, because

### DEBIT DOES NOT EQUAL CREDIT

It is important to realize that the trial balance is unlikely to disclose precisely where the error lies: it simply will not balance, and this will draw attention to the fact that the books contain at least one error.

The following errors associated with the trial balance itself will prevent it from balancing:

(a) a balance may be entered on the wrong side of the trial balance;
(b) an account balance may have been omitted from the list of balances;
(c) there may be an error in totalling the trial balance columns.

In addition, there will be errors contained in the accounts themselves, which will affect the balancing of the trial balance:

(i) only a single entry has been made;
(ii) double entry has been inaccurate (different figures recorded in the two accounts);
(iii) the transaction has resulted in two debit entries, or two credit entries, instead of one debit and one credit;
(iv) the book of original entry has been posted incorrectly, either for individual items or for the total of the book.

## CORRECTION OF ERRORS

The six types of error (COPCOR) illustrated above will have to be corrected. So will the other errors which *do* affect the balancing of the trial balance. Questions concentrate on the mechanics of correction, and the first task is to identify which type of error requires correction.

## Errors which are not disclosed by the trial balance

If the error is one which is not disclosed by the trial balance, correction of that error will not involve the Suspense account (see below).

We need to identify:

(a) what *has* happened (which accounts have been used);
(b) what *should have* happened.

We can use the six types of error above to illustrate this procedure.

1. With an error of COMMISSION, an incorrect personal account has been used. Because there is an entry in F. Jones account which should not be there, it has to be cancelled by making an opposite entry. We must then identify the correct debtor account, and update it:

'Sold goods to J. Jones, £50'

| Sales a/c | | F. Jones a/c | | J. Jones a/c | |
|---|---|---|---|---|---|
| | 50 | 50 | (50) | (50) | |

(the ringed entries are those made to correct the error)

2. The error of OMISSION involved the transaction being missed out of both accounts. If one account had been updated, this would have been disclosed by the trial balance. To correct the error, we have to enter the transaction in both accounts: thus:

'Cash sales £50'

| Cash a/c | | Sales a/c | |
|---|---|---|---|
| 50 | | | 50 |

3. The error of PRINCIPLE involved an asset account being debited, instead of an expense account. The asset account entry requires cancelling by making a credit entry, and the expense account is debited, as it should have been originally:

'Paid motor expenses, £50'

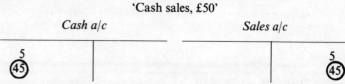

| Bank a/c | | Motor vehicles a/c | | Motor expenses a/c | |
|---|---|---|---|---|---|
| | 50 | 50 | (50) | (50) | |

4. COMPENSATING errors will be corrected according to the exact nature of the error. It is difficult to give hard and fast rules here, though we must follow the general principle of comparing what has been done with what should have been done.

5. Errors of ORIGINAL ENTRY require us to correct the amount which has been entered in both accounts. If the incorrect figure is smaller than the correct one, an entry on the same side of the account is needed: if the wrong figure is larger than the correct one, an entry is required on the other side of the account:

'Cash sales, £50'

| Cash a/c | | Sales a/c | |
|---|---|---|---|
| 5 (45) | | | 5 (45) |

6. REVERSAL errors are commonly found in examination questions on this topic. The original incorrect entry must be cancelled by an entry on the opposite side of the account, for double the amount (entering the original amount only would merely cancel the error):

'Cash sales, £50'

| Cash a/c | | Sales a/c | |
|---|---|---|---|
| (100) | 50 | 50 | (100) |

**Errors disclosed by the trial balance**

For these errors, a *Suspense account* will have to be used to correct the error. The suspense account has been created to make the trial balance totals agree. If the debit column of the trial balance is larger in total than the credit side, suspense will have a *credit* balance (to make the totals agree). If the credit side of the trial balance is the greater, the suspense account will be opened with a *debit* balance representing the difference in the trial balance totals.

The trial balance does not balance because there are errors where debit does not equal credit. Typically, one account contains an error which needs correcting. An entry is made in the account to correct this error. The other entry (because we are still operating in double entry) is made in the suspense account.

| Use of the Journal | Questions commonly ask for the Journal to be used in the correction of errors. In section E, the answers to questions 5 and 6 illustrate the use of the Journal in this way, and also reinforce the basic layout points originally explained in section F of Chapter 3. |
|---|---|

## ERRORS AND NET PROFIT

Some questions ask you to correct a given profit figure, which is incorrect as a result of a number of errors.

Assets and liabilities will not affect profit calculation, and therefore any errors involving asset or liability accounts are ignored when we adjust profit. Having said this, we must not forget that there are 'linked' accounts, e.g. provision for depreciation or for doubtful debts, which will affect profit. In addition, the stock account – classed as an asset – features in the trading account and therefore will affect the profit calculation.

The major accounts involved in correcting profit will be the expense and revenue accounts. We must calculate whether the error has resulted in the expense or revenue being overstated or understated.

| Error | Effect | Action |
|---|---|---|
| Expense overstated | profit understated | increase profit |
| Expense understated | profit overstated | reduce profit |
| Revenue overstated | profit overstated | reduce profit |
| Revenue understated | profit understated | increase profit |

## C. USEFUL APPLIED MATERIALS

All businesses want to reduce – and if possible to eliminate – errors, whether these errors are the type we study in accounting, or whether they involve incorrect buying, employing the wrong calibre of people, mistakes in marketing, and so on.

Businesses will set up systems to improve the accuracy of their paperwork; either paperwork in the traditional sense, or computerized 'paperwork'. A major task is to ensure that *data capture* takes place: in accounting, this means that each transaction is recorded and not overlooked. Documents such as bank statements (as shown in Fig. 6.1) can be used in practice to check whether errors or omissions have occurred.

## D. RECENT EXAMINATION QUESTIONS

There are seven questions in this section. Questions 1, 2 and 3 are multiple choice in style and should take less than five minutes to answer. Questions 4–7 are either descriptive or computational.

Question 4 is an essay-type question on the topic of correction of errors. Question 5 also involves error correction, but with this question you are required to correct the given errors by identifying the relevant ledger accounts.

Questions 6 and 7 test your understanding of how profit is affected by errors, linking profit correction to the use of the suspense account: *question 7 (answered in full in section F)* also includes balance sheet correction.

**Objective questions**

**1**  If a posting is made to the correct class of account and on the correct side, but in the wrong account, it is an error of
A  omission
B  principle
C  commission
D  compensation

(AEB Specimen Accounting O level Paper, 1980)

**2**  A suspense account can be used as a temporary measure to balance the
A  trading and profit and loss account
B  manufacturing account
C  trial balance
D  appropriation account

(AEB Specimen Accounting O level Paper, 1980)

**3**  A trial balance fails to agree by £40. Which one of the following errors, subsequently discovered, could have caused the disagreement?
A  A sale of goods, £40, to A. Brown had been debited to B. Brown's account
B  A cheque for £20 received from C. Green had been debited to C. Grey's account
C  A machine sold for £40 had been credited to the sales account
D  A payment for rent £40 had been debited to the wages account.

(AEB Specimen Accounting O level Paper, 1980)

**Essay and computational questions**

**4**
(a)  Define a trial balance and explain its purposes.

(5 marks out of 200)

(b)  Write down five types of errors, with examples, which could have been made in the books, but would not be revealed by the trial balance.

(15 marks out of 200)

(JMB Bookkeeping and Accounting, June 1984)

**5**  R. Blackett's trial balance, extracted at 30 April 1982, failed to agree. In early May the following errors were discovered.
1.  The total of the returns outward book £124 had not been posted to the ledger.
2.  An invoice received from W. Dawson, £100, had been mislaid. Entries for this transaction had, therefore, not been made.
3.  A payment for repairs to the motor van £36 had been entered in the vehicle repairs account as £30.
4.  When balancing the account of R. Race in the ledger, the debit balance had been brought down in error as £26, instead of £62.

(a) (i) Journal entries, complete with suitable narrations, to correct each of the above errors.

(6 marks)

(ii) A suspense account indicating the nature and extent of the original difference in the books.

(4 marks)

(iii) The incorrect total of the trial balance credit column, given that the incorrect total of the debit column was £10 000.

(2 marks)

*REQUIRED:*

(b) Four types of errors which do not affect the agreement of the trial balance, giving an example of each.

(8 marks)

(AEB Accounting O level, June 1982)

**6** To enable work to proceed on a firm's draft year end accounts a difference found in the trial balance was entered into a suspense account opened for the purpose. The draft Profit and Loss Account subsequently showed a profit for the year of £102 108 and the Suspense Account was shown in the draft balance sheet.

During audit the following errors were found which when corrected eliminated the Suspense Account entry:

(i) one of the pages of the Sales Day Book totalling £5 138 had not been posted to Sales Account;

(ii) the year-end stock sheets had been over-cast by £1 100;

(iii) the last page of the Purchases Day Book totalling £7 179 had been posted to Purchases Account as £1 779;

(iv) no account had been taken of electricity consumed since the last meter reading, the estimated amount being £246;

(v) an invoice for £64 entered correctly in the Sales Day Book had been posted to the customer's account as £164;

(vi) an entry in the Purchases Day Book of £82 had not been posted to the supplier's account;

(vii) an error had been made in balancing the Petty Cash Book, the correct amount being £250, not £25;

(viii) Loan Interest paid amounting to £500 had been posted to the Loan Account.

*REQUIRED:*

(a) Frame the necessary journal entries to clear the Suspense Account (narratives not required).

(7 marks)

(b) Prepare the Suspense Account showing the amount of the original difference.

(6 marks)

(c) Prepare a statement showing the corrected profit/loss for the year.

(7 marks)

(Total 20 marks)

(AAT Numeracy and Accounting, December 1983)

**7** The following is the Balance Sheet of A. Blower & Co as at 31 December 1981:

| | £ | | | £ |
|---|---|---|---|---|
| Capital | 42 000 | Fixed assets | | |
| Add net profit for year | 10 500 | Premises | | 25 000 |
| | ——— | Machinery | | 10 000 |
| | 52 500 | | | ——— |
| Less drawings | 8 000 | | | 35 000 |
| | ——— | | | |
| | 44 500 | | | |
| Current liabilities | | Current assets | | |
| Sundry creditors | 3 400 | Stock | 4 400 | |
| | | Debtors | 2 822 | |
| | | Bank | 4 900 | |
| | | Cash | 554 | |
| | | | ——— | 12 676 |
| | | Suspense account | | 224 |
| | ——— | | | ——— |
| | £47 900 | | | £47 900 |

Although the trial balance of the business did not agree, the above balance sheet was prepared and a suspense account opened for the difference. At a later date an audit of the books revealed the following errors:

1. The sales day book had been overcast by £200.
2. A payment by a debtor of £56 had not been posted from the cash book to the personal account.
3. A discount allowed by J. Tree of £15 had been posted to the wrong side of the personal account.
4. Bank charges of £85 had not been entered into the books.
5. The stock book had been undercast at 31 December 1981 by £1 000.
6. An invoice for £85 for repairs to A. Blower's private home had been paid by the business and posted to sundry expenses account.
7. A cash float of £50 in the shop had not been included in the trial balance.

*REQUIRED:*
Take this information into account and show:
(a) the suspense account, written up and balanced,
(b) a statement showing the calculation of the corrected net profit,
(c) an amended balance sheet as at 31 December 1981.

(50 marks out of 200)
(JMB Bookkeeping and Accounting, June 1982)

---

**E. OUTLINE ANSWERS**

1. An error of commission (C) has been made.
2. The suspense account is used to get the trial balance (C) to balance.

3.  With alternatives (A), (C) and (D), debit equals credit. Alternative (B), we should have credited C. Green £20 but have debited C. Grey £20: Dr is £40 (two entries of £20) greater than Cr.

**4** Your definition for 4 (a) should mention a list of balances from the ledger (also, not an account); purpose is to check the arithmetical accuracy of the books. For (b), any five of the six errors described in section B of the chapter, together with appropriate examples, would provide a satisfactory answer.

**5**

(a)  Your Journal should be laid out correctly, and should contain relevant narratives. The entries are:

|   |   |   |   |
|---|---|---|---|
| 1. | Suspense | 124 |  |
|  | Returns outwards |  | 124 |
| 2. | Purchases | 100 |  |
|  | W. Dawson |  | 100 |
| 3. | Vehicle repairs | 6 |  |
|  | Suspense |  | 6 |
| 4. | R. Race | 36 |  |
|  | Suspense |  | 36 |

The suspense account contains the above entries:

*Suspense account*

| £ | £ |
|---|---|
| 124 | 6 |
|  | 36 |

The difference (Cr balance) is £82, which represents the original balance on the account.

If the trial balance Dr column totalled £1 000, the Cr total must have been £82 less (the value of the suspense balance): Cr total £918.

(b)  Any four errors selected from the six explained in section B, together with appropriate examples, would provide a satisfactory answer.

**6**

(a)

| | **Journal** | £ | £ |
|---|---|---|---|
| (i) | Suspense | 5 138 |  |
|  | Sales |  | 5 138 |
| (iii) | Purchases | 5 400 |  |
|  | Suspense |  | 5 400 |
| (v) | Suspense | 100 |  |
|  | Debtor |  | 100 |
| (vi) | Suspense | 82 |  |
|  | Creditor |  | 82 |
| (vii) | Petty Cash | 225 |  |
|  | Suspense |  | 225 |

In each case, Dr does not equal Cr:
(i) Sales (Cr) too small by £5 138; (iii) Purchases (Dr) too small by the amount of the difference; (v) Debtor balance (Dr) too large; (vi) Creditor balance (Cr) too small; (vii) PCB balance (Dr) too small by the amount of the difference.

(b)  Entering the above in suspense account leaves a Dr balance on the account of £305; this represents the original difference in the trial balance.

*Suspense account*

|  | £ |  | £ |
|---|---|---|---|
| Sales | 5 138 | Purchases | 5 400 |
| Debtor | 100 | Petty cash | 225 |
| Creditor | 82 |  |  |
| Balance | 305 |  |  |
|  | 5 625 |  | 5 625 |

|  |  | £ | £ |
|---|---|---|---|
| (c) | Profit from draft accounts |  | 102 108 |
|  | Add: sales understated (i) |  | 5 138 |
|  |  |  | 107 246 |
|  | Less: closing stock overstated (ii) | 1 100 |  |
|  | purchases understated (iii) | 5 400 |  |
|  | accrued expense omitted (iv) | 246 |  |
|  | loan interest omitted (viii) | 500 |  |
|  |  |  | 7 246 |
|  | Net Profit for the year: |  | 100 000 |

# F. A TUTOR'S ANSWER

Question 7 is a wide-ranging question testing knowledge of how errors are corrected using a suspense account, how these errors affect profit, and also how they affect balance sheet items.

(a)                              *Suspense account*

|  | £ |  | £ |
|---|---|---|---|
| Original Balance | 224 | Sales (1) | 200 |
| Debtor (2) | 56 | J. Tree (3) | 30 |
|  |  | Cash (7) | 50 |
|  | 280 |  | 280 |

(b)                    **A. Blower & Co**

*Statement of corrected net profit for period ended*
*31 December 1981*

|  | £ | £ |
|---|---:|---:|
| Balance as per Balance Sheet |  | 10 500 |
| Add: |  |  |
|   Closing stock understated | 1 000 |  |
|   Expenses overstated | 85 |  |
|  |  | 1 085 |
|  |  | 11 585 |
| Less: |  |  |
|   Sales overcast | 200 |  |
|   Charges understated | 85 | 285 |
| Corrected Net Profit |  | 11 300 |

(c)                    **A. Blower & Co**

*Balance Sheet at 31 December 1981*

|  | £ | £ |
|---|---:|---:|
| *Fixed Assets* |  |  |
| Premises |  | 25 000 |
| Machinery |  | 10 000 |
|  |  | 35 000 |
| *Current Assets* |  |  |
| Stock | 5 400 |  |
| Debtors | 2 766 |  |
| Bank | 4 815 |  |
| Cash | 604 |  |
|  | 13 585 |  |
| *Less Current Liabilities* |  |  |
| Creditors | 3 370 |  |
|  |  | 10 215 |
|  |  | 45 215 |
| *Financed by:* |  |  |
| Capital |  | 42 000 |
| Net Profit | 11 300 |  |
| less Drawings | 8 085 |  |
|  |  | 3 215 |
|  |  | 45 215 |

**Workings**

Here are the effects of the errors, listed in order of error, on suspense, profit and balance sheet.

1. (a) Suspense involved because error of addition in one account (sales, the total of the sales book being posted to sales account). Sales overstated by £200, so debit the account to reduce this credit balance and credit suspense.
    (b) Profit also affected: sales is a revenue item: revenue overstated, so profit overstated. Deduct £200 from net profit.
    (c) Balance Sheet affected through correction of net profit.

2. (a) Suspense involved, with one entry only being made. Missing entry is a credit in the debtor account (debtor has given payment): the account needs crediting, and suspense is therefore debited.
    (b) No effect on profit: asset account affected.
    (c) Balance sheet is affected. By crediting the debtor with the payment, amount owed by total debtors is reduced by £56.

3. (a) Suspense involved, because two entries made on the same side. J. Tree is a creditor (discount allowed by him): discount always recorded on the same side as bank/cash in a personal account. Tree is debited with receiving money, so he should have been debited with discount £15. A credit entry of £15 has been made: cancelled by debiting the account with £30, to give the net effect of £15 debit. The credit entry is in suspense.
    (b) No effect on net profit, even though discount is involved (no mention of incorrect entry in profit and loss account).
    (c) Tree's balance is £30 too great, because the credit side is £15 too much and debit side £15 too small (the creditor account has a credit balance). Creditors are £30 too much, and £30 is deducted from the balance sheet total.

4. (a) No effect on suspense (Error of Omission: Dr = Cr).
    (b) Profit is £85 overstated, because an expense has been omitted. Deduct £85 from net profit.
    (c) Bank account in the balance sheet is £85 overstated: deduct £85.

5. (a) No effect on suspense (closing stock not in trial balance).
    (b) Closing stock £1 000 understated, so cost of sales is £1 000 overstated. Cost of sales too much, gross profit too small and so net profit also too small. Add £1 000 to net profit.
    (c) In the balance sheet, the stock figure is £1 000 too small.

6. (a) No effect on suspense: the wrong account used, but Dr = Cr.
    (b) Profit is affected: business expenses are overstated by £85, so increase net profit by £85.
    (c) Drawings are involved ('private home'): understated by £85, so add £85 to the balance sheet figure for drawings.

7. (a) Omission of the cash float has affected trial balance balancing, and suspense is involved. Cash (Dr balance) is £50 too small, so effectively a debit to the account: credit suspense.

(b)  No effect on profit.

(c)  The balance sheet figure for cash needs increasing by £50.

N.B. My balance sheet layout is in vertical format: no layout is stipulated in the question, so do not be concerned if your answer is in the traditional horizontal form.

---

## G.  A STEP FURTHER

The topic of correcting errors is a very difficult one to master. Most books on accounting contain a separate chapter dealing with the workings of the suspense account, together with an explanation of the types of errors that do or do not affect the balancing of the trial balance. Here is a selection of books which you may find useful:

Castle and Owens, *Principles of Accounts* (7th edn) (M & E). Ch. 15.

Garbutt, *Carter's Advanced Accounts* (7th edn) (Pitman). Ch. 03.

Harrison, *Stage One Financial Accounting* (Northwick). Ch. 15.

Whitehead, *Bookkeeping Made Simple* ('Made Simple' series). Ch. 9.

Wood, *Business Accounting 1* (4th edn) (Longman). Chs 29 and 30.

| Chapter 10 | # Control accounts |
|---|---|

## A. GETTING STARTED

Questions on control accounts give the examiner the chance to test your knowledge of the construction and the use of these accounts. The typical question will provide a list of balances associated with debtors and creditors, from which Sales Ledger and Purchase Ledger Control accounts must be constructed. Although most questions are computational, it is possible to be asked to explain the function of control accounts. These essay questions allow the examiner to check that you understand why certain procedures are followed.

What accounting knowledge do you need to study this topic? Because control accounts are based on the ledger being divided into its four main areas, you should be familiar with this division. A knowledge of the books of original entry is required, together with an understanding of the construction of debtor and creditor accounts.

## B. ESSENTIAL PRINCIPLES

### CONSTRUCTION OF CONTROL ACCOUNTS

Many transactions in accounting involve purchases or sales. The two aspects of the transaction are recorded, once *in* the sales or purchases ledger, and once *outside* the sales or purchases ledger. For example:

1. Credit sale : (a) debit debtor a/c in sales ledger (SL)
   (b) record in Sales Book outside SL
2. Purchases returns : (a) debit creditor a/c in purchases ledger (PL)
   (b) record in Purchases Returns Book outside PL

It is this principle that allows control accounts to be constructed.

## The sales ledger control account

How does the double entry work with a sales ledger control account? The totals of the various books of original entry are used:

*Sales Book*

Dr SL Control a/c                                    Cr Sales a/c

*Sales Returns Book*

Dr Sales Returns a/c                                 Cr SL Control a/c

*Cash Book*

Dr Bank a/c and record                               Cr SL Control a/c
discount

We are used to recording transactions in the sales account, the sales returns account and the cash book. Instead of making the other entry in the relevant debtor account, the total sales, sales returns, and bank/discount will be recorded in the sales ledger control account. Analysis columns will be used in practice to obtain these totals: for example, the cash book could have an analysis column recording all payments received from debtors.

The SL control account is recorded from this and other information such as bad debts, which relate to debtors. The debtor 'accounts' in the sales ledger still exist, but not as accounts proper because they no longer form part of the 'debit-credit' double entry. The individual debtor records are updated from the source documents or books of original entry, very much as before.

## The control

Everything should still agree: if, for example, we were to total the entries for sales in the individual debtor records, this total should be the same as the total for sales shown in the SL control account. The total of returns, cash/bank and discount allowed in the various debtor accounts should equal the totals in sales ledger control. If we total the closing balances on the individual debtor records, this total should equal the closing balance on the sales ledger control account.

If these closing balances agree, it would suggest that no errors have occurred, either in updating the debtor records or in constructing the sales ledger control account. If the balances do not agree, then errors are present which need to be identified and corrected.

## The purchases ledger control account

The *Purchases Ledger Control Account* is constructed using the same basic procedures. The totals from the various books of original entry – the purchases book, the returns outwards book, the cash book (credit side) and the discount received column – are posted to the relevant accounts in the general ledger (purchases, returns outwards and discount received). The other entry is made in the purchases ledger control account.

The creditor 'accounts' are updated from source documents such as the purchases invoice, or from the relevant book of original entry, independently of the totals of these books. At the end of the period, the closing balance of the PL control account should equal the total of the balances obtained from the individual creditor records.

| Control account layout | Here are sales ledger and purchases ledger control accounts, without amounts but with their typical entries: |
| --- | --- |

### Sales Ledger Control account

|  | £ |  | £ |
| --- | --- | --- | --- |
| Opening balance b/d |  | Bank |  |
| Sales |  | Discount allowed |  |
|  |  | Sales returns |  |
|  |  | Bad debts |  |
|  |  | Closing balance c/d |  |

### Purchases Ledger Control account

|  | £ |  | £ |
| --- | --- | --- | --- |
| Bank |  | Opening balance b/d |  |
| Discount received |  | Purchases |  |
| Returns outwards |  |  |  |
| Closing balance c/d |  |  |  |

The *sales ledger control* account looks the same as an *individual debtor* account: this is because its 'totals' entries replace the individual entries made in the debtor accounts. Similarly, the *purchases ledger control* account is, in appearance, the same as an *individual creditor* account.

**Contra entries**

Where a business trades with a firm which acts as both a debtor and a creditor, the two balances in the books of the business may be 'set off' against each other. If, for example, a firm is a debtor for £50, and the same firm is also a creditor for £40, the lesser balance may be transferred from the purchase ledger to the sales ledger, leaving a 'net indebtedness' (i.e. a net balance) of £10 in the sales ledger record:

| SALES LEDGER *Debtor (firm X)* | | | | PURCHASES LEDGER *Creditor (firm X)* | | | |
| --- | --- | --- | --- | --- | --- | --- | --- |
| £ | | £ | | £ | | £ | |
| (Balance 50) | To PL | 40 | | To SL | 40 | (Balance 40) | |
| debit balance £10 | | | | zero balance | | | |

With these 'set-offs', there will be two entries to make, one in each control account. The purchases ledger control account will be debited, since the credit balance is being transferred, and the *contra entry* is in the sales ledger control account which is credited (the debit balance being transferred).

## C. USEFUL APPLIED MATERIALS

**Figure 10.1** is an example of a sales ledger control account organized using a three-column approach. It contains a running balance, and entries are made on a regular basis, following the completion and totalling of individual pages of the source books (as illustrated in its 'Ref.' column).

**SALES** Ledger Control Account

| Date | Ref. | Details | Debits | | Credits | | Balance | |
|------|------|---------|--------|------|---------|------|---------|------|
| Aug. 1 | | Brought Forward | | | | | 12370 | 26 |
| Aug. 4 | SDB 168 | Sales | 1451 | 13 | | | 13821 | 39 |
| Aug. 4 | CB 108 | Cash & Disc. | | | 716 | 49 | 13104 | 90 |
| Aug. 20 | SDB 169 | Sales | 391 | 79 | | | 13496 | 69 |
| Aug. 22 | SDB 170 | Sales | 846 | 57 | | | 14343 | 26 |
| Aug. 28 | CB 109 | Cash & Disc. | | | 5110 | 15 | 9233 | 11 |
| Sept. 1 | SDB 171 | Sales | 958 | 36 | | | 10191 | 47 |
| Sept. 2 | SDB 172 | Sales | 1230 | 25 | | | 11421 | 72 |
| Sept. 3 | SDB 173 | Sales | 680 | 02 | | | 12101 | 74 |
| Sept. 7 | CB 110 | Cash & Disc. | | | 1173 | 72 | 10928 | 02 |
| Sept. 8 | SDB 174 | Sales | 862 | 56 | | | 11790 | 58 |
| Sept. 10 | SDB 175 | Sales | 476 | 23 | | | 12266 | 81 |
| Sept. 11 | SDB 176 | Sales | 1898 | 26 | | | 14165 | 07 |
| Sept. 13 | SDB 177 | Sales | 1042 | 26 | | | 15207 | 33 |
| Sept. 15 | SDB 178 | Sales | 839 | 48 | | | 16046 | 81 |
| Sept. 16 | SDB 179 | Sales | 1337 | 41 | | | 17384 | 22 |
| Sept. 18 | SDB 180 | Sales | 2068 | 56 | | | 19452 | 78 |

*Fig. 10.1    Sales Ledger Control account*
Courtesy: Kalamazoo Business Systems

## D. RECENT EXAMINATION QUESTIONS

Question **1** is multiple choice, testing your understanding of the relationship between day books, ledgers and control accounts. Question **2** is an example of a descriptive question on the topic of control accounts: it also asks you to create a sales ledger control account.

Questions **3–6** are typical questions asked on this topic. You have to construct control accounts from given information; question **5** is also part descriptive. *Question 4 is fully answered in section F of the chapter.*

Question **6** is more advanced, and tests your knowledge of the relationship between the purchases ledger accounts and the relevant control account.

**1** In the totalling of the purchases day book an error is made and the resulting total is £100 more than it should have been.

Assuming that no other errors have been made, the effect of this error will be that the balance of the creditors' control account will be:

A £100 less than the net total of creditors' accounts
B equal to the net total of creditors' accounts
C £100 more than the net total of creditors' accounts
D £200 more than the net total of creditors' accounts.

(AEB Specimen Accounting O level Paper, 1980)

**Essay and computational questions**

**2** What is a control account? Give an example of a sales (debtors') ledger control account of a firm which has a large number of customers. Your control account should contain at least four different entries and should be balanced at the period end. (7 marks)

(AEB Accounting O level, June 1983)

**3** Chilvers & Co. balanced its purchases and sales ledger control accounts monthly. From the following information for the month of May 1983 you are required to complete the SALES Ledger Control Account, and bring down the balance at 1 June 1983.

| 1983 | | | £ |
|---|---|---|---:|
| May | 1 | Credit balance in purchases ledger | 988 |
| | 1 | Credit balance in sales ledger | 154 |
| | 1 | Debit balance in purchases ledger | 63 |
| | 1 | Debit balance in sales ledger | 3 699 |
| | 31 | Purchases for month | 2 963 |
| | 31 | Sales for month | 8 503 |
| | 31 | Returns inward for month | 183 |
| | 31 | Returns outward for month | 110 |
| | 31 | Credit notes sent to debtors for faulty goods not returned to Chilvers & Co | 46 |
| | 31 | Cash paid to creditors | 2 649 |
| | 31 | Cash paid by customers | 6 964 |
| | 31 | Discounts received | 60 |
| | 31 | Discounts allowed | 95 |
| | 31 | Bad debts written off during month | 10 |
| | 31 | Debit balance on sales ledger set off against balances in the purchases ledger | 50 |
| | 31 | Debit balances in purchases ledger | nil |
| | 31 | Credit balances in sales ledger | nil |

(20 marks out of 200)
(JMB Bookkeeping and Accounting, June 1983)

**4** Stream Ltd maintains control accounts for its sales and purchases ledgers. Balances at 31 December 1982 were:

| | Debit £ | Credit £ |
|---|---:|---:|
| Sales ledger | 45 862 | 348 |
| Purchases ledger | 619 | 36 941 |

Details of transactions during 1983 were as follows:

|  | £ |
|---|---|
| Sales | 422 987 |
| Purchases | 284 142 |
| Receipts from credit customers | 394 281 |
| Cash sales | 241 652 |
| Payments to suppliers for goods purchased on credit | 276 110 |
| Cash purchases | 560 |
| Returns inwards | 3 048 |
| Returns outwards | 2 361 |
| Bad debts written off | 4 668 |
| Debts settled by contra between ledgers | 1 862 |
| Increase in provision for bad debts | 1 150 |

At 31 December 1983 credit balances on the sales ledger were £384 and debit balances on the purchases ledger were £450.

*REQUIRED:*
Prepare the sales ledger control account and purchases ledger control account of Stream Ltd for 1983.

(20 marks)
(RSA II Accounting, June 1984)


**5**
(a) What are the purposes of control accounts?

(8 marks)
(b) The following information is provided for Monkton Ltd which maintains separate control accounts for its sales ledger and purchases ledger:

|  | Debit | Credit |
|---|---|---|
| Balances at 1 January 1982 | £ | £ |
| Sales ledger | 25 160 | 350 |
| Purchases ledger | 110 | 16 360 |

Details of transactions during 1982 are as follows:

|  | £ |
|---|---|
| Purchases | 126 300 |
| Credit sales | 279 280 |
| Cash sales | 3 150 |
| Payments to suppliers | 119 680 |
| Receipts from customers | 256 390 |
| Refund to customer in respect of overpayment | 310 |
| Discounts received | 1 960 |
| Discounts allowed | 2 320 |
| Returns inwards | 14 600 |
| Returns outwards | 3 570 |
| Bad debts written off | 2 100 |
| Debit balance on purchases ledger transferred to sales ledger | 850 |

At 31 December 1982 the debit balances on suppliers accounts totalled £460 and the credit balances on customers accounts totalled £820.

*REQUIRED:*

(i)   The sales ledger control account, and
(ii)  The purchase ledger control account of Monkton Ltd for 1982

(22 marks)

(RSA II Accounting, May 1983)


**6**  The following information relates to Roxy Limited for the year to 31 May 1983:

Extract from the Purchases Ledger Control Account at 31 May 1983

|  | £ |
|---|---|
| Trade creditors as at 1 June 1982 | 20 000 |
| Credit purchases | 240 000 |
| Payments made to trade creditors | 232 000 |
| Discounts received | 6 000 |

The accountant has extracted a list of credit balances which total £23 800. There were no debit balances.

In checking these credit balances the following errors were discovered:

1.   Goods costing £1 500 had been omitted from Collin's Account.
2.   Discounts received for January 1983 amounting to £500 had not been entered in any of the personal accounts.
3.   The credit side of Brown's Account had been undercast by £1 000.
4.   A cash payment of £200 to Almond had been credited to his account.
5.   A bank payment to Martin of £750 had been omitted from his account.
6.   Ashton's balance of £2 000 had not been included in the list of balances.
7.   The entry for a motor car purchased from Gill, and costing £5 000 should not have appeared in the Purchases Ledger.
8.   Discounts Allowed totalling £350 had been debited to Crosby's Account.

*REQUIRED:*

(a)  Prepare the Purchases Ledger Control Account for the year to 31 May 1983.

(4 marks)

(b)  Prepare a statement showing the necessary corrections to the list of Purchase Ledger balances as originally extracted at 31 May 1983.

(16 marks)

(Total 20 marks)

(AAT Accounting 2, June 1983)

# E. OUTLINE ANSWERS

The answer to question **1** is (C). Purchases Book total is posted to PL Control; closing PL Control balance is £100 more than should be (purchases increase the balance), i.e. £100 more than total creditors from the purchases ledger.

**2** Your answer should mention that a control account checks the accuracy of the (purchases and sales) ledgers, by taking totals from the subsidiary records and comparing its balance with the total of the debtor or creditor balances extracted from the sales or purchases ledgers.

Your example of SL Control should contain an opening Dr balance; total sales (Dr); Cr items such as returns outwards, cash, discount allowed or bad debts; and a closing balance (Dr, recorded on the Cr side).

**3** Your first task is to identify sales ledger control items from the list: i.e. debtor-related items. These items are then entered in SL Control account.

Dr items:   opening balance £3 699; sales.
Cr items:   opening balance £154; returns in; credit notes; cash (£6 964); discount allowed; bad debts; set-offs (£50).

This leaves a closing balance of £4 700 (totals £12 202).

**5**
(a) Your answer should identify the purpose of checking and controlling the various ledgers through the use of control accounts; the control account acts as a sort of trial balance for these ledgers (only those ledgers whose control accounts do not balance need checking).
(b) Here are the summarized control accounts: note that cash sales are not included in a control account.

### SL Control

| | £ | | £ |
|---|---|---|---|
| Balance | 25 160 | Balance | 350 |
| Sales | 279 280 | Cash | 256 390 |
| Refund | 310 | Discount | 2 320 |
| Transfer | 850 | Returns | 14 600 |
| Balance | 820 | Bad debts | 2 100 |
| | | | 30 660 |
| | | Balance | |
| | 306 420 | | 306 420 |

### PL Control

| | £ | | £ |
|---|---|---|---|
| Balance | 110 | Balance | 16 360 |
| Cash | 119 680 | Purchases | 126 300 |
| Discount | 1 960 | Transfer | 850 |
| Returns | 3 570 | Balance | 460 |
| Balance | 18 650 | | |
| 143 970 | | 143 970 | |

Closing balances (£30 660 and £18 650) calculated in the normal manner.

**6**
(a) The PL Control a/c is straightforward: opening (Cr) balance, add purchases, less payments and discount. This gives a closing balance of £22 000.

(b) There is a difference between the PL Control balance and the total of the creditor balances. Each error affects a creditor account (and not control a/c): your task is to calculate whether the error results in the £23 800 total being overstated or understated:

| Error | Effect | Action |
|---|---|---|
| 1. | Balance too small (purchases increase the balance) | Add £1 500 |
| 2. | Balances too large (discount reduces a creditor balance) | Deduct £500 |
| 3. | Brown's balance too small (Cr balance as a creditor) | Add £1 000 |
| 4. | Balance £400 too large (the £200 should reduce Almond's balance; it has increased it) | Deduct £400 |
| 5. | Balance too large (payment will reduce it) | Deduct £750 |
| 6. | Total balances understated | Add £2 000 |
| 7. | Gill's balance too great (transaction recorded as 'purchases') | Deduct £5 000 |
| 8. | Not a PL item ('allowed' in debtor accounts): Crosby's a/c balance too small (debit entry reduces it) | Add £350 |

Your statement should commence with the £23 800 balance; then add items 1, 3, 6 and 8, totalling £4 850; finally, deduct items 2, 4, 5 and 7, totalling £6 650. This brings the balance to £22 000, as per the PL Control balance in (a).

## F. A TUTOR'S ANSWER

Question 4 tests your understanding of how control accounts are constructed, which item is recorded in which control account, and which items are omitted from these accounts. Here is the suggested answer:

### Stream Ltd

*Sales Ledger Control account*

| 1983 | | £ | 1983 | | £ |
|---|---|---|---|---|---|
| 1 Jan | Balance b/d | 45 862 | 1 Jan | Balance b/d | 348 |
| 31 Dec | Sales | 422 987 | 31 Dec | Bank | 394 281 |
| | Balance c/d | 384 | | Returns inwards | 3 048 |
| | | | | Bad debts | 4 668 |
| | | | | Contra items | 1 862 |
| | | | | Balance c/d | 65 026 |
| | | 469 233 | | | 469 233 |

| 1984 | | | 1984 | | |
|---|---|---|---|---|---|
| 1 Jan | Balance b/d | 65 026 | 1 Jan | Balance b/d | 384 |

**Stream Ltd**

*Purchases Ledger Control account*

| 1983 | | £ | 1983 | | £ |
|---|---|---|---|---|---|
| 1 Jan | Balance b/d | 619 | 1 Jan | Balance b/d | 36 941 |
| 31 Dec | Bank | 276 110 | 31 Dec | Purchases | 284 142 |
| | Returns outwards | 2 361 | | Balance c/d | 450 |
| | Contra items | 1 862 | | | |
| | Balance c/d | 40 581 | | | |
| | | 321 533 | | | 321 533 |

| 1984 | | | 1984 | | |
|---|---|---|---|---|---|
| 1 Jan | Balance b/d | 450 | 1 Jan | Balance b/d | 40 581 |

**Workings**

In these control accounts, cash sales and purchases are not recorded. Also ignore the increase in bad debts provision, as this is not a control account item.

Enter the closing balances on the wrong sides before bringing down to their correct sides.

Once all items are included, the final balance can be calculated in each account.

## G.  A STEP FURTHER

The topic of control accounts requires careful study. Here is a selection of textbooks that you might find useful in your study of control accounts:

Eve and Forth, *Accounting: an Insight* (Pitman). Ch. 5.

Garbutt, *Carter's Advanced Accounts* (7th edn) (Pitman). Ch. 05.

Whitehead, *Success in Principles of Accounting* (John Murray). Unit 34.

Wood, *Business Accounting 1* (4th edn) (Longman). Ch. 31.

Wood, *Bookkeeping and Accounts* (Longman). Ch. 33.

**Chapter 11**

# Manufacturing accounts and departmental accounts

## A. GETTING STARTED

Final accounts, in their various forms, appear on all the major accounting syllabuses. In this chapter we shall examine two different forms of final accounts: *Manufacturing accounts* and *Departmental accounts*.

The questions on these topics usually take the form of a trial balance, or a list of account balances not in trial balance form, from which the manufacturing account or the departmental account must be constructed. The account balances will usually have a series of notes attached, requiring appropriate adjustments to be made.

Before studying the chapter or attempting the questions, you should be familiar with the layout and construction of the final accounts of a sole trader, including how to make adjustments for items such as prepaid expenses or provision for depreciation.

## B. ESSENTIAL PRINCIPLES

### MANUFACTURING ACCOUNTS

We have assumed until now that an organization has been buying and selling finished goods, rather than manufacturing them. The trading account has been our starting point for work on the final accounts. A trading account will still be required where a firm manufactures goods to sell, but it will be preceded by the *Manufacturing* account.

### Costs

A major problem in constructing manufacturing accounts involves the classification of *costs* under their relevant headings. Here are the categories of cost found in questions on manufacturing accounts:

| | name of cost | elements of cost | account used |
|---|---|---|---|
| 1 | PRIME COST | *Direct* costs of production:<br>Direct labour<br>Direct materials<br>Direct expenses | Manufacturing |
| 2 | FACTORY OVERHEADS | *Indirect* costs of production, e.g. supervisory wages, factory rent and rates. | Manufacturing |
| 3 | ADMINISTRATION COSTS and SELLING AND DISTRIBUTION COSTS | *Office* costs, e.g. office rent/rates, salesmen's salaries. | Profit and Loss |

**Stocks**

Questions on manufacturing accounts will involve stocks of *raw materials*, stocks of *work in progress*, and stocks of *finished goods* (the stock we have always shown in the trading account).

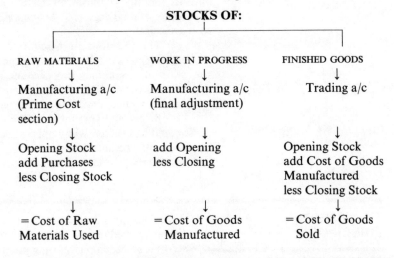

**STOCKS OF:**

| RAW MATERIALS | WORK IN PROGRESS | FINISHED GOODS |
|---|---|---|
| ↓ | ↓ | ↓ |
| Manufacturing a/c (Prime Cost section) | Manufacturing a/c (final adjustment) | Trading a/c |
| ↓ | ↓ | ↓ |
| Opening Stock add Purchases less Closing Stock | add Opening less Closing | Opening Stock add Cost of Goods Manufactured less Closing Stock |
| ↓ | ↓ | ↓ |
| = Cost of Raw Materials Used | = Cost of Goods Manufactured | = Cost of Goods Sold |

The principle of commencing with opening stock and deducting closing stock, which we first met in Chapter 5, will still apply to the two new types of stock found in questions on manufacturing accounts.

**Layout**

Regardless of the type or complexity of the question, the layout of the manufacturing account is very important. Use of subheadings and a two-column approach on the debit side should result in a neat and well-organized account, and is likely to help you to avoid errors of addition and omission.

A typical manufacturing account (Dr side) could be laid out as shown below:

|  | £ | £ |
|---|---|---|
| *Raw Materials* | | |
| Opening stock | | x |
| Purchases | | x |
| | | x |
| Less closing stock | | x |
| Cost of materials used | | x |
| Direct labour | | x |
| Direct expenses | | x |
| PRIME COST | | x |
| *Factory Overheads* | | |
| Factory rent | x | |
| Factory rates | x | |
| Indirect labour | x | |
| Depreciation of machinery | x | |
| TOTAL OVERHEADS | | x |
| | | x |
| Add Opening Work in Progress | | x |
| | | x |
| Less Closing Work in Progress | | x |
| | | x |

One common error is to forget to add the total overheads to the prime cost. By displaying the individual overhead items to the left of the prime cost total, you should avoid making this error.

## DEPARTMENTAL ACCOUNTS

Departmental accounts, unlike manufacturing accounts, do not involve the construction of a new final account. Rather, a question will require us to restructure trading and profit and loss accounts in columnar format in order to calculate the profit or loss on separate departments.

### Costs

The majority of questions set on this topic give clear instructions on how to allocate or apportion costs to the various departments. Sales volume, floor area or number of employees per department are commonly used bases in these questions. Occasionally, we have to use our judgement as to which basis to use: it is a case of selecting the most appropriate base.

Layout is very important in questions on departmental accounts. The layout problem is as much one of arithmetic as appearance, because of the volume of figures typically involved. The answer illustrated in section F demonstrates an appropriate layout.

## C.  USEFUL APPLIED MATERIALS

**Figure 11.1** provides a good example of how a major department store analyses the weekly sales of its branches. From this analysis, the profitability of the individual departments can be established.

## D.  RECENT EXAMINATION QUESTIONS

Questions **1–3** (objective) are on manufacturing accounts. They are followed by three computational questions which are also on this topic: question **4** requires a manufacturing account to be constructed; questions **5** and **6** ask for manufacturing and trading accounts.

Questions **7**, **8** and **9** test your knowledge of departmental accounts.

The most demanding question is probably question **10**, because it combines elements of manufacturing and departmental accounts. *Question 10 is answered in full in section F.*

### Objective questions

1   The total of raw materials consumed and the direct wages is called
. . . . . .

(London Board Principles of Accounts O level,<br>January 1983)

2   The factory cost of production is found by adding the prime cost to the . . . . . .

(London Board Principles of Accounts O level,<br>January 1983)

3   A manufacturing account is drawn up by:
A   firms engaged solely in the buying and selling of goods
B   firms providing personal services
C   non-trading organizations
D   firms which make and sell articles

(AEB Specimen Accounting O level Paper, 1980)

| DEPARTMENT | Wolverhampton | Birkenhead | Solihull | Dudley | Sutton Coldfield | Northampton | Group |
|---|---|---|---|---|---|---|---|
| | | | | SALES FOR WEEK | | | |
| Soft Furnishings | 8,445 47+ 70+ | 4,168 13+ 34+ | 1,929 25+ 12− | 731 32− 23− | 1,198 39− 15− | 1,127 39− 45− | 17,599 11+ 20+ |
| Linens | 3,689 2− 5− | 1,470 19+ 17− | 1,696 13+ 5+ | 546 9− 54− | 1,426 1− 24− | 1,546 28+ 1+ | 10,373 7+ 13− |
| Christy's | 1,308 18− 17− | | | | | | 1,308 18− 17− |
| Furnishing Accessories | 1,370 5− 32− | 846 17+ 3+ | 672 28− 31− | 330 58− 24+ | 797 16− 20− | 580 5− 9− | 4,595 16− 19− |
| China/Glass | 1,854 25− 18− | 1,039 36− 46− | 1,396 5+ 1− | 1,322 3− 5+ | 1,356 7+ 34− | 750 29− 32− | 7,716 15− 23− |
| Royal Worcester | 1,047 9− 38+ | 827 12− 55+ | 764 5+ 10− | | 572 6+ 12− | 935 135+ 69+ | 4,145 10+ 3− |
| Wedgwood | 1,954 34+ 85+ | | 1,116 6+ 26+ | 767 4+ − | 798 28− 44− | 1,140 30+ 41+ | 5,775 10+ 17+ |
| Royal Doulton | 2,220 14− 3+ | | 915 18− − | | 1,898 11+ − | 1,030 35− 4− | 6,064 13− 18+ |
| Denby/Dema | 1,538 44+ 23+ | | | | | | 1,538 44+ 23+ |
| Stuart Crystal | 540 51− 49− | 997 28− 23− | 729 10− 46− | (PY 288) | 701 38− 49− | 482 33− 5− | 3,448 33− 42− |
| Royal Brierley & Poole | 1,103 16− 8+ | | 756 41+ − | | | | 1,859 − 83+ |
| Cutlery | 1,612 40− 34− | 677 1− 44− | 1,292 10− 22− | 460 18− 148+ | 771 67+ 94+ | 404 42− 40− | 5,216 20− 21− |
| Cannon | 1,213 126+ − | | | | | | 1,213 126+ − |
| Clocks | 970 31− 25− | 514 4+ 23+ | 631 153+ 110+ | 201 48− 18− | 145 58− 31− | 200 46− 31− | 2,660 18− 3− |
| Lighting | 4,054 13+ 12+ | 1,349 27+ 21+ | 1,369 19− 78+ | 781 29− 3− | 1,685 7− 4− | 1,355 23+ 40+ | 10,592 2+ 17+ |
| Electrical | 6,765 16− 13+ | 1,775 6− 27+ | 2,993 5− 4+ | 695 51− 50− | 2,775 13+ 49+ | 1,750 38+ 1+ | 16,753 8− 10+ |
| Home & Garden | (PY 2,186) | | | | | | |
| K.G.B. | 7,023 3− 25+ | 1,304 3− 1− | 2,587 5− 2− | 1,033 32− 1− | 2,387 5− 10− | 1,517 20− 17− | 15,850 8− 8− |
| Service Bar | 579 6− 19+ | | | | | | 579 6− 19+ |
| Toys | 3,109 − 2+ | 1,142 8− 11+ | 1,448 3− 1+ | 886 22− 11− | 2,191 25+ 18+ | 859 30− 7− | 9,637 3− 4+ |
| Garden Furniture | | | | | | | |

*Fig. 11.1   Departmental sales analysis*
Courtesy: James Beattie PLC

4   The following balances, relating to 1982, are extracted from the books of Wadham Ltd:

|  | £ |
|---|---:|
| Stock raw materials 1 Jan 1982 | 116 980 |
| Stock raw materials 31 Dec 1982 | 139 810 |
| Stock manufactured goods 1 Jan 1982 | 182 790 |
| Stock manufactured goods 31 Dec 1982 | 181 190 |
| Purchases of raw materials | 1 017 260 |
| Fixed factory expense | 217 760 |
| Depreciation of plant | 105 000 |
| Transport vehicle costs (inc. depreciation) | 25 000 |
| Rent, rates factory | 60 000 |
| Rent, rates office | 35 000 |
| Manufacturing wages | 912 840 |
| Sales | 3 014 610 |
| Work in progress, 1 Jan 1982 | 154 210 |
| Work in progress, 31 Dec 1982 | 171 890 |

Transport vehicles are used to the extent of $\frac{1}{5}$ for inward raw materials and $\frac{4}{5}$ for the delivery of goods to customers.

*REQUIRED:*
A Manufacturing Account for Wadham Ltd for 1982. You should pay particular attention to the proper description of balances and sub-totals.

Note: A Trading Account is *not* required.

(20 marks)
(RSA II Accounting, May 1983)

5   H. Pearson is a manufacturer of wooden toys.
The following information was extracted from the books of H. Pearson at 31 December 1983:

|  | £ |
|---|---:|
| Sales | 291 700 |
| Machinery at cost | 60 000 |
| Materials: Stock at 1 Jan 1983 | 6 200 |
| Purchases | 77 500 |
| Returns inwards – manufactured goods | 1 900 |
| Returns outwards – raw materials | 3 200 |
| Manufacturing wages – direct | 103 600 |
| Work in progress | |
| valued at factory cost at 1 Jan 1983 | 3 400 |
| Stock of finished goods at 1 Jan. 1983 | 7 400 |
| Carriage inwards | 5 900 |
| Factory power | 8 800 |
| Factory expenses | 8 400 |
| Carriage outwards | 11 100 |
| Maintenance of machinery | 3 800 |

Notes:
Depreciation is to be provided on machinery at the rate of 10% per annum on cost.
The market value of the goods completed during the year was £243 000, at which figure they are to be charged to the Trading Account.
Stocks at 31 December 1983: Raw Materials £5 800; work in progress valued at factory cost £4 600; finished goods £10 600.

*REQUIRED:*
(i) Prepare a Manufacturing Account for H. Pearson for the year ended 31 December 1983, to show the cost of raw materials consumed, the prime cost and the cost of goods manufactured.
(ii) Prepare a Trading Account for the year ended 31 December 1983.

(30 marks)
(LCCI Intermediate Bookkeeping, Winter 1984)


**6** W. Wilkins manufactures concrete ornamental bird baths in one standard pattern.

The following information relates to the manufacture of 1 000 birdbaths during the month ended 31 May 1984, and to his sales, during that month.

|  |  | £ |
|---|---|---|
| 1 May | Stock of finished bird baths: 150 valued at | 375 |
|  | Stock of: sand | 100 |
|  | cement | 1 300 |
|  | gravel chippings | 70 |
|  | Purchases during month: sand | 75 |
|  | cement | 1 200 |
|  | gravel chippings | 100 |
| 31 May | Stock of: sand | 90 |
|  | cement | 1 450 |
|  | gravel chippings | 95 |
|  | Carriage inwards paid during month | 85 |
|  | Workshop wages paid | 900 |
|  | Workshop rent and rates | 150 |
|  | Workshop heating and lighting | 75 |
|  | Power used by mixing machines etc. | 140 |
|  | Water charges for mixer | 25 |

During the month 1 000 birdbaths were completed and 950 sold for £3 each.

(a) Prepare a manufacturing account and a trading account for the month of May 1984. (Show clearly your calculations of the number and value of birdbaths in stock at the end of the month.)
(b) After having completed the accounts for the month W. Wilkins learns that his employees' union has negotiated a wage increase

backdated to 1 May 1984. This will increase his wages bill for the month to £1 000. Recalculate:

(i) Prime cost,
(ii) Cost of production,
(iii) Value of closing stock,
(iv) Cost of goods sold,
(v) Gross profit.

(24 marks)<br>(London Board Principles of Accounts O level,<br>June 1984)

**7** The business of XYZ Ltd is carried on in three departments, X, Y, and Z. The following information relates to the year ended 30 April 1983:

|  | Dept. X | Dept. Y | Dept. Z |
|---|---|---|---|
|  | £ | £ | £ |
| Sales | 176 400 | 352 800 | 529 200 |
| Purchases | 110 000 | 216 700 | 299 800 |
| Stock, 1 May 1982 | 26 800 | 40 300 | 38 700 |
| Stock, 30 April 1983 | 24 300 | 42 000 | 43 600 |

Overhead expenses for the year, to be apportioned on the bases indicated, are:

| Overhead expense | | Basis for apportionment |
|---|---|---|
|  | £ |  |
| Rent and rates | 126 000 | Floor area |
| Wages and salaries | 192 000 | Number of employees |
| Insurance | 5 290 | Value of opening stock |
| Administration | 31 325 | Purchases |
| Advertising | 31 752 | Sales |

Statistical information relating to the three departments is appended:

| Department | Floor area square metres | Number of employees |
|---|---|---|
| X | 5 000 | 8 |
| Y | 7 000 | 11 |
| Z | 8 000 | 13 |

*REQUIRED:*
Prepare accounts in columnar form showing the trading results of the departments for the year.

(20 marks)<br>(AAT Numeracy and Accounting, June 1983)

**8** Gold and Silver Ltd is a wholesale jeweller and silversmith operating two distinct departments, namely Jewellery and Silver.
The firm's Balance Sheet at 1 July 1981 was:

|                                | £ '000 |                        | £ '000 |
|--------------------------------|--------|------------------------|--------|
| Authorized Capital             | 500    | Fixed Assets           |        |
| 200 000 10%                    |        | Fixtures and fittings  | 45     |
| Shares of £1                   |        | Equipment              | 12     |
| 300 000 £1 Ordinary Shares     |        |                        |        |
| Issued and paid-up Capital:    |        | Current Assets         |        |
| 10% Preference Shares          | 140    | Stock of silver        | 124    |
| £1 Ordinary Shares             | 220    | Stock of jewellery     | 215    |
| Profit and Loss Account        | 64     | Debtors                | 57     |
| Current Liabilities            |        | Balance at bank        | 67     |
| Creditors                      | 96     |                        |        |

The following information was available at 30 June 1982:

|                          | Silver £ '000 | Jewellery £ '000 |
|--------------------------|---------------|------------------|
| Purchases during the year | 362          | 519              |
| Sales for the year        | 617          | 927              |
| Sales returns             | 17           | 27               |
| Purchases returns         | 28           | 62               |
| Stock at 30 June 1982     | 141          | 256              |

|                        | £ '000 |
|------------------------|--------|
| Rent                   | 48     |
| Administration expenses | 65    |
| Advertising            | 80     |
| Selling expenses       | 105    |
| Carriage on sales      | 125    |

Unallocated expenses and provisions are to be allocated to each department in the proportion of its net turnover, with the exception of rent which is to be divided equally.

Notes:
A provision of £5 000 is to be created for bad debts.
Provide £10 000 for a legal claim which is pending.

*REQUIRED:*
Prepare the Trading and Profit and Loss Accounts of Gold and Silver Ltd for the year ended 30 June 1982, *in columnar form.*

Notes:
Prepare separate columns for each department (Jewellery and Silver) and a Total column.
Use £'000 sub-headings, as above, instead of writing numbers out in full.

(20 marks)
(LCCI Intermediate Bookkeeping, Winter 1983)

**9** D. Bird owns a retail store with two departments, one dealing in electrical goods and the other in furniture. The following information has been extracted from his books for the year ended 31 December 1982.

|  | £ |
|---|---|
| Premises at cost | 26 000 |
| Capital | 50 400 |
| Drawings | 9 500 |
| Fixtures and fittings at cost | 12 000 |
| Motor vehicles at cost | 11 000 |
| Provisions for depreciation: | |
|     Fixtures and fittings | 4 000 |
|     Motor vehicles | 5 000 |
| Purchases: | |
|     Electrical goods | 27 050 |
|     Furniture | 50 850 |
| Sales: | |
|     Electrical goods | 40 000 |
|     Furniture | 80 000 |
| Debtors | 3 430 |
| Creditors | 5 330 |
| Salaries and wages | 21 150 |
| Rates and insurance | 1 500 |
| Motor vehicle expenses | 3 000 |
| Heating and lighting | 2 500 |
| Cash at bank | 3 850 |
| Stock (1 January 1982): | |
|     Electrical goods | 5 100 |
|     Furniture | 7 800 |

*REQUIRED:*
Prepare Trading and Profit and Loss Accounts, in columnar form, to show the Gross Profit and Net Profit for each department for the year ended 31 December 1982 and a Balance Sheet for the whole business as at that date, taking into account the following additional information:

(a) Stocks at 31 December 1982 were: Electrical goods £6 400
                                        Furniture £8 700

(b) Fixtures and fittings should be depreciated at 15% on cost and the motor vehicles at 20% on cost.

(c) The floor area occupied by the Electrical Goods Department is 120 square metres and that of the Furniture Department is 180 square metres.

(d) Expenses are to be allocated between the departments on the following basis:
    (i)   Rates and insurance and Heating and lighting in proportion to the departments' floor areas.
    (ii)  Salaries and wages and Motor vehicle expenses, other than depreciation, in proportion to the turnover of each department.

(iii) Depreciation of fixtures and fittings and motor vehicles to be shared equally by the two departments.

(28 marks)

(Cambridge Board Principles of Accounts O level, Summer 1983)

10   T. Morgan is the proprietor of a manufacturing business, making two products (Brand X and Brand Y). On 30 April 1982, the following Trial Balance was prepared:

|  | £ | £ |
|---|---|---|
| Trade debtors and trade creditors | 32 950 | 11 680 |
| Bank interest | 4 300 | |
| Cash discounts allowed | 1 260 | |
| Carriage outwards | 12 750 | |
| Manufacturing wages: Brand X | 78 640 | |
| Brand Y | 66 900 | |
| Sundry manufacturing expenses: Brand X | 9 100 | |
| Brand Y | 10 250 | |
| Office salaries | 14 570 | |
| Sundry office expenses | 7 260 | |
| Selling expenses | 21 540 | |
| Raw material purchases | 88 500 | |
| Sales: Brand X | | 189 940 |
| Brand Y | | 165 870 |
| Stocks, 1 May 1981: Raw materials | 14 260 | |
| Brand X | 25 200 | |
| Brand Y | 17 900 | |
| Land and buildings | 61 000 | |
| Machinery and plant | 28 800 | |
| Office equipment | 4 640 | |
| Vehicles | 8 600 | |
| Capital | | 118 870 |
| Drawings | 23 500 | |
| Petty cash | 340 | |
| Bank overdraft | | 45 900 |
| | 532 260 | 532 260 |

*REQUIRED:*

Prepare T. Morgan's Manufacturing, Trading and Profit and Loss Accounts for the year to 30 April 1982, showing the net profit or loss made on each brand, and the Balance Sheet at 30 April 1982, taking the following into account:

(a)   Stocks at 30 April 1982: Raw materials £22 400
       Brand X       £21 300
       Brand Y       £17 400

(b)   Of the total cost of raw materials consumed in manufacturing, £46 300 applies to Brand X and the remainder to Brand Y.

(c) Allow for depreciation at the following rates (all on book value): Machinery and plant 20%, Vehicles 30%, Office equipment 10%. All the amounts are to be charged in equal proportions to Brand X and Brand Y. The vehicles are used for transporting goods to customers.

(d) Each brand is to be charged with one-half of any non-manufacturing expenses.

(24 marks)
(Oxford Board Principles of Accounts O level, Summer 1982)

---

**E.  OUTLINE ANSWERS**

**1** and **2**: the sentences test your recall of terminology, the gaps being 'Prime cost' and 'Overheads' respectively.

**3**: alternative (D) is correct; firms that *make* and sell items.

**4**: You have to ignore the trading and profit and loss items in the list, since a manufacturing account only is required. The manufacturing account is (Dr side):

|  | £ | £ |
|---|---:|---:|
| *Raw materials:* | | |
| Opening stock | | 116 980 |
| Purchases | | 1 017 260 |
| Transport ($\frac{1}{5}$) | | 5 000 |
| | | 1 139 240 |
| Less closing stock | | 139 810 |
| Cost of raw materials used | | 999 430 |
| Direct wages | | 912 840 |
| PRIME COST | | 1 912 270 |
| *Factory Overheads:* | | |
| Fixed expense | 217 760 | |
| Depreciation of plant | 105 000 | |
| Rent and rates | 60 000 | |
| | | 382 760 |
| | | 2 295 030 |
| Work in Progress at start | | 154 210 |
| | | 2 449 240 |
| deduct Work in Progress at close | | 171 890 |
| | | 2 277 350 |

**5** Your manufacturing and trading accounts should produce £33 000 profit on manufacture and £50 000 profit on trading.

Manufacturing account:

Prime cost £184 200; raw materials (opening stock + purchases − returns + carriage in − closing stock) and direct wages.

Overheads £27 000; m/c depreciation, power, expenses, maintenance.

Add opening W.I.P.; deduct closing W.I.P.

Factory cost (Dr total) £210 000; Market value (Cr side) £243 000; balance of £33 000.

Trading: the normal stock and sales (and returns out) entries, with the £243 000 market value total used in place of purchases, produces a £50 000 profit on trading.

**6**

(a) Your manufacturing account should produce a prime cost of £2 195 (stock of the three raw materials + purchases and carriage less closing stock; add direct wages). Overheads are £390; rent/rates, heat/light, power and water charges. Factory cost is £2 585.

Including factory cost in trading, produces a gross profit of £407. The calculation for closing stock is:

150 bird baths at start + 1 000 made − 950 sold = 200 in stock at end of month.

1 000 have been produced at a cost of £2 585.

Closing stock is one fifth (200 out of 1 000); so value of closing stock = $\frac{1}{5}$ × £2 585 = £517.

(b) Wages have increased by £100. Your prime cost and factory cost (cost of production) totals also should have increased by £100.

Closing stock: one-fifth of new factory cost total = $\frac{1}{5}$ × £2 685 = £537.

Using the new closing stock and factory cost totals in trading produces £2 523 cost of sales and £327 gross profit.

**7** One method of presentation of the departmental accounts is shown below.

**XYZ Ltd**

*Trading and Profit and Loss accounts year ended 30 April 1983*

|  | Department X | | Department Y | | Department Z | |
|---|---|---|---|---|---|---|
|  | £ | £ | £ | £ | £ | £ |
| Sales |  | 176 400 |  | 352 800 |  | 529 200 |
| Less cost of sales: |  |  |  |  |  |  |
|   Opening stock | 26 800 |  | 40 300 |  | 38 700 |  |
|   Purchases | 110 000 |  | 216 700 |  | 299 800 |  |
|  | 136 800 |  | 257 000 |  | 338 500 |  |
| Less closing stock | 24 300 |  | 42 000 |  | 43 600 |  |
|  |  | 112 500 |  | 215 000 |  | 294 900 |

|  | Department X | | Department Y | | Department Z | |
|---|---|---|---|---|---|---|
|  | £ | £ | £ | £ | £ | £ |
| Gross Profit | | 63 900 | | 137 800 | | 234 300 |
| Less: | | | | | | |
| Rent and rates | 31 500 | | 44 100 | | 50 400 | |
| Wages and salaries | 48 000 | | 66 000 | | 78 000 | |
| Insurance | 1 340 | | 2 015 | | 1 935 | |
| Administration | 5 500 | | 10 835 | | 14 990 | |
| Advertising | 5 292 | | 10 584 | | 15 876 | |
| Total expenses | | 91 632 | | 133 534 | | 161 201 |
| Net Profit/Loss | | (27 732) | | 4 266 | | 73 099 |

Apportionment (in order of X, Y, Z):

Rent and rates $\frac{5}{20}$, $\frac{7}{20}$, $\frac{8}{20}$ ($\frac{1}{20} = £6\,300$)

Wages/salaries $\frac{8}{32}$, $\frac{11}{32}$, $\frac{13}{32}$ ($\frac{1}{32} = £6\,000$)

Insurance: $\frac{26\,800}{105\,800} \times £5\,290$; $\frac{40\,300}{105\,800} \times £5\,290$; $\frac{38\,700}{105\,800} \times £5\,290$.

Admin: $£31\,325 \times \frac{110\,000}{626\,500}$, $\times \frac{216\,700}{626\,500}$, $\times \frac{299\,800}{626\,500}$

Advertising: $£31\,752 \times \frac{176\,400}{1\,058\,400}$, $\times \frac{352\,800}{1\,058\,400}$, $\times \frac{529\,200}{1\,058\,400}$

**8** The proportion of turnover is $\frac{3}{5}$ jewellery and $\frac{2}{5}$ silver. The trading account yields a gross profit total of £767 (000), of which £484 is for jewellery and £283 for silver. Your profit and loss account should include the £5 000 bad debts provision and the £10 000 for the legal claim in the list of expenses (no revenues). All expenses other than rent are divided three-fifths jewellery, two-fifths silver. Resultant net profit totals are (£000):

Jewellery £226; Silver £103; Total £329.

**9** The trading account is without complication; your gross profits should be £14 250 (electrical) and £30 050 (furniture). The profit and loss (Dr side) is:

|  | Electrical (£) | Furniture (£) |
|---|---|---|
| Depreciation: Fixtures | 900 | 900 |
| Vehicles | 1 100 | 1 100 |
| Salaries and wages ($\frac{1}{3} : \frac{2}{3}$) | 7 050 | 14 100 |
| Rates and insurance ($\frac{2}{5} : \frac{3}{5}$) | 600 | 900 |
| Motor expenses ($\frac{1}{3} : \frac{2}{3}$) | 1 000 | 2 000 |
| Heat and light ($\frac{2}{5} : \frac{3}{5}$) | 1 000 | 1 500 |
| Net Profit | 2 600 | 9 550 |

Balance sheet totals: Capital (+ profit, less drawings) £53 050; current liabilities £5 330; current assets £22 380; fixed assets £36 000 (depreciation on fixtures is £4 000 + £1 800, and on vehicles £5 000 + £2 200).

Question **10** involves both manufacturing and departmental accounts, combining them in order to test your understanding of both. Here is the suggested answer:

### T. Morgan

*Manufacturing, Trading and Profit and Loss accounts for the year to 30 April 1982*

| | Brand X £ | Brand Y £ | | Brand X £ | Brand Y £ |
|---|---|---|---|---|---|
| Cost of raw materials used | 46 300 | 34 060 | Factory cost of goods produced c/d | 136 920 | 114 090 |
| Direct wages | 78 640 | 66 900 | | | |
| | | | | | |
| Prime cost | 124 940 | 100 960 | | | |
| Overheads: | | | | | |
| Sundry expenses | 9 100 | 10 250 | | | |
| Depreciation (Plant) | 2 880 | 2 880 | | | |
| | | | | | |
| | 136 920 | 114 090 | | 136 920 | 114 090 |
| | | | | | |
| Finished Goods: | | | Sales | 189 940 | 165 870 |
| Opening stock | 25 200 | 17 900 | | | |
| Factory cost b/d | 136 920 | 114 090 | | | |
| | | | | | |
| | 162 120 | 131 990 | | | |
| Closing stock | 21 300 | 17 400 | | | |
| | | | | | |
| | | | | | |
| Cost of sales | 140 820 | 114 590 | | | |
| Gross profit c/d | 49 120 | 51 280 | | | |
| | | | | | |
| | 189 940 | 165 870 | | 189 940 | 165 870 |
| | | | | | |
| | | | Gross profit b/d | 49 120 | 51 280 |
| Depreciation: | | | | | |
| Vehicles | 1 290 | 1 290 | | | |
| Equipment | 232 | 232 | | | |
| Bank interest | 2 150 | 2 150 | | | |
| Discount allowed | 630 | 630 | | | |
| Carriage outwards | 6 375 | 6 375 | | | |
| Salaries | 7 285 | 7 285 | | | |
| Office expenses | 3 630 | 3 630 | | | |
| Selling expenses | 10 770 | 10 770 | | | |
| Net profit | 16 758 | 18 918 | | | |
| | | | | | |
| | 49 120 | 51 280 | | 49 120 | 51 280 |

**Workings**

Cost of raw materials used calculated in total, i.e. opening stock + purchases − closing stock. The total is £80 360, of which £46 300 is for Brand X, leaving £34 060 for Brand Y.

## G.  A STEP FURTHER

The analysis of costs that is undertaken when drawing up manufacturing accounts is developed in the subject of *Cost Accounting*. Costs are analysed as Direct and Indirect or as Fixed and Variable, and areas such as Standard Costing and Variance Analysis, Break-Even Analysis and Marginal Costing are featured. This area is outside the scope of the book, but it is of great importance in practice. If you want to study any of the topics from this field, there are many books available, and a selection is given below.

Budgetary Control is an accounting technique which is relevant to departmental accounting. Using this technique, budgets are prepared by individual departments, these budgets acting as a target for the departments to aim at. The budgeted performance is checked against the actual performance, to see whether the relevant department is achieving its set target. This particular technique is also outside the scope of the book: but if you are interested in studying Budgetary Control there are books which cover this topic in some detail, some of which are listed below.

Here is a selection of books which include chapters on manufacturing accounts ('M') and on departmental accounts ('D'). Also listed here are books which are either exclusively on cost accounting, or which contain chapters on cost accounting ('CA') and budgetary control ('BC').

Bright, *Practical Accounts 2* (Pan 'Breakthrough' series). Ch. 3 (M) and 12 (BC).

Castle and Owens, *Principles of Accounts* (7th edn) (M & E). Ch. 19 (M) and 24 (D).

Garbutt, *Carter's Advanced Accounts* (7th edn) (Pitman). Ch. 13 (D) and 15 (CA).

Owler and Brown, *Wheldon's Cost Accounting* (15th edn) (M & E). (CA).

Tubb, *Teach Yourself Cost Accounting* ('Teach Yourself' series). (CA).

Whitehead, *Bookkeeping Made Simple* ('Made Simple' series). Ch. 27 (D) and 28 (M).

Whitehead, *Success in Principles of Accounting* (John Murray). Units 29 (M) and 33 (D)

Wood, *Business Accounting 2* (4th edn) (Longman). Ch. 26 (BC).

# Chapter 12

# Income and expenditure accounts

## A.  GETTING STARTED

Questions on the accounts of clubs and societies are mainly computational in character. A question will typically provide you with a cash account or bank account for the club (or society), together with supporting notes. From this information you have to prepare final accounts.

Within this common approach a number of variations are found. You may be asked to construct a ledger account, to calculate the opening capital, or to establish how much profit is made by the club running a bar for its members.

What background knowledge and skills do you need? Firstly, an understanding of basic double entry principles is required. Secondly, you will need to understand the nature of both cash accounts and final accounts, and to be able to construct final accounts. Thirdly, a clear understanding of the distinction between capital and revenue expenditure is required. Finally, you need to understand the accruals concept.

## B.  ESSENTIAL PRINCIPLES

### THE BALANCE SHEET

This remains a record of the organization's assets, liabilities and capital (i.e. accumulated fund). It follows the same principles of construction and layout that we have already met in earlier chapters.

**Subscriptions in the balance sheet**

With *subscriptions in advance*, we have an example of income which has been received in the current year, but which refers to next year. The members concerned have paid for something – next year's membership – which they have not yet received. The club therefore owes these members the value of their subscriptions paid in advance, and they must be treated as a (current) liability.

If there are *subscriptions in arrears* at the end of the year – in other words, the club was owed money by some members, rather than it owing money to members – these are treated as a current asset, the members being thought of as a form of debtor (they have enjoyed the privilege of a year's membership of the club, for which they have not paid).

In practice a club may decide to adopt the principle of *conservatism* and choose to ignore the subscriptions owed. Examination questions should state whether subscriptions in arrears are to be treated as a current asset in a closing balance sheet. Where the subscriptions are given, and no guidance is given in the question, the usual practice is to treat them as a current asset in answering the question.

We will shortly see how to adjust amounts for subscriptions in the income and expenditure account.

---

## THE RECEIPTS AND PAYMENTS ACCOUNT

This account is a cash or bank account containing the receipts and payments of the relevant club or society. Here is a sample account:

| RECEIPTS | £ | PAYMENTS | £ |
|---|---|---|---|
| Opening balance b/d | 180 | Purchases of new | |
| Subscriptions received | 1 410 | equipment | 1 000 |
| Dance receipts | 450 | Light and heat | 360 |
| Refreshment receipts | 220 | Dance expenses | 210 |
| | | Cost of refreshments | 70 |
| | | Insurance premium | 15 |
| | | Rates | 305 |
| | | Closing balance c/d | 300 |
| | 2 260 | | 2 260 |

*Notes:*
(a) At the end of the financial year rates were prepaid £15.
(b) There was an opening stock of refreshments, £10 and there is no closing stock.

---

### Limitations of the account

When we come to examine this account in more detail, we can see its limitations.

1. It contains both capital and revenue expenditure: e.g. the credit side may contain payment for new equipment (capital) and insurance premium (revenue).

| **Revenue expenditure** | **Capital expenditure** |
|---|---|
| ↓ | ↓ |
| Income and expenditure account | Balance sheet |

2. A cash account records the receipt and payment of cash, and does not classify the items in the way that we need to when constructing final accounts.

The purpose of a cash account is to record receipts and payments of cash, and it does not classify these receipts and payments into *the time period* to which they refer. The final accounts include details relating only to the year (or other period) in question: but a receipts and payments account will record cash inflows and outflows regardless of the period to which they refer.

The accruals concept is relevant here, and is used to allocate costs or revenues to the period to which they refer. For instance, there has been £305 paid during the year for rates, but £15 of this amount does not apply to this year. It has been paid in advance, and therefore refers to next year. The cost of rates to be recorded in the income and expenditure account is £290.

Cash paid for refreshments, on the credit side of the account, amounts to £70, but the true cost of refreshments sold is £80. The opening stock (£10) has been used this year and must be included in the total cost. Had there been any closing stock, this would have been deducted from the total cost, because it would refer to stock to be used next year.

Note that there is a closing balance on a receipts and payments account. This is the closing bank or cash balance, and is required for completion of the closing balance sheet.

## INCOME AND EXPENDITURE ACCOUNTS

The purpose of constructing an *income and expenditure account* is to establish whether or not a surplus has been made. Adjustments similar to those met in profit and loss accounts may have to be made.

Some confusion may arise from the fact that the credit side of the income and expenditure account contains items recorded on the debit side of the receipts and payments account, and vice versa. Cash received (and therefore debited in the receipts and payments account) is usually in the form of income which is recorded on the credit side of the income and expenditure account. Cash paid out and credited to the receipts and payments account is usually for expenses, which are shown on the debit side of the income and expenditure account.

There are two quite difficult areas:

1. preparing a separate trading account;
2. constructing a subscriptions account.

### Preparing a separate trading account

Many clubs or societies carry out secondary activities that will lead to profit being made. The most common example is where a club operates a bar for the benefit of its members, any profit from this operation being used for the furtherance of the main activity.

We need to calculate the relevant profit (or loss) in a separate trading account. The profit calculated is then transferred to the income and expenditure account. The standard trading account procedures are used here. There may be additional expenses associated with the profit-making activity: for example, if a bar is being run, the wages of the bar staff need including (in the cost of sales) since they apply specifically to this activity.

The true values of purchases and sales may not be given. Should the receipts and payments account be the main source of information, we need to remember that the amounts included in this account may not be the accurate purchases or sales figures. This is another example of the need to match revenues and expenses to the period to which they relate, and this has a close link with the topic of Incomplete Records (see Ch. 16). Here is an example:

A club runs a bar to help finance its main activity.

(a) Bar stocks in the year were:
opening stock £540
closing stock £470

(b) Payments to suppliers during the year (from the receipts and payments account) totalled £2 450.

(c) Cash received from sales at the bar was £6 490.

(d) Creditors for bar stocks at the start of the year were £145, and at the end of the year were £225.

(e) Wages of the bar staff totalled £515.

If a *Bar Trading Account* is required, some adjustments must be made to calculate the actual cost of purchases.

£2 450 was paid to bar suppliers, but £145 of this was for goods relating to last year's trading (the opening creditors total). We therefore have £2 305 as the value of goods relating to this year and which are paid for.

There are also goods bought during this year for which no money has been paid (the closing creditors figure), and which will not be included in the £2 305 total. The goods refer to this trading period, and must be included in the value of purchases: £2 305 + £225, giving £2 530 as the true value of purchases.

The bar trading account can now be constructed.

*Bar trading account*

|  | £ |  | £ |
|---|---|---|---|
| Opening stock | 540 | Sales | 6 490 |
| Purchases | 2 530 |  |  |
|  | 3 070 |  |  |
| Less closing stock | 470 |  |  |
| Cost of goods sold | 2 600 |  |  |
| Staff wages | 515 |  |  |
|  | 3 115 |  |  |
| Profit | 3 375 |  |  |
|  | 6 490 |  | 6 490 |

The profit of £3 375 is shown on the credit side of the income and expenditure account, as an income for the club.

**Constructing a subscriptions account**

To calculate the correct amount of subscriptions to record in the income and expenditure account, we need to identify the true value of subscriptions for the period. For income and expenditure purposes, it does not matter *when* the money was received, or *whether* the subscriptions have been received or not: if they relate to *this* accounting period, they are included. Here is an illustration to help explain this point:

Calculate the subscriptions amount to be shown in the income and expenditure account for the year to 31 December 1986:

(a)   1986 subscriptions paid in advance at 31 December 1985: £45.

(b)   1986 cash received from subscriptions: £685 (this includes £15 received in 1986 for 1985 subscriptions, and £10 paid in advance for 1987).

(c)   Unpaid 1986 subscriptions at 31 December 1986: £35.

Because we are interested in the 1986 subscriptions total, we only include amounts referring to 1986:

| £ | |
|---|---|
| 45 | received 1985 for 1986 subscriptions |
| 660 | received in 1986 for 1986 subscriptions (685 − 15 − 10) |
| 35 | still owed for 1986 |
| 740 | figure for subscriptions in the income and expenditure account. |

**The subscriptions account**

The *subscriptions account* is a revenue account. The above information is now shown in the form of a subscriptions account:

*Subscriptions account* (1986)

| | | £ | | | £ |
|---|---|---|---|---|---|
| 1 Jan | Subs in arrears b/d | 15 | 1 Jan | Subs in advance b/d | 45 |
| 31 Dec | Subs in advance c/d | 10 | | Cash received from members | 685 |
| | | | 31 Dec | Subs in arrears c/d | 35 |

1.   The opening balances represent an asset (a debit balance for subscriptions in arrears) and a liability (credit balance for subscriptions in advance).

2.   Cash received for subscriptions is debited to the receipts and payments account, the matching credit entry being shown in the account above. Note that this total includes the closing accrued and prepaid amounts.

3.   The closing accrued and prepaid balances are also shown. Because these balances are 'above the line' (before the account totals are included and ruled off), they are recorded on the 'wrong' side. After the account is closed off, the balances are brought down to the correct side.

This account has another balance, as we see when we total the two sides. The difference represents the value of 1986 subscriptions to be shown in the income and expenditure account. In our example, it is £740 (which we know from our arithmetical calculation of 1986 subscriptions made earlier). Here is the remaining information for the account:

|  |  | £ |  |  | £ |
|---|---|---|---|---|---|
| 31 Dec | Transfer to | | | | |
| | I and E account | 740 | | | |
| | | 765 | | | 765 |
| 1987 | | | 1987 | | |
| 1 Jan | Subs in | | 1 Jan | Subs in | |
| | arrears b/d | 35 | | advance b/d | 10 |

The completed account now contains the totals and the balances brought down to their correct sides. The accrued subscriptions are shown as an asset (debit) balance, and subscriptions in advance appear as a credit (liability) balance.

## C.  USEFUL APPLIED MATERIALS

**Figure 12.1** illustrates part of a set of final accounts, excluding supporting notes. As can be seen, the Society has to meet a variety of 'Charges' (items of expenditure) from its income, which is comprised of subscriptions, registration and transfer fees, and examining fees.

## D.  RECENT EXAMINATION QUESTIONS

The questions in this section on the various aspects of club accounts are computational, the typical method of testing your understanding of this topic. Question **1** is a simple multiple choice item on the accumulated fund, while question **2** tests your knowledge of the receipts and payments area.

Questions **3–6** concentrate on final accounts. Question 3 is relatively straightforward, being based on the income and expenditure account; while the remaining questions require a balance sheet to be constructed as well. Question 6 involves an additional trading account, and question 4 requires the accumulated fund to be calculated.

*Question 6 is answered fully in the section 'A tutor's answer'.*

## The Society of Company and Commercial Accountants

# Income and Expenditure Account for the year ended 31st December 1983

| Income | 1983 £ | £ | 1982 £ | £ |
|---|---|---|---|---|
| Annual subscriptions: | | | | |
| Members | 195,484 | | 196,688 | |
| Students | 38,567 | | 41,597 | |
| BAAA members | — | 234,051 | 13,118 | 251,403 |
| Registration and transfer fees | 14,882 | | 28,519 | |
| Examinations | 23,001 | 37,883 | 28,696 | 57,215 |
| | | 271,934 | | 308,618 |

| Charges | | | | |
|---|---|---|---|---|
| Staff costs | 81,459 | | 100,535 | |
| Depreciation | 17,670 | | 14,683 | |
| Other operating charges: | | | | |
| Accommodation | 9,969 | | 10,360 | |
| Office services | 41,202 | | 45,113 | |
| Council and Committee expenses | 25,471 | | 21,160 | |
| Audit fees | 5,268 | | 3,750 | |
| Legal fees | 2,396 | | 2,295 | |
| Publications | 41,442 | | 52,468 | |
| Examinations | 21,436 | | 24,093 | |
| Car and travelling expenses | 4,821 | | 10,205 | |
| Local Centre expenses | 5,171 | | 6,000 | |
| Irish Association | — | | 750 | |
| European Diploma expenses | 4,671 | | 5,756 | |
| Promotion and development | 19,420 | 280,396 | 25,368 | 322,536 |
| Operating deficit | | (8,462) | | (13,918) |
| Property letting | 1,514 | | 2,097 | |
| Investment income | 8,883 | | 8,760 | |
| Interest receivable | 8,954 | 19,351 | 9,785 | 20,642 |
| Surplus on ordinary activities before taxation | | 10,889 | | 6,724 |
| Taxation | | 5,715 | | 7,498 |
| Surplus/(Deficit) after taxation transferred to accumulated fund | | £5,174 | | £(774) |

*Fig. 12.1   Income and Expenditure account*
Courtesy: Society of Company and Commercial Accountants

1  The balance on the accumulated fund of a club can be established at any date by:

A    preparing a balance sheet
B    looking only at the bank statement
C    preparing an income and expenditure account
D    calculating the current balance on the subscription account.
(AEB Specimen Accounting O level Paper, 1980)

**Computational questions**

2  The following information relates to the affairs of the Sexton Social Club for the year ended 29 February 1984:

|  | £ |
|---|---|
| Balance in bank 1 March 1983 | 125 |
| Subscriptions received for current year | 4 000 |
| Cash paid for catering supplies | 7 326 |
| Unpaid accounts for catering supplies | 78 |
| Cash takings for sales of food and drink | 9 324 |
| Stocks of food at cost 29 February 1984 | 104 |
| Rates paid for current year | 750 |
| Insurance premium for year 1984 | 250 |
| Purchase of new furniture at cost of £3 000, of which one half had been paid | 1 500 |
| Payment of wages to catering staff | 2 000 |
| Sales of Christmas draw tickets | 925 |
| Expenses of Christmas draw paid | 450 |

(a)  Select the necessary items from the list above and prepare the club's Receipts and Payments account for the year ended 29 February 1984.
(b)  What information is conveyed to you by the closing balance?
(12 marks)
(RSA I Bookkeeping, March 1984)

3  The following is the summarized Receipts and Payments Account of the Junior Gannymede Social Club for the year ended 30 June 1983.

| Receipts | £ | Payments | £ |
|---|---|---|---|
| Balance at 1 July 1982 | 840 | Rent of gaming machines | 895 |
| Bar takings | 10 570 | Raffle prizes | 280 |
| Sale of raffle tickets | 395 | Payments for bar supplies | 7 040 |
| Receipts from gaming | | Purchase of new furniture | |
| machines | 2 105 | for the club house | 2 190 |
| Subscriptions | 2 320 | Wages | 2 050 |
| | | General expenses | 2 105 |
| | | Rates and insurances | 714 |
| | | Balance at 30 June 1983 | 956 |
| | 16 230 | | 16 230 |

*Note:*
There was a small stock of raffle prizes valued at £40 on 30 June 1983. There were no bar stocks at the beginning or end of the year.

*REQUIRED:*
From the information given above prepare an Income and Expenditure Account for the Club for the year ended 30 June 1983, showing clearly the profit or loss on the bar, gaming machines and raffle.

(12 marks)
(RSA I Bookkeeping, February 1984)

**4** The assets and liabilities of the Scotgate Social Club on 1 April 1982 were:

|  | £ |
|---|---|
| Freehold premises | 30 000 |
| Furniture, fittings and fixtures | 12 000 |
| Bar stock | 150 |
| Balance at bank | 600 |

The following is a summary of the receipts and payments for the club for the year ended 31 March 1983.

| Receipts | £ | Payments | £ |
|---|---|---|---|
| Balance at bank | 600 | Bar supplies | 4 300 |
| Subscriptions | 480 | Raffle prizes | 60 |
| Bar sales | 4 750 | Expenses of annual dance | 130 |
| Sale of raffle tickets | 150 | Cost of refreshments for | |
| Annual dance | 200 | sale on club nights | 80 |
| Sale of refreshments | 160 | Rates | 250 |
|  |  | Electricity | 500 |
|  |  | Repairs to equipment | 200 |
|  |  | New tables for use in bar | 200 |
|  |  | Balance at 31.3.83 | 620 |
|  | 6 340 |  | 6 340 |

On 31 March 1983 bar stocks were £200; £80 was owing for electricity and rates were prepaid by £45.

*REQUIRED:*
Calculate the accumulated fund as at 1 April 1982.
Prepare an Income and Expenditure Account for the year ended 31 March 1983 and a Balance Sheet as at that date.

(26 marks)
(RSA I Bookkeeping, May 1983)

**5** Oxbridge Social Club was formed on 10 April 1983. The honorary treasurer presented to the members the following report covering the first year's activities of the Club.

'Our first year has proved a satisfactory one financially.

80 seniors joined the Club and I received from them the full annual subscription (£12 each). In addition, 16 of these senior

members paid me their subscriptions for the second year (£12 each) before 10 April 1984. 156 juniors also joined, but only 150 had paid their annual subscriptions (£3 each) by 9 April 1984 and I think it is very unlikely that we shall receive the 6 junior subscriptions outstanding.

Our thanks are due to Mr T. Murray, who lent the Club £1 000 for 3 years, free of interest.

Our socials and dances proved very successful: receipts were £4 240, compared with expenses £1 720. The £1 720 expenses includes some outstanding bills totalling £115 which remained unpaid at 9 April 1984 but will be paid in the near future.

We spent £1 760 on equipment and in this year's accounts we have allowed £360 for depreciation on this equipment.

Payments for general running expenses totalled £2 054, consisting of: rent £980, lighting and heating £412, postage and stationery £241, miscellaneous expenses £421. In addition, we have some outstanding bills to pay relating to our first year's activities: rent £60, lighting and heating £85, miscellaneous expenses £92.

We have £1 200 in a savings bank account and the remainder of our cash is in a bank current account. In addition to the £1 200 in our savings bank account, I estimate that we have earned £70 interest during the year on these savings, but I have not yet been notified of the exact amount.'

You are asked to prepare the Club's Income and Expenditure Account for the year ended 9 April 1984 and Balance Sheet as at 9 April 1984.

*Note:*
There are no liabilities, assets, payments or receipts to consider other than those mentioned in the report.                              (16 marks)
(Oxford Board Principles of Accounts O level, Summer 1984)


**6**    You are asked to prepare the annual accounts of the Leisure Social Club for the year to 31 December 1983.

You ascertain that some expenses are paid in cash out of the takings and the balance of these takings and other receipts are paid into the bank. You prepare a summary of the bank account from the bank statements and it appears as follows:

|  | £ |  | £ |
|---|---|---|---|
| Balance at bank 1 Jan 1983 | 6 000 | Payments for bar supplies | 54 000 |
| Cash paid into the bank |  | Rent | 3 600 |
| during the year | 72 000 | Repairs | 1 320 |
|  |  | New furniture | 3 700 |
|  |  | Gas, electricity and fuel | 1 440 |
|  |  | New billiard table | 1 200 |
|  |  | General expenses | 4 800 |
|  |  | Balance at bank, |  |
|  |  | 31 Dec 1983 | 7 940 |
|  | 78 000 |  | 78 000 |

No adequate records of actual cash in hand have been kept, but bar takings are recorded and show a total of £81 600. Receipts from games amount to £1 560 and from subscriptions to £2 040.

You obtain the following information regarding the disposal of the cash receipts not lodged at the bank:

(a) Weekly wages, for bar staff, amounting to £80 are paid in cash.
(b) Tobacco and cigarettes are purchased for the bar in small quantities, always for cash, and you ascertain from suppliers' invoices that the total so paid in 1983 amounted to £5 200.
(c) The secretary and members of the committee received honorariums, paid in cash, which amounted to £1 200.
(d) The balance of cash not accounted for is assumed to be for general expenses.

Details of the opening and closing assets and liabilities, apart from those otherwise mentioned, are:

|  | 1 Jan 1983 £ | 31 Dec 1983 £ |
|---|---|---|
| Creditors for bar purchases | 3 600 | 3 000 |
| Bar stock | 7 200 | 8 400 |
| Furniture and equipment | 4 800 | see below |

10% for depreciation is to be written off all furniture and equipment and off the new billiard table.

*REQUIRED:*
(a) A bar trading account and an Income and Expenditure Account for 1983. (19 marks)
(b) A Balance Sheet as at 31 Dec 1983. (11 marks)

(RSA II Accounting, May 1984)

---

**E. OUTLINE ANSWERS**

Question **1** tests your understanding of the accumulated fund; as 'capital', it can be found by constructing a balance sheet, and therefore (A) is the correct answer.

**2**

(a) Receipts and Payments account records cash received (Dr) and paid (Cr). The Dr side of your account should include: opening balance, subscriptions received, food and drink takings, Christmas draw ticket sales; total £14 374.

The Cr side of the account includes cash paid for catering supplies, rates paid, insurance paid, purchase of new furniture (£1 500), wages paid and expenses of Christmas draw. Total payments £12 276.

Balance of cash £14 374 − £12 276 = £2 098.

All other items do not involve cash receipt or payment.

(b) The closing balance is cash in hand (or at bank): it represents excess of receipts over payments, and is a current asset.

**3** You are required to calculate profit/loss on the bar, on gaming and on the raffle. Calculations are:

    Bar:       takings less cost of supplies = £3 530 profit.
    Gaming:  receipts less rent of machines = £1 210 profit.
    Raffle:    sale of tickets less net cost of prizes (£280 − £40 stock left) = £155 profit.

The income and expenditure account is summarized below:

| | £ | | £ |
|---|---|---|---|
| Wages | 2 050 | Subscriptions | 2 320 |
| General expenses | 2 105 | Profits on: | |
| Rates and insurance | 714 | Bar | 3 530 |
| SURPLUS | 2 346 | Gaming | 1 210 |
| | | Raffle | 155 |
| | 7 215 | | 7 215 |

The purchase of new furniture is capital expenditure, and the opening and closing (cash) balances are ignored for the purposes of the I & E account.

**4**

(a) Your accumulated fund total should be £42 750. There are four opening assets and no opening liabilities.

(b) Even though the question does not ask for it, a Bar Trading account can be prepared, to show profit/loss on the bar. Sales are £4 750; cost of sales (opening stock + purchases less closing stock) £4 250; profit £500.

    Here is the income and expenditure account for the year:

| | £ | | £ |
|---|---|---|---|
| Rates (250 − 45) | 205 | Bar profit | 500 |
| Electricity (500 + 80) | 580 | Subscriptions | 480 |
| Repairs | 200 | Raffle profit (150 − 60) | 90 |
| Surplus | 235 | Dance profit (200 − 130) | 70 |
| | | Refreshment profit (160 − 80) | 80 |
| | 1 220 | | 1 220 |

In the balance sheet you should have £42 200 for fixed assets (£200 new furniture) and current assets of closing stock, closing bank balance and prepaid rates.

    Accumulated fund plus surplus totals £42 985, and there is one current liability, £80 accrued electricity.

**5** This question is laid out in an untypical way, and requires you to search for the various items. Here are the effects of the individual items:

| | |
|---|---|
| Subscriptions: | 80 × £12 and 150 (not 156) × £3 to I&E as subs for the year. The prepaid 16 subs to the balance sheet (current liability). |
| Loan: | Balance Sheet liability. |

| | | |
|---|---|---|
| Socials/dances: | receipts as income, expenses (£1 720) as expenditure, in I&E. The £115 accrual to B/S as liability. |
| Equipment: | shown in B/S as an asset; depreciation deducted on B/S and also charged as expenditure in I&E. |
| Expenses: | shown in I&E, including the accrued amounts; the various accruals shown in B/S as liabilities. |
| Savings a/c: | Balance Sheet asset; interest also an asset (accrued revenue) and shown in I&E as income. |

You also have to calculate the closing cash balance, by constructing a receipts and payments account. This account records cash receipts and payments regardless of which accounting period the receipts and payments refer to.

| | |
|---|---|
| Receipts are: | subs £960 + £192 + £450; loan £1 000; socials £4 240; total receipts £6 842. |
| Payments are: | social expenses £1 605 (deduct the unpaid bills); equipment £1 720; running expenses £2 054 (the cash paid figure is required); transfer to savings a/c £1 200; total payments £6 579. |
| Closing balance: | £6 842 − £6 579 = £263. |

The summarized Income and Expenditure account is:

| | £ | | £ |
|---|---|---|---|
| Depreciation | 360 | Subscriptions: full | 960 |
| Rent (+60) | 1 040 | junior | 450 |
| Light/heat (+85) | 497 | Socials profit: | 2 520 |
| Postage | 241 | (4 240 − 1 720) | |
| Miscellaneous (+92) | 513 | Accrued interest | 70 |
| Surplus | 1 349 | | |
| | ———— | | ———— |
| | 4 000 | | 4 000 |

The balance sheet of the Oxbridge Social Club is:

| | £ | £ | | £ | £ |
|---|---|---|---|---|---|
| *Fixed Assets:* | | | *Accumulated Fund:* | | |
| Equipment | | 1 720 | Surplus | | 1 349 |
| Less depreciation | | 360 | *Long-term Liability:* | | |
| | | ———— | Loan | | 1 000 |
| | | 1 360 | *Current Liabilities:* | | |
| *Current Assets:* | | | Prepaid revenue | 192 | |
| Savings account | 1 200 | | Accrued expenses | | |
| Accrued interest | 70 | | (115 + 60 + 85 + 92) | 352 | |
| Current account | 263 | | | | ———— |
| | ———— | | | | 544 |
| | 1 533 | | | | |
| | ———— | | | | ———— |
| | 2 893 | | | | 2 893 |

## F. A TUTOR'S ANSWER

Question **6** is a difficult one on this topic, requiring you to identify and adjust various expense and asset totals. Here is the suggested answer:

**Leisure Social Club**

*Bar Trading account for year to 31 December 1983*

|  | £ |  | £ |
|---|---|---|---|
| Opening stock | 7 200 | Takings | 81 600 |
| Purchases | 53 400 |  |  |
|  | 60 600 |  |  |
| Less closing stock | 8 400 |  |  |
|  | 52 200 |  |  |
| Wages | 4 160 |  |  |
| Tobacco | 5 200 |  |  |
|  | 61 560 |  |  |
| Profit to I & E account | 20 040 |  |  |
|  | 81 600 |  | 81 600 |

*Workings:*

£

Purchases: 54 000 payment
  − 3 600 opening creditors
  + 3 000 closing creditors
Wages: £80 × 52 weeks

**Leisure Social Club**

*Income and Expenditure account for year to 31 December 1983*

|  | £ |  | £ |
|---|---|---|---|
| Rent | 3 600 | Bar takings | 20 040 |
| Repairs | 1 320 | Receipts from games | 1 560 |
| Gas | 1 440 | Subscriptions | 2 040 |
| General expenses | 4 800 |  |  |
| Depreciation | 970 |  |  |
| Honorariums | 1 200 |  |  |
| Surplus of income over expenditure | 10 310 |  |  |
|  | 23 640 |  | 23 640 |

**Workings**

£

Depreciation: asset value = 4 800 opening balance
3 700 new furniture
1 200 new table

---

9 700 at 10%

### Leisure Social Club

*Balance Sheet at 31 December 1983*

| | £ | £ | | £ |
|---|---|---|---|---|
| *Fixed Assets:* | | | *Accumulated Fund:* | |
| Furniture and equipment | 9 700 | | Opening balance | 14 400 |
| Less depreciation | | 970 | Add surplus | 10 310 |
| | | 8 730 | | 24 710 |
| *Current Assets:* | | | *Current Liabilities:* | |
| Stock | 8 400 | | Creditors | 3 000 |
| Bank | 7 940 | | | |
| Cash | 2 640 | 18 980 | | |
| | | 27 710 | | 27 710 |

**Workings**

Opening Accumulated Fund: Assets £7 200 + £4 800 + £6 000 less
Liabilities £3 600

| Cash: | Receipts | Payments |
|---|---|---|
| | £ | £ |
| | 81 600 | 4 160 |
| | 1 560 | 5 200 |
| | 2 040 | 1 200 |
| | | 72 000 |
| | 85 200 | |
| | | 82 560 |

Net balance £2 640

---

## G.  A STEP FURTHER

Many textbooks contain clearly written and well illustrated chapters on club accounts. Here is a selection:

Bright, *Practical Accounts 2* (Pan 'Breakthrough' series). Ch. 6.

Castle and Owens, *Principles of Accounts* (7th edn) (M & E). Ch. 18.

Garbutt, *Carter's Advanced Accounts* (7th edn) (Pitman). Ch. 10.

Whitehead, *Bookkeeping Made Simple* ('Made Simple' series). Ch. 24.

Wood, *Business Accounting 1* (4th edn) (Longman). Ch. 34.

# Chapter 13

**Partnership accounts**

## A. GETTING STARTED

Questions set on partnership accounts can be either computational or descriptive in character. The computational questions are normally based on the problem that all partnerships face – that of dividing a single net profit between more than one partner. These questions typically test:

1. your ability to construct partners' *Current accounts*, showing details of profit and drawings;
2. your knowledge of the construction of the *Appropriation account*; or
3. your ability to construct *full final accounts*, using an acceptable layout.

Essay questions may also be set on this topic. Such questions may ask you to describe the function and construction of the current accounts, or the purpose of the appropriation account.

To study this topic effectively, you need to know how to construct the final accounts of a sole trader, and you should also be familiar with the structure of a sole trader's capital account.

## B. ESSENTIAL PRINCIPLES

### APPROPRIATION OF PROFITS

A question may ask why profit is shared out under the various headings found in the appropriation account.

*Interest on capital* is one of the principal methods used to share partnership profits: it is a reward to the partners for investing their private money in the business. Since the partner investing the most is taking the greatest risk, interest on capital will reward that partner with the greatest return.

*Partnership salaries* are given for investing more time (rather than more money) in a partnership. If only one of the partners works in the partnership, he or she may receive a salary allocated from profits.

Salary and interest on capital are taken from the net profit: the *balance of the remaining profit* is shared according to the partnership agreement.

*Interest on drawings* may also be present in a partnership agreement. It acts as a penalty to the partners (being charged on drawings), to deter them from taking out more money from the partnership in anticipation of profits than is necessary.

## The appropriation account

It is the role of the *Appropriation account* to record how the profit is to be shared between the partners. The credit side shows the profit available for distribution: the debit side shows how the profit is actually shared out. For example:

### Appropriation account

| | £ | | | £ |
|---|---|---|---|---|
| Salary: Partner X | | (Net Profit b/d) | | |
| Interest on Capitals: | | Interest on Drawings: | | |
| Partner X | | Partner X | | |
| Partner Y | | Partner Y | | |
| Partner Z | | Partner Z | | |
| Balance of Profits: | | OR Balance of Losses: | | |
| Partner X | | Partner X | | |
| Partner Y | | Partner Y | | |
| Partner Z | | Partner Z | | |

## Handling a loss

Some questions result in the partnership making a loss, and this loss must be appropriated. We have to go through the normal appropriation procedure in the appropriation account:

(a) net loss b/d (debit side of the account);
(b) credit any interest on drawings to the account;
(c) debit any salary or interest on capital.

This will leave a debit balance on the account: 'Balance of Loss', which is then shared between the partners in their agreed profit/loss sharing ratio (credit the appropriation account as shown above, and debit individual current accounts).

## Where there is no partnership agreement

Some questions may ask for an explanation of the rules for appropriating profit where there has been no agreement drawn up by the partners. The provisions of the Partnership Act give guidance in these situations. Here is the list of points:

1. Profits and losses are shared equally.
2. There is no interest on capital (or interest on drawings).
3. There is no entitlement to a partnership salary.
4. Any partnership loan receives 5% interest per annum.

These rules will only apply where there is no agreement to the contrary.

## CURRENT AND CAPITAL ACCOUNTS

A sole trader's capital account is relatively straightforward:

*Capital account*

| | £ | | £ |
|---|---|---|---|
| | | Existing Balance | |
| Drawings | | Net Profit | |

The current account of a partner effectively takes over the lower part of the sole trader capital account:

| | £ | | £ | |
|---|---|---|---|---|
| | | Existing Balance | | } Partner's Capital account |
| Drawings | | Net Profit | | } Partner's Current account |

The partner's capital account holds the value of capital invested by the partner: it is not affected by profits or drawings, but only by increases or withdrawals of capital. The credit side of the current account records gain (in the form of profits), while the debit side records drawings on profit.

## Links with appropriation

There is a close link between the current account and the appropriation account. Using the example appropriation account earlier, here is Partner X's Current account (the entries matching those in the appropriation account are in capitals):

*Current account: Partner X*

| | £ | | £ |
|---|---|---|---|
| Balance b/d | | PARTNERSHIP SALARY | |
| Drawings | | INTEREST ON CAPITAL | |
| INTEREST ON DRAWINGS | | BALANCE OF PROFIT | |
| Balance c/d | | | |
| | | Balance b/d | |

## Links with the balance sheet

The opening debit balance in the current account above would be shown in last period's balance sheet as an asset: partner X owes the value of this balance to the partnership. There is a closing credit balance (brought down to the credit side of the account), which would be shown in this period's balance sheet as a liability: it represents the balance of undrawn profits.

| **Goodwill** | *Goodwill* may be featured in a partnership question, particularly one involving some form of change in the partnership. It is: |
|---|---|

(a) the difference between the value of the business as a 'going concern' and the value of its net assets;
(b) an intangible asset, shown by (or within) the fixed assets on a balance sheet;
(c) written off from profits made.

Its valuation, and the technicalities associated with it, do not concern us here, but we may be asked to define 'goodwill' and to show its basic treatment in the accounts.

| **Amalgamation** | A question concerning the amalgamation of sole traders usually requires us to proceed as follows: |
|---|---|

(a) adjust the values of the assets/liabilities for each trader, remembering to omit those which are not to be brought into the new partnership;
(b) calculate the new capitals for each (new) partner;
(c) construct the new balance sheet.

As with the rest of this 'partnership alteration' work, there are many complications, and more advanced accounting syllabuses require a much more detailed knowledge of the creation or dissolution of partnerships. Some advice, if you have to study this topic at greater depth, is given in section G of the chapter.

## C. USEFUL APPLIED MATERIALS

Information on partnership accounts, like sole trader accounts, is not readily available because partnerships are not legally required to publish their accounts. Partnerships remain an important and a common form of business ownership; checking the streets in your local town or city centre will demonstrate this, with solicitors, estate agents, accountants and other professions providing real-life examples.

## D. RECENT EXAMINATION QUESTIONS

Questions **1–3** are objective questions on partnership accounts. They should take less than five minutes to complete.

Question **4** is descriptive and tests your knowledge of specific partnership accounts (notably current and appropriation accounts).

Question **5** requires appropriation and current accounts to be constructed. Questions **6** and **7** are based on full final accounts for a partnership. *The answer to question 7 is provided in section F of the chapter.*

Question **8** involves amalgamation into a new partnership.

**1**   Interest on capital appears on the . . . . . . side of a partner's
. . . . . . account.

(JMB Bookkeeping and Accounting O level, June 1984)

**2**   In a partnership, the Profit and Loss Appropriation Account
shows how the net profit will be shared.

Which one of the following items could also appear on the credit
side of that account?

A   Interest on capital
B   Partners' capital
C   Interest on drawings
D   Partners' drawings.

(AEB Specimen Accounting O level Paper, 1980)

**3**   The purchaser of a business pays £15 000 for the business, taking
over £12 000 worth of assets and £2 000 worth of liabilities. The value
of the goodwill is:

A   £3 000
B   £5 000
C   £10 000
D   £12 000

(AEB Specimen Accounting O level Paper, 1980)

**4**

(a)   (i)   What is the purpose of the appropriation section of the Profit
and Loss Account to a partnership?

(1 mark)

(ii)   Name four items that can be found in the appropriation
section and explain, in each case, where the double entry would be
found.

(8 marks)

(b)   A partner withdraws goods valued at £200 cost price.
(i)   How would this item be entered in the ledger accounts?

(2 marks)

(ii)   How would these drawings be shown in the final accounts?

(1 mark)

(c)   In the absence of a partnership agreement, how would partners
resolve disputes with respect to:
(i)   share of profit;
(ii)   partners' salaries;
(iii)   interest on loan by a partner?

(3 marks)

(AEB Accounting O level, November 1983)

**5**   Pen and Ink are in partnership, and in 1983 their firm made a
profit of £25 000. The partners have agreed to share profits as follows:

(a)   Each partner is to receive 10% interest on the balance on his
capital account at 1 January.

(b)  A salary of £3 000 per annum is to be paid to Pen, and one of £9 000 to Ink.

(c)  During 1983 Pen withdrew £10 000 and Ink £12 000. Interest is to be charged on drawings; the charges for 1983 are Pen £300 and Ink £350.

(d)  Any residue of profit is to be shared Pen three-fifths and Ink two-fifths.

At 1 January 1983 the balances shown in the firm's books were:

|  | Pen | Ink |
|---|---|---|
|  | £ | £ |
| Capital account | 50 000 | 15 000 |
| Current account (Credit Balances) | 3 000 | 4 500 |

The capital account balances are to remain unchanged.

*REQUIRED:*
Prepare the firm's Appropriation Account and the separate Current Account of each partner for 1983.

(20 marks)
(RSA II Accounting, March 1984)


**6**  The following is the Trial Balance of Jack and Jill, who trade in partnership, at 31 March 1983:

|  | £ | £ |
|---|---|---|
| Capital Account Balances 1 April 1982 |  |  |
| Jack |  | 15 000 |
| Jill |  | 5 000 |
| Current Account Balances 1 April 1982: |  |  |
| Jack |  | 1 500 |
| Jill |  | 2 500 |
| Sales |  | 75 000 |
| Stock 1 April 1982 | 15 000 |  |
| Wages | 7 250 |  |
| Rent | 2 500 |  |
| Expenses | 1 500 |  |
| Heat and light | 600 |  |
| Debtors/creditors | 7 000 | 5 750 |
| Delivery costs | 2 650 |  |
| Drawings: |  |  |
| Jack | 3 500 |  |
| Jill | 4 500 |  |
| Cash | 2 250 |  |
| Fixed assets | 3 000 |  |
| Purchases | 55 000 |  |
|  | 104 750 | 104 750 |

*Notes:*

1. Stock at 31 March 1983 was valued at £20 000.
2. Depreciation of £750 is to be written off the Fixed Assets for the year to 31 March 1983.
3. At 31 March 1983 wages accrued amounted to £250, and rent of £500 was prepaid.
4. On 1 February 1983 the partnership ordered and paid for goods costing £350. These were recorded as purchases but were never received as they were lost by the carrier responsible for their delivery. The carrier accepted liability for the loss during March 1983 and paid full compensation of £350 in April 1983. No entries had been made in the books in respect of the loss or claim.
5. Jack took goods which had cost the firm £170 for his own use during the year. No entry has been made in the books to record this.
6. The Partnership Agreement provided that profits and losses should be shared equally between the partners after:

   (a) allowing annual salaries of £1 000 to Jack and £2 000 to Jill;
   (b) allowing interest of 5% per annum on the balance of each partner's capital account; and
   (c) charging Jack £100 and Jill £150 interest on drawings.
7. The balances on the Capital Accounts shall remain unchanged, all adjustments being recorded in the Current Accounts.

*REQUIRED:*
Prepare the Trading, Profit and Loss and Appropriation Accounts for the Jack and Jill Partnership for the year to 31 March 1983 and the Balance Sheet as at that date.

(30 marks)
(RSA II Accounting, June 1983)

**7** Ben, Ken and Len are in partnership sharing profits and losses in the ratio 3:2:1. The following is the trial balance of the partnership as at 30 September 1983:

|  | £ | £ |
|---|---|---|
| Bad debts provision (at 1 Oct 1982) |  | 1 000 |
| Bank and cash in hand | 2 500 |  |
| Capital Accounts: |  |  |
| Ben |  | 18 000 |
| Ken |  | 12 000 |
| Len |  | 6 000 |
| Current Accounts: |  |  |
| Ben |  | 700 |
| Ken | 500 |  |
| Len |  | 300 |
| Debtors and creditors | 23 000 | 35 000 |

|  | £ | £ |
|---|---|---|
| Depreciation (at 1 Oct 1982): | | |
| Land and buildings | | 12 000 |
| Motor vehicles | | 8 000 |
| Drawings: | | |
| Ben | 4 000 | |
| Ken | 3 000 | |
| Len | 3 000 | |
| Land and buildings, at cost | 60 000 | |
| Motor vehicles, at cost | 20 000 | |
| Office expenses | 4 000 | |
| Purchases | 85 000 | |
| Rates | 4 000 | |
| Sales | | 150 000 |
| Selling expenses | 14 000 | |
| Stock (at 1 Oct 1982) | 20 000 | |
| | 243 000 | 243 000 |

You are provided with the following additional information:
1. Stock at 30 September 1983 was valued at £30 000.
2. Fixed assets are written-off at the following rates:
   Land and buildings       5% per annum on cost
   Motor vehicles             20% per annum on cost
3. At 30 September 1983 an amount of £1 775 was owing for selling expenses.
4. Rates were prepaid by £2 000 as at 30 September 1983.
5. A certain bad debt of £500 is to be written-off.
6. The bad debts provision is to be made equal to 5% of outstanding debtors as at 30 September 1983.
7. The partnership agreement covers the following appropriations:
   (a) Len is to be allowed a salary of £6 000 per annum;
   (b) Interest of 10% per annum is allowed on the partners' capital account balances;
   (c) No interest is allowed on the partners' current accounts;
   (d) No interest is charged on the partners' drawings.

*REQUIRED:*
(a) Prepare the partners' trading, profit and loss and profit and loss appropriation accounts for the year to 30 September 1983;

(9 marks)
(b) Write-up the partners' current accounts for the year to 30 September 1983, and bring down the balances as at 1 October 1983;

(5 marks)
(c) Prepare the partnership balance sheet at 30 September 1983.

(6 marks)
(Total 20 marks)
(AAT Accounting 2, December 1983)

**8** C. Walters and R. Strange are the proprietors of two separate businesses. Their Balance Sheets on 31 December 1983 are given below.

### C. Walters. Balance Sheet as at 31 December 1983

|  | £ |  | £ |
|---|---|---|---|
| Capital | 86 880 | Premises | 65 000 |
| Creditors | 2 140 | Delivery vans | 15 000 |
|  |  | Stock | 7 400 |
|  |  | Bank | 1 500 |
|  |  | Cash | 120 |
|  | 89 020 |  | 89 020 |

### R. Strange. Balance Sheet as at 31 December 1983

|  | £ |  | £ |
|---|---|---|---|
| Capital | 98 410 | Premises | 80 000 |
| Creditors | 1 470 | Furniture | 12 000 |
|  |  | Stock | 4 700 |
|  |  | Debtors | 1 400 |
|  |  | Bank | 1 700 |
|  |  | Cash | 80 |
|  | 99 880 |  | 99 880 |

They decide to amalgamate into a partnership running two branches from 1 January 1984. Profits and losses will be shared equally.
The following valuations and revaluations were agreed by the partners:

|  | C. Walters £ | R. Strange £ |
|---|---|---|
| Goodwill | 20 000 | 15 000 |
| Premises | 120 000 | 90 000 |
| Furniture |  | 8 000 |

R. Strange will not bring his debtors into the partnership.

(a)  Calculate the capital each partner is introducing into the business.
(b)  Write off the goodwill.
(c)  Set out the Balance Sheet of the new business as at 1 January 1984, after writing off the goodwill.
(d)  On 2 January 1984 Walters and Strange agreed to bring in extra or take out cash so that their capitals should be equal at £125 000. This was done immediately.

Write up the partners' capital accounts from 1 January 1984 showing the capital adjustments, and the bank columns of the cash book showing the resultant bank balance.
(Assume no other transactions take place.) (24 marks)

(London Board Principles of Accounts O level, January 1984)

**1**  Interest on capital is an appropriation of profit; it appears on the credit side of the current account.

**2**  The credit side of appropriation account records net profit b/d and interest on drawings; alternative (C) is therefore correct.

**3**  Since the net value of the business is £10 000 and the price paid for it is £15 000, goodwill must be £5 000 (B).

**4**  Your answer to (a) (i) should state that the purpose is to show how the one net profit is shared between the partners. Your answer to (a) (ii) should identify any four of the items found (see question 5 below): the double entry for the debit appropriation items is in the relevant current account, and the matching entry for interest on drawings is also in the current account (Dr side).

(b)  Your answer should show drawings debited and purchases credited and, for (ii), should state that drawings are shown as a deduction from the current account balance which is shown in the balance sheet.

(c)  This section refers to the Partnership Act provisions; your answers should be:
(i)  equally;
(ii)  no salaries to be awarded;
(iii)  5%.

**5**  The appropriation account is as follows:

|  | £ | £ | £ |
|---|---|---|---|
| Net profit b/d |  |  | 25 000 |
| Interest on drawings: Pen |  |  | 300 |
| Ink |  |  | 350 |
|  |  |  | 25 650 |
| Less: Interest on capitals: |  |  |  |
| Pen | 5 000 |  |  |
| Ink | 1 500 | 6 500 |  |
| Salaries: Pen | 3 000 |  |  |
| Ink | 9 000 | 12 000 |  |
| Balance of profit: Pen | 4 290 |  |  |
| Ink | 2 860 | 7 150 |  |
|  |  |  | 25 650 |

Current accounts: opening Cr balances; credit the three forms of profit appropriations shown in the appropriation account; total Cr side, £15 290 Pen and £17 860 Ink.
On the Dr, record drawings and interest on drawings; your closing balances should then be £4 990 Pen and £5 510 Ink.

**6** In the trading account, your purchases total should be £54 480, after deducting £350 (not received) and £170 (goods for own use). The gross profit is £25 520.

In the profit and loss account there are no additional revenues; expenses are wages ( + 250), rent ( − 500), expenses, heat/light, delivery costs and depreciation; total of £15 000, giving a net profit of £10 520 to be appropriated.

Here is the appropriation account:

|  | £ | £ |  | £ |
|---|---|---|---|---|
| Salaries: Jack | 1 000 |  | Net profit b/d | 10 520 |
| Jill | 2 000 | 3 000 | Interest on |  |
|  |  |  | drawings: Jack | 100 |
| Interest on |  |  | Jill | 150 |
| capitals: Jack | 750 |  |  |  |
| Jill | 250 | 1 000 |  |  |
| Balance of |  |  |  |  |
| profits: Jack | 3 385 |  |  |  |
| Jill | 3 385 | 6 770 |  |  |
|  |  | 10 770 |  | 10 770 |

The balance sheet for the partnership is shown below:

|  | £ | £ |  | £ | £ |
|---|---|---|---|---|---|
| *Capital accounts:* |  |  | *Fixed Assets:* |  |  |
| Jack |  | 15 000 | Total (less depr.) |  | 2 250 |
| Jill |  | 5 000 |  |  |  |
|  |  | 20 000 | *Current Assets:* |  |  |
| *Current accounts:* |  |  | Stock | 20 000 |  |
| Jack | 2 865 |  | Debtors | 7 000 |  |
| Jill | 3 485 | 6 350 | Carrier | 350 |  |
|  |  |  | Prepaid expense | 500 |  |
| *Current liabilities:* |  |  | Cash | 2 250 |  |
| Creditors | 5 750 |  |  |  | 30 100 |
| Accrued expense | 250 |  |  |  |  |
|  |  | 6 000 |  |  |  |
|  |  | 32 350 |  |  | 32 350 |

Workings for the current accounts:

Jack, opening balance + salary + interest on capital + balance of profit − drawings − goods own use − interest on drawings.

Jill, opening balance + salary + interest on capital + balance of profit − drawings − interest on drawings.

**8**

(a)   Capitals are calculated from (revalued) assets less liabilities:

|  | Walters £ | Strange £ |
|---|---|---|
| Goodwill | 20 000 | 15 000 |
| Premises | 120 000 | 90 000 |
| Furniture | — | 8 000 |
| Vans | 15 000 | — |
| Stock | 7 400 | 4 700 |
| Bank | 1 500 | 1 700 |
| Cash | 120 | 80 |
|  | 164 020 | 119 480 |
| Less: Creditors | 2 140 | 1 470 |
|  | 161 880 | 118 010 |

(b)   Writing off the goodwill reduces the capital balances: Walters £141 880 and Strange £103 010.

(c)   **Walters and Strange**

*Balance Sheet at 1 January 1984*

|  | £ | £ |
|---|---|---|
| *Capital Employed:* Walters |  | 141 880 |
| Strange |  | 103 010 |
|  |  | 244 890 |
| *Utilization of Capital:* |  |  |
| *Fixed Assets:* Premises |  | 210 000 |
| Furniture |  | 8 000 |
| Vans |  | 15 000 |
|  |  | 233 000 |
| *Current Assets:* |  |  |
| Stock | 12 100 |  |
| Bank | 3 200 |  |
| Cash | 200 |  |
|  | 15 500 |  |
| *Less Current Liabilities:* |  |  |
| Creditors | 3 610 |  |
|  |  | 11 890 |
|  |  | 244 890 |

(d) Your capital accounts should contain the balances (Cr) shown in part (a) of the question, and goodwill written off on the Dr side (Walters £20 000 and Strange £15 000). To get each account equal to £125 000, Walters must be debited with £16 880 (£141 880 − £125 000) and Strange credited with £21 990 (£125 000 less £103 010). Both accounts now contain the required balance. The bank account balance is £3 200 Dr. It is debited with £21 990 received from Strange, and credited with £16 880 paid to Walters. The closing Dr balance at bank is £8 310.

## F.  A TUTOR'S ANSWER

Question **7** is a typical final accounts partnership question. It includes a section testing your understanding of the operation of current accounts.

(a) **Ben, Ken and Len**

*Trading and Profit and Loss accounts for the year to 30 September 1983*

|  | £ | £ |
|---|---:|---:|
| Sales |  | 150 000 |
| Less Cost of sales: |  |  |
| Opening stock | 20 000 |  |
| Purchases | 85 000 |  |
|  | 105 000 |  |
| Less Closing stock | 30 000 |  |
|  |  | 75 000 |
| Gross Profit |  | 75 000 |
| Less Expenses: |  |  |
| Depreciation – Land and buildings | 3 000 |  |
|  – Motor vehicles | 4 000 |  |
| Office expenses | 4 000 |  |
| Rates | 2 000 |  |
| Selling expenses | 15 775 |  |
| Bad debt | 500 |  |
| Increase in bad debts provision | 125 |  |
|  |  | 29 400 |
| Net Profit |  | 45 600 |
| Less Appropriations: |  |  |
| Salary: Len | 6 000 |  |
| Interest on capitals: Ben | 1 800 |  |
| Ken | 1 200 |  |
| Len | 600 |  |
| Balance of profits: Ben | 18 000 |  |
| Ken | 12 000 |  |
| Len | 6 000 |  |
|  |  | 45 600 |

**Workings**

1. Rates, deduct £2 000 prepaid: selling expenses, add £1 775 accrued.
2. Bad debts provision: closing debtors are £22 500 (deducting the £500 bad debts), and so closing provision is £1 125, an increase of £125 on the existing provision.
3. Balance of profits is £36 000, shared 3/6, 2/6 and 1/6.

(b) Current accounts:

|  | Ben £ | Ken £ | Len £ |  | Ben £ | Ken £ | Len £ |
|---|---|---|---|---|---|---|---|
| Balance b/d |  | 500 |  | Balances b/d | 700 | — | 300 |
| Drawings | 4 000 | 3 000 | 3 000 | Salary | — | — | 6 000 |
| Balances c/d | 16 500 | 9 700 | 9 900 | Interest on capital | 1 800 | 1 200 | 600 |
|  |  |  |  | Balance of profit | 18 000 | 12 000 | 6 000 |
|  | 20 500 | 13 200 | 12 900 |  | 20 500 | 13 200 | 12 900 |
|  |  |  |  | Balances b/d | 16 500 | 9 700 | 9 900 |

(c)

**Ben, Ken and Len**

*Balance Sheet at 30 September 1983*

*Fixed Assets:*

|  | Cost £ | Depreciation £ | Net £ |
|---|---|---|---|
| Land and buildings | 60 000 | 15 000 | 45 000 |
| Motor vehicles | 20 000 | 12 000 | 8 000 |
|  | 80 000 | 27 000 | 53 000 |

*Current Assets:*

| Stock | 30 000 |
|---|---|
| Debtors | 21 375 |
| Prepaid expense | 2 000 |
| Bank and cash | 2 500 |
|  | 55 875 |

*Less Current Liabilities:*

| Creditors | 35 000 |  |
|---|---|---|
| Accrued expense | 1 775 |  |
|  | 36 775 |  |
|  |  | 19 100 |
|  |  | 72 100 |

| Financed by: | £ | £ |
|---|---|---|
| *Capital Accounts:* | | |
| Ben | | 18 000 |
| Ken | | 12 000 |
| Len | | 6 000 |
| | | 36 000 |
| *Current Accounts:* | | |
| Ben | 16 500 | |
| Ken | 9 700 | |
| Len | 9 900 | |
| | | 36 100 |
| | | 72 100 |

**Workings**  Debtors total £23 000 − £500 bad debt − £1 125 provision.

## G.  A STEP FURTHER

Partnership accounts can be quite complicated, particularly where a new partner is being introduced or where the partnership has been dissolved because of the death or retirement of one of the partners. Some of these complications are outside the scope of the book, because they are not normally featured on basic accounting syllabuses. The more advanced textbooks will provide full details of these areas: for example, Garbutt's *Carters Advanced Accounts* (7th edn) (Pitman), and Wood's *Business Accounting 2* (4th edn) (Longman), examine partnership dissolution.

Here is a selection of books containing details on the areas of partnership accounts covered in this chapter:

Bright, *Practical Accounts 2* (Pan 'Breakthrough' series). Ch. 1.

Castle and Owens, *Principles of Accounts* (7th edn) (M & E). Ch. 21.

Harrison, *Stage One Financial Accounting* (Northwick). Chs 20 and 22.

Piper, *Teach Yourself Bookkeeping* ('Teach Yourself' series), Ch. 16.

Whitehead, *Success in Principles of Accounting* (John Murray). Units 27 and 35.

Wood, *Business Accounting 1* (4th edn) (Longman). Chs 38 and 40.

Wood, *Bookkeeping and Accounts* (Longman). Chs 30 and 31.

# Chapter 14

# The accounts of limited companies

---

## A. GETTING STARTED

This chapter gives an introduction to the basic principles of company final accounts. Examination questions which are set at this level tend to be computational. These questions are usually (but not exclusively) in the form of a trial balance or a list of balances, from which the final accounts must be constructed. It is worth noting that more and more essay-based questions are being asked. With the essay questions, you may be asked to describe or to distinguish between various 'company-specific' items, such as shares or dividends on shares.

---

## B. ESSENTIAL PRINCIPLES

### INTRODUCTION

In recent years there have been major developments in accountancy, and probably the most important areas of change concern the final accounts of limited companies. There has been the development of 'Inflation Accounting', which attempts to take account of money values which have changed as a result of inflation. In addition, the 'SSAP' (Statements of Standard Accounting Practice) area has influenced the nature and construction of company accounts. Because of these and other developments, it is difficult to provide comprehensive guidelines. This section will therefore outline the traditional, 'historical cost' aspect of company accounts: this remains a necessary area of study, and provides a basis for the examination questions set at this level.

We need to be familiar with the difference between shares and debentures (and the difference between different types of shares) when studying limited company accounts. We also require a knowledge of how shares and debentures affect the final accounts.

## PROFIT AND LOSS APPROPRIATION

In brief, the profit and loss appropriation section is the same as that for partnerships, in that

| THE DEBIT SIDE | THE CREDIT SIDE |
|---|---|
| shows *where the profit goes to* when it is appropriated | shows *how much profit* is available for appropriation |

**Links with the balance sheet**

Once the appropriation account has been constructed, it will contain information to be included in a balance sheet. Here is a diagram illustrating the likely links:

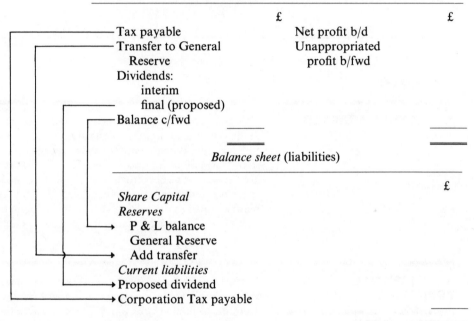

*Appropriation account*

| | £ | | £ |
|---|---|---|---|
| Tax payable | | Net profit b/d | |
| Transfer to General Reserve | | Unappropriated profit b/fwd | |
| Dividends: | | | |
| interim | | | |
| final (proposed) | | | |
| Balance c/fwd | | | |

*Balance sheet* (liabilities)

| | £ |
|---|---|
| *Share Capital* | |
| *Reserves* | |
| P & L balance | |
| General Reserve | |
| Add transfer | |
| *Current liabilities* | |
| Proposed dividend | |
| Corporation Tax payable | |

**The credit side**

Net profit is brought down to the credit side, because it is a credit balance (as explained in Ch. 5). Unlike partnerships, where the profit is always fully appropriated each year, there will be an *existing balance of profit* to be added to this year's net profit. This is known as *retained profits*, and represents profits deliberately held back by the company as a reserve. We need to examine the question set to check whether a (credit) balance, usually referred to as 'Profit and Loss appropriation balance', 'Profit and Loss account balance' or 'Retained profits', has last year's (or the start of this financial year's) date recorded by it. If so, this balance from last year's appropriation account is added to this period's profit, in order to obtain the total profit available for distribution.

| **The debit side** | The debit side of the appropriation account identifies where the profit goes to. It may stay *in* the company, in the form of transfers to reserves such as the General Reserve, or as retained profits (the balance on the appropriation account). Some of it will be transferred *out* of the company; for example, in the form of Corporation Tax, or as dividends on shares. The treatment of Corporation Tax is very complicated; at this level, we are required to record amounts due for Corporation Tax on the debit side of the appropriation account. |
|---|---|
| | Dividends may be either *paid* or *proposed*. As far as the appropriation account is concerned, there is no real distinction to be made: both are debited. We have to check the Preference Share dividend (if there is one); it will be expressed as a fixed percentage, e.g. '£1 000 8% Preference shares issued'. Here, assuming profits are sufficient, the dividend payable will be 8% of £1 000 (£80). The question must be checked to see if the dividend has been fully or partly paid, or not paid at all. |

| **Balance** | Finally, we are left with a closing balance on the account. This will be a credit balance, because it represents undistributed profit. This will need recording in the balance sheet, in the 'Reserves' section. |
|---|---|

## BALANCE SHEETS

Published accounts of limited companies follow the rules that exist regarding layout and disclosure of information. At this level of study, a detailed knowledge of the provisions of the relevant (Companies) Acts is not required. We still, however, need to produce a balance sheet using an acceptable layout.

| **Layout** | The *vertical* form of balance sheet is widely used nowadays. Also, many questions require *Working Capital* to be shown in the balance sheet. Various forms of presentation and layout have already been introduced in the book, and we will continue to use them. |
|---|---|

*Balance sheet at 31 December 1986*

£

| *Authorized Share Capital* | (shown as a note) |
|---|---|
| CAPITAL EMPLOYED: | |
| *Issued Share Capital* | (Ordinary and Preference shares) |
| *Reserves* | (including P & L balance) |
| *Loan Capital* | (Debentures) |
| | |
| UTILIZATION OF CAPITAL: | |
| *Fixed Assets* | (showing total cost, total depreciation and net book value) |
| *Current Assets* | |
| *Less: Current Liabilities* | (CA − CL to show Working Capital) |

## Variations on layout

We could easily reorganize this layout, to commence with the fixed assets and working capital (i.e. 'net assets'), following this with a 'financed by' section containing the information on capital employed.

It is advisable to become accustomed to presenting balance sheet information using more than one layout, so that you will be in a position to display this information in whatever form is required by a question.

## Content

Most of the new items to be found in company balance sheets have been mentioned. Many of these originate in the appropriation account; notably the current liabilities of:

(a) proposed dividend;
(b) Corporation tax payable.

The appropriation account also contains the closing profit balance (unappropriated profit), which is recorded in the Reserves section of the balance sheet. The reserves commonly met in company accounts questions are:

1. General Reserve.
2. Fixed Assets Replacement Reserve.
3. Share Premium account.
4. Retained Profit (P & L Appropriation balance).

You may be asked to *describe* balance sheet or related items. Two popular areas of questioning involve the following.

## Share premium account

Where shares have been issued at a premium, i.e. above the nominal value, the value of the premium is recorded in a Share Premium account which is recorded in the Reserves section of the balance sheet.

## Share capital terms

(a) *Authorized* share capital refers to the maximum share capital that can be issued by the company.
(b) *Issued* share capital identifies the value of shares actually issued by the company (this may be equal to or less than authorized capital).
(c) *Called-up* capital refers to situations where shares have been issued at less than the total value to be called at a later date: it is the amount actually called up on each share (e.g. 1 000 shares of a nominal value of £1 issued initially at 75p each, the value of called-up capital is £750).
(d) *Uncalled* capital also refers to situations where shares are issued at less than the value to be called at a later date (in the above example, the value of uncalled capital is 25p × 1 000 shares = £250).

Unlike the final accounts of sole traders and of partnerships, company accounts (i.e. those which have to be published by law) are available for study by members of the public. As we mentioned in Chapter 8, public limited companies hold copies of their published accounts, which can often be obtained by writing to these companies. Some libraries, such as those of local colleges, may have copies of published company accounts available for study by students. **Figures 14.1 and 14.2** are good examples of the summarized final accounts presented in published form.

| | | 1984 £m | 1983 £m |
|---|---|---|---|
| **Group profit and loss account** for the year ended 31st March 1984 | Turnover | 1832·8 | 1670·0 |
| | **Trading profit** | 155·6 | 137·8 |
| | Share of profit of related companies | 1·8 | 3·5 |
| | | 157·4 | 141·3 |
| | Interest | 7·7 | (1·2) |
| | **Profit on ordinary activities before taxation** | 165·1 | 140·1 |
| | Taxation on profit on ordinary activities | (59·8) | (46·9) |
| | **Profit on ordinary activies after taxation** | 105·3 | 93·2 |
| | Minority interests | (·9) | (·7) |
| | | 104·4 | 92·5 |
| | Extraordinary items after taxation | 23·9 | (3·2) |
| | **Profit for the financial year attributable to shareholders** | 128·3 | 89·3 |
| | **Dividends** | (40·0) | (34·5) |
| | **Profit retained** | 88·3 | 54·8 |
| | **Earnings per share before taxation** | 22·4p | 19·1p |
| | **Earnings per share after taxation** | 14·4p | 12·7p |

*Fig. 14.1   Group profit and loss account*
Courtesy: The Boots Company PLC, from their annual report ending March 31, 1984

**Balance sheet**
31st March 1984

| | 1984 £m | 1983 £m |
|---|---|---|
| **Fixed assets** | | |
| Tangible assets | 453·2 | 431·9 |
| Investments | 4·4 | 49·3 |
| | 457·6 | 481·2 |
| | | |
| **Current assets** | | |
| Stocks | 339·5 | 307·8 |
| Debtors | 112·2 | 107·5 |
| Investments | 143·3 | 46·5 |
| Cash at bank and in hand | 11·2 | 4·7 |
| | 606·2 | 466·5 |
| Creditors: amounts falling due within one year | (338·7) | (298·1) |
| **Net current assets** | 267·5 | 168·4 |
| | | |
| **Total assets less current liabilities** | 725·1 | 649·6 |
| Creditors: amounts falling due after more than one year | (13·3) | (11·6) |
| Provision for liabilities and charges | (21·7) | — |
| **Net assets** | 690·1 | 638·0 |
| | | |
| **Capital and reserves** | | |
| Called up share capital | 182·0 | 90·8 |
| Share premium | 1·5 | 11·3 |
| Revaluation reserve | 8·9 | 9·9 |
| Profit and loss account | 495·0 | 523·5 |
| | 687·4 | 635·5 |
| Minority interests | 2·7 | 2·5 |
| | 690·1 | 638·0 |

*Fig. 14.2    Group balance sheet*
Courtesy: The Boots Company PLC

## D.   RECENT EXAMINATION QUESTIONS

The majority of questions on company accounts are computational in character, although many of these questions include a descriptive element.

Questions **1–4** are either multiple choice or sentence completion types, and should take approximately five minutes to answer. Question **5** is computational, and concentrates on appropriation of profit. Question **6** tests your understanding of balance sheet construction, while questions **7** and **8** involve both appropriation of profits and construction of balance sheets. *The answer to question 8 is given in section F.*

**Objective questions**

1   The appropriation account of a limited company shows:

A   depreciation
B   directors' remuneration
C   debenture interest
D   proposed dividends

(AEB Specimen Accounting O level Paper, 1980)

**2** The following items appear in the balance sheet of a limited company.

*Authorized Share Capital*
200 000 £1 Ordinary Shares                                    £200 000

*Issued Share Capital*
150 000 £1 Ordinary Shares – fully paid                      £150 000
A dividend of 10% is declared.
The amount shown in the appropriation account as due to the ordinary shareholders for dividends is:

A   £15 000
B   £20 000
C   £30 000
D   £35 000

(AEB Specimen Accounting O level Paper, 1980)


**3** The . . . . . . is the amount by which the money paid for a share exceeds the nominal value.

(London Board Principles of Accounts O level, January 1983)


**4** The amount of share capital registered with the Registrar of Companies is known as:

A   fixed capital
B   uncalled capital
C   authorized capital
D   issued capital

(AEB Specimen Accounting O level Paper, 1980)

---

**Essay and Computational questions**

**5** During the year ended 31 December 1982, the Kingston Supplies Company Limited made a Net Profit of £66 250. Its Authorized Capital is 500 000 Ordinary Shares of 50p each and 100 000 10% Preference Shares of £1 each. The Preference Shares have been issued in full but only 400 000 of the Ordinary Shares have been issued. All the issued shares are paid up in full.

The balance of unallocated profit brought forward from the previous year is £2 500.

An interim dividend of 5% was paid on the Ordinary Shares earlier in the year.

The directors of the company now propose to pay one year's dividend on the Preference Shares, to transfer £15 000 to General Reserve and to recommend a final dividend of 15% on the Ordinary Shares.

*REQUIRED:*
Prepare the Profit and Loss Appropriation Account for the year ended 31 December 1982 (ignore taxation).                    (13 marks)

(Cambridge Board Principles of Accounts O level, Summer 1983)

**6**  Common Ltd is a limited company with an Authorized Capital of 200 000 12% Preference Shares of £1 each and 300 000 Ordinary Shares of £1 each. 100 000 Preference Shares have been issued and 100 000 Ordinary Shares have been issued at a premium of 10%. All shares are fully paid.

The following balances appeared in the books of the company at 30 June 1983, after the Profit & Loss Account had been prepared:

|  | £ |
|---|---|
| Premises (at cost) | 180 000 |
| Machinery (at cost) | 85 000 |
| Creditors | 63 000 |
| Debtors | 92 000 |
| Stock | 45 000 |
| Furniture | 22 000 |
| Investments | 10 000 |
| Bank overdraft | 17 000 |
| Profit & Loss Account | 62 000 |
| Provision for depreciation of machinery | 12 000 |
| Provision for depreciation of furniture | 2 000 |
| 15% Debentures issued | 60 000 |
| Motor Vehicles (at cost) | 30 000 |
| Provision for depreciation of motor vehicles | 12 000 |
| Provision for bad debts | 8 000 |
| Bills receivable | 22 000 |
| Bills payable | 38 000 |
| Payments in advance | 11 000 |
| Cash in hand | 2 000 |
| General reserve | 15 000 |

*Notes:*
The Debenture Interest and the Preference Share dividend for the year ended 30 June 1983 have not been provided for.
The directors have recommended a dividend of 8p per share on the Ordinary Share Capital.

*REQUIRED:*
Prepare a Balance Sheet, preferably in vertical form, as at 30 June 1983, showing clearly the figures for Shareholders' Funds and the amount of Working Capital.

(25 marks)
(LCC I Intermediate Bookkeeping, Autumn 1983)


**7**  Ogden Limited had an authorized capital of £100 000, divided into 75 000 ordinary shares of £1 each and 25 000 8% Preference shares of £1 each. The following balances remained in the accounts of the company after the trading and profit and loss accounts had been prepared for the year ended 31 December 1982.

|  | Debit £ | Credit £ |
|---|---|---|
| Ordinary share capital: fully paid | | 50 000 |
| 8% Preference shares: fully paid | | 15 000 |
| Machinery and plant at cost | 40 000 | |
| Provision for depreciation on machinery and plant | | 19 000 |
| Premises at cost | 50 000 | |
| Profit and loss account balance (1 January 1982) | | 5 600 |
| Net profit (for year ended 31 December 1982) | | 9 026 |
| Light and heat | | 280 |
| Cash at bank | 3 508 | |
| Stock | 3 860 | |
| Debtors and Creditors | 2 300 | 894 |
| Insurance | 132 | |
| | 99 800 | 99 800 |

The directors have recommended an ordinary dividend of 12% and wish to provide for payment of the year's preference share dividend.

*REQUIRED:*
The profit and loss appropriation account for year ended 31 December 1982.

(3 marks)

The balance sheet as at 31 December 1982, in a form which shows clearly the shareholders' funds and the working capital.

(13 marks)

An explanation of the term 'limited liability'.

(1 mark)

A statement of three differences between an ordinary share and a debenture.

(3 marks)
(AEB Accounting O level, June 1983)

**8** The trial balance extracted from the books of Flower Ltd, a wholesaling company, at 31 December 1983 was:

|  | £ | £ |
|---|---|---|
| Share capital | | 150 000 |
| Share premium | | 50 000 |
| 10% debentures | | 150 000 |
| Fixed assets at cost: | | |
| Freehold land and buildings | 290 000 | |
| Plant and equipment | 40 000 | |
| Motor vehicles | 150 000 | |

| | £ | £ |
|---|---|---|
| Provisions for depreciation at 1.1.83: | | |
| Freehold land and buildings | | 20 000 |
| Plant and equipment | | 16 000 |
| Motor vehicles | | 20 000 |
| Sales | | 526 500 |
| Purchases | 317 400 | |
| Debtors and creditors | 35 600 | 20 700 |
| Bad debts | 1 900 | |
| Provision for doubtful debts at 1.1.83 | | 1 600 |
| Wages and salaries | 46 200 | |
| Rates | 7 100 | |
| Debenture interest | 15 000 | |
| Profit and loss account 1.1.83 | | 75 100 |
| Directors' salaries | 36 000 | |
| Motor expenses | 16 800 | |
| General expenses | 1 200 | |
| Stock in trade 1.1.83 | 74 500 | |
| Balance at bank | | 1 800 |
| | 1 031 700 | 1 031 700 |

The following additional information is provided:

(a) Share capital is divided into 150 000 shares of £1 each which are all issued and fully paid.

(b) Stock in trade at 31 December 1983 was £81 200.

(c) The provision for doubtful debts is to be increased to £1 800.

(d) Motor expenses due but unpaid at 31 December 1983 £2 100.

(e) Rates paid in advance at 31 December 1983 £1 500.

(f) Provision is to be made for depreciation on:
   (i) plant at 10% per annum of cost;
   (ii) motor vehicles at 20% per annum of cost;
   (iii) freehold buildings are to be depreciated by £4 000.

(g) A dividend is proposed for 1983 at the rate of 10p per share.

*REQUIRED:*
A Trading and Profit and Loss Account for 1983 and a Balance Sheet at 31 December 1983.
*Note:* Ignore taxation.

(30 marks)
(RSA II Accounting, June 1984)

---

## E.  OUTLINE ANSWERS

1 and 2: both questions are on company appropriation accounts. The answer to question 1 is (D); the other items appear in the profit and loss account. Question 2 tests your understanding of the calculation of share dividends; it is based on issued shares and not on authorized capital, so the answer is (A).

3 and 4: these questions concentrate on shares. For question 3, you should have stated 'premium'; the answer to question 4 is (C).

## 5                         Kingston Supplies Co Ltd

*Appropriation account for year ended 31 December 1982*

| | £ | | £ |
|---|---|---|---|
| Interim dividend (5% Ord.) | 10 000 | Net profit b/d | 66 250 |
| Transfer to General Reserve | 15 000 | P&L balance b/fwd | 2 500 |
| Proposed dividends: | | | |
|     Pref. (10%) | 10 000 | | |
|     Ord. (15%) | 30 000 | | |
| Balance carried forward | 3 750 | | |
| | 68 750 | | 68 750 |

## 6                         Common Ltd

*Balance Sheet at 30 June 1983*

| CAPITAL EMPLOYED | £(000) | £(000) | £(000) |
|---|---|---|---|
| *Issued Share Capital:* | | | |
| 100 000 Preference | | | 100 |
| 100 000 Ordinary | | | 100 |
| | | | 200 |
| *Reserves:* | | | |
| Share Premium account | | 10 | |
| General Reserve | | 15 | |
| Retained profits | | 33 | 58 |
| Shareholders' Funds | | | 258 |
| *Loan Capital:* | | | |
| 15% Debentures | | | 60 |
| | | | 318 |
| UTILIZATION OF CAPITAL | | | |
| *Fixed Assets:* | Cost | Depr. | Net |
| Premises | 180 | | 180 |
| Machinery | 85 | 12 | 73 |
| Furniture | 22 | 2 | 20 |
| Vehicles | 30 | 12 | 18 |
| | 317 | 26 | 291 |
| Investments | | | 10 |
| *Current Assets:* | | | |
| Stock | | 45 | |
| Debtors | 92 | | |
| Less provision | 8 | 84 | |

| | £ | £ | £ |
|---|---|---|---|
| Bills receivable | | 22 | |
| Prepayments | | 11 | |
| Cash | | 2 | |
| | | 164 | |
| *Less Current Liabilities:* | | | |
| Creditors | 63 | | |
| Overdraft | 17 | | |
| Bills payable | 38 | | |
| Debenture interest accrued | 9 | | |
| Proposed dividends | 20 | 147 | |
| Working Capital | | | 17 |
| | | | 318 |

The share premium account comes from the issue of ordinary shares at the stated premium. Profit and loss balance has been adjusted, taking into account the debenture interest and the two proposed dividends.

**7**

(a)                                  **Ogden Ltd**

*Appropriation account for year ended 31 December 1982*

| | £ | | £ |
|---|---|---|---|
| Proposed dividends: | | Net profit b/d | 9 026 |
| Preference | 1 200 | P&L balance b/fwd | 5 600 |
| Ordinary | 6 000 | | |
| Balance c/fwd | 7 426 | | |
| | 14 626 | | 14 626 |

(b)                                  **Ogden Ltd**

*Balance Sheet at 31 December 1982*

| | £ | £ | £ |
|---|---|---|---|
| *Fixed Assets:* | Cost | Depr. | Net |
| Premises | 50 000 | | 50 000 |
| Machinery | 40 000 | 19 000 | 21 000 |
| | 90 000 | 19 000 | 71 000 |
| *Current Assets:* | | | |
| Stock | | 3 860 | |
| Debtors | | 2 300 | |
| Prepayment | | 132 | |
| Bank | | 3 508 | |
| | | 9 800 | |

|  | £ | £ | £ |
|---|---|---|---|
| *Less Current LIabilities:* | | | |
| Creditors | 894 | | |
| Proposed dividends | 7 200 | | |
| Accrual | 280 | | |
| | | 8 374 | |
| | | | 1 426 |
| | | | 72 426 |

|  | £ |
|---|---|
| **Financed by:** | |
| *Share Capital:* | |
| Authorized Preference | 25 000 |
| Authorized Ordinary | 75 000 |
| | 100 000 |
| Issued Preference | 15 000 |
| Issued Ordinary | 50 000 |
| | 65 000 |
| *Reserves:* | |
| Unappropriated profit | 7 426 |
| Shareholders' Funds | 72 426 |

(c) Your answer should state that *liability* of the shareholders for debts of the business is *limited* to the value of shares held (no personal possessions can be taken to pay business debts).

(d) Your answer should include any three of the differences outlined below:

| *Ord. Share* | *Debenture* |
|---|---|
| Voting right | No vote |
| Dividend | Interest |
| Owner of co. | Creditor of co. |

## F.   A TUTOR'S ANSWER

Question **8** is a comprehensive company final accounts question asking for Trading and Profit and Loss accounts, and the Balance Sheet. It includes a number of adjustments. Here is the suggested answer:

**Flower Ltd**

*Trading and Profit & Loss account for the year to 31 December 1983*

|  | £ | £ | £ |
|---|---|---|---|
| Sales | | | 526 500 |
| Less Cost of Goods Sold: | | | |
| Opening stock | | 74 500 | |
| Purchases | | 317 400 | |
| | | 391 900 | |
| Less Closing stock | | 81 200 | |
| | | | 310 700 |
| Gross Profit | | | 215 800 |
| Less Expenses: | | | |
| Bad debts | | 1 900 | |
| Wages and salaries | | 46 200 | |
| Rates | 7 100 | | |
| Less prepayment | 1 500 | 5 600 | |
| Debenture interest | | 15 000 | |
| Directors' salaries | | 36 000 | |
| Motor expenses | 16 800 | | |
| Add accrual | 2 100 | 18 900 | |
| General expenses | | 1 200 | |
| Depreciation: Plant | 4 000 | | |
| Vehicles | 30 000 | | |
| Buildings | 4 000 | 38 000 | |
| Increase in bad debts provision | | 200 | |
| | | | 163 000 |
| Net Profit | | | 52 800 |
| Profit and loss balance 1.1.83 | | | 75 100 |
| | | | 127 900 |
| Less Appropriations: | | | |
| Proposed dividend | | | 15 000 |
| Balance carried forward | | | 112 900 |

# Flower Ltd

*Balance Sheet at 31 December 1983*

| CAPITAL EMPLOYED | £ | £ | £ |
|---|---:|---:|---:|
| *Authorised and issued* | | | |
| *Share Capital:* | | | |
| 150 000 £1 shares, fully paid | | | 150 000 |
| *Reserves:* | | | |
| Share premium account | | 50 000 | |
| Retained profits | | 112 900 | |
| | | | 162 900 |
| Shareholders' funds | | | 312 900 |
| *Loan Capital:* | | | |
| 10% Debentures | | | 150 000 |
| | | | 462 900 |

| UTILIZATION OF CAPITAL: | | | |
|---|---:|---:|---:|
| *Fixed Assets:* | Cost | Depr. | Net |
| Land and buildings | 290 000 | 24 000 | 266 000 |
| Plant and equipment | 40 000 | 20 000 | 20 000 |
| Motor vehicles | 150 000 | 50 000 | 100 000 |
| | 480 000 | 94 000 | 386 000 |
| *Current Assets:* | | | |
| Stock | | 81 200 | |
| Debtors | 35 600 | | |
| Less provision | 1 800 | 33 800 | |
| Prepaid expense | | 1 500 | |
| | | 116 500 | |
| *Less Current Liabilities:* | | | |
| Creditors | 20 700 | | |
| Bank overdraft | 1 800 | | |
| Accrued expense | 2 100 | | |
| Proposed dividend | 15 000 | | |
| | | 39 600 | |
| | | | 76 900 |
| | | | 462 900 |

## G. A STEP FURTHER

The published accounts of companies can be obtained by writing to the relevant company. Information on company operations and news can be obtained from papers such as *The Financial Times*, *The Times* or *The Guardian*. The Prestel service of British Telecom, the BBC's Ceefax and the IBA's Oracle service contain bulletins on company performance.

If you need to study other aspects of company accounts, such as share issue or redemption, or amalgamation procedures, you will need to consult an advanced textbook. There are several detailed textbooks available such as:

Castle and Owens, *Principles of Accounts* (7th edn) (M & E). Ch. 27 on published accounts.

Garbutt, *Carter's Advanced Accounts* (7th edn) (Pitman). Ch. 22 (published accounts); Chs 23 and 24 (redemption).

Oldcorn, *Understanding Company Accounts* (Pan 'Breakthrough' series).

Wood, *Business Accounting 2* (4th edn) (Longman). Chs 18 and 19.

Here is a selection of books which contain chapters on limited company accounts:

Bright, *Practical Accounts 2* (Pan 'Breakthrough' series). Ch. 2.

Castle and Owens, *Principles of Accounts* (7th edn) (M & E). Ch. 26.

Whitehead, *Bookkeeping Made Simple* ('Made Simple' series). Ch. 29.

Wood, *Business Accounting 1* (4th edn) (Longman). Ch. 41.

# Chapter 15

# Interpreting and forecasting

## A. GETTING STARTED

This chapter differs from what has gone before by concentrating on the interpretation of information that has already been prepared. The function of analysing and commenting on information is an essential part of accounting: the role of bookkeeping is to *provide* the information to be interpreted.

Questions set in this area will make candidates interpret accounting information, and use accounting-related facts and figures to forecast future profitability. We can identify three topics associated with interpretation and forecasting:

1.  *Source and Application of Funds* statements which analyse movements of cash and working capital.
2.  The preparation of *forecast final accounts* and/or *projected profit* statements.
3.  *Accounting ratios*, which must be calculated and described.

Syllabuses vary widely as regards which of these areas you are required to study, so check with your teacher.

To benefit from studying this chapter, you need to be familiar with the layout of final accounts and with the nature of working capital. Many of the questions will involve calculations, and you will have to undertake calculations involving percentages, fractions and ratios.

## B. ESSENTIAL PRINCIPLES

### SOURCE AND APPLICATION OF FUNDS

*Statements of sources and applications of funds* (funds flow statements) normally consist of two parts. The first part analyses the sources and applications of funds resulting from items which do not influence working capital: changes in current assets or current liabilities are therefore not featured here. The second part details the increases and decreases in working capital: it identifies and lists the changes in current asset and current liability values that have taken place.

| Working capital | To answer questions on funds flow statements, we have to recall how working capital is affected by changes in current assets and current liabilities. Working capital is the difference between total current assets (CA) and total current liabilities (CL). |

*Increases* in working capital: through

(i)   an increase in C.A.:       STOCKS       +
                                 DEBTORS      +
                                 CASH/BANK +

and/or

(ii)  a decrease in C.L.:        CREDITORS  −

*Decrease* in working capital: through

(i)   a decrease in C.A.:        STOCKS       −
                                 DEBTORS      −
                                 CASH/BANK −

and/or

(ii)  an increase in C.L.:       CREDITORS +

| Layout | Here is a common layout used for funds flow statements. The example statement includes items which are typically to be found in such statements: |

*Statement of Sources and Applications of Funds:*

£

*Sources of Funds:*
Profit before tax
Adjustment for items not
 involving a movement of funds:
    Depreciation

*Application of Funds:*
Dividend payments
Tax payments
Purchase of fixed assets

Increase (Decrease)

*Changes in Working Capital:*
*Increases:*   increase in stocks
               increase in bank
               decrease in creditors
*Decreases:*   decrease in debtors
               decrease in bank

the
amounts
AGREE

## FORECASTING

Some questions require you to make some form of forecast. These questions may ask you:

(a) to construct a statement of *forecast profit*; or
(b) to draw up complete *forecast final accounts*.

### Cash forecast

Cash forecasts, which are a form of cash budget, are relatively easy to prepare. Questions sometimes include *non-cash items* in the information: we must identify and ignore these items. We must follow a recognized method of presenting the forecast. One common form used for presentation is summarized below:

|  | **Month** | | |
|---|---|---|---|
|  | Jan | Feb | Mar |
| *Opening Cash Balance* | | | |
| *Receipts:* | | | |
| (listed) | | | |
| | | | |
| *Payments:* | | | |
| (listed) | | | |
| | | | |
| *Closing Balance* | | | |

Individual receipts and payments could be detailed in the forecast itself, or they could be detailed elsewhere, leaving the total receipts and payments displayed in the forecast.

### Projected profit and final accounts

Questions which are based on the projected profit and/or final accounts of a business usually require you to make a series of calculations. An existing cost or income is typically given, this amount having to be adjusted (usually increased) by a given percentage. The new (forecast) amounts are then used in calculating the projected profit. Questions 4 and 5 in section D (and their answers in section E) illustrate the nature of these forecasts.

## ACCOUNTING RATIOS

To answer questions on accounting ratios, we need to be able to recall

(i) *how* the relevant ratio is calculated; and
(ii) *why* it is calculated (i.e. what it tells us).

### Categories of interested parties

1. *Creditors* are interested in liquidity ratios, to check how easily the business can meet its debts owed to them.
2. *Lenders* (e.g. banks or debenture holders) are interested in liquidity ratios and profitability ratios (to see how likely the business is to make future profits or to pay interest and dividends).
3. The *management* of the business will be interested in both liquidity and profitability ratios, as well as those ratios on investment, the use of the firm's assets, and capital structure.

4. *Shareholders* will also be interested in company performance as measured by the investment, use of assets and capital structure ratios: and they will naturally be interested in the performance of the business as measured by the liquidity ratios and the profitability ratios.

**The ratios**

The ratios that we shall concentrate on relate to:

(a) liquidity;
(b) profitability;
(c) use of assets.

Those ratios linked with investment (such as the Earnings Per Share and Price/Earnings ratios), and those involving capital structure (Gearing) have not been included since they are associated with more advanced syllabuses.

**Summary**

Here is a summary of the important ratios found in our three categories: (P = Profitability; L = Liquidity; A = Use of Assets)

| Ratio | Calculation | Type |
|---|---|---|
| Gross profit margin (%) | $\dfrac{\text{Gross profit}}{\text{Turnover}} \times \dfrac{100}{1}$ | P |
| Net profit margin (%) | $\dfrac{\text{Net profit}}{\text{Turnover}} \times \dfrac{100}{1}$ | P |
| Expenses (%) | $\dfrac{\text{Expense}}{\text{Turnover}} \times \dfrac{100}{1}$ | P |
| Rate of stock turnover ('stockturn') | $\dfrac{\text{Cost of sales}}{\text{Average stock}}$ | A |
| Return on capital employed (%) ('ROCE') | $\dfrac{\text{Net profit}}{\text{Capital employed}} \times \dfrac{100}{1}$ | P |
| Working capital ('current' ratio) | C.A.: C.L. | L |
| Liquid capital ('acid test') | C.A. − stock: C.L. | L |
| Sales/fixed assets | $\dfrac{\text{Sales}}{\text{Fixed assets}}$ | A |
| Sales/current assets | $\dfrac{\text{Sales}}{\text{Current assets}}$ | A |
| Debtors' collection period | $\dfrac{\text{Debtors} \times 365}{\text{Sales}}$ | A |
| Creditors' collection period | $\dfrac{\text{Creditors} \times 365}{\text{Sales}}$ | A |

Questions do not normally give the methods of calculation for these ratios, and you will therefore have to memorize these.

We must remember that on their own, these ratios are relatively meaningless. A debtors' collection period of 27 days, a stockturn of 6 times per month, or a net profit margin of 8.25% all need further information for comparison before they can really tell us anything. If *last year's* debtor collection period was 24 days, if *last month's* stockturn was 9 times, if *last period's* net profit margin was 6.9%: this additional information now gives us a basis for comparison and comment. Of course, as well as comparing with *other time periods*, we can compare with *other companies* in the *same* industrial sector, or in *different* sectors altogether.

## C.  USEFUL APPLIED MATERIALS

Public limited companies include in their published accounts a statement of the source and application of funds for the financial year: like the final accounts, last year's figures are also included for comparison.

**Source and application of funds**
for the year ended 31st March 1984

| | 1984 £m | 1984 £m | 1983 £m | 1983 £m |
|---|---|---|---|---|
| **Source** | | | | |
| Group trading: | | | | |
| Profit on ordinary activities before taxation | | 165·1 | | 140·1 |
| Share of profit of related companies | | (1·8) | | (3·5) |
| | | 163·3 | | 136·6 |
| Distributions from related companies | | 6·0 | | ·3 |
| Depreciation less net surplus on disposal of tangible fixed assets | | 15·5 | | 13·6 |
| Proceeds on disposal of tangible fixed assets | | 21·7 | | 19·6 |
| Loans | | 2·9 | | – |
| Issue of ordinary shares | | 2·0 | | ·9 |
| | | 211·4 | | 171·0 |
| Extraordinary loss | | – | | (4·5) |
| **Proceeds on disposal:** | | | | |
| Investment in related company | 54·9 | | | |
| Surplus houseware premises | 14·0 | | | |
| | | 68·9 | | – |
| | | 280·3 | | 166·5 |
| **Application** | | | | |
| Capital expenditure | | 59·9 | | 58·0 |
| Investments: | | | | |
| Related companies | 1·8 | | ·1 | |
| Goodwill | 1·6 | | – | |
| Subsidiaries | – | | 17·4 | |
| | | 3·4 | | 17·5 |
| Increase in creditors falling due after more than one year | | (·3) | | (·4) |
| Repayment of loans | | 1·4 | | 5·6 |
| Dividends paid | | 36·3 | | 33·1 |
| Taxation paid | | 52·4 | | 40·1 |
| **Working capital:** | | | | |
| Increase (decrease) in stocks | 32·3 | | (13·2) | |
| Increase (decrease) in debtors | 16·3 | | (·4) | |
| Increase in creditors falling due within one year | (32·0) | | (18·9) | |
| | | 16·6 | | (32·5) |
| Other items | | 1·2 | | ·9 |
| | | 170·9 | | 122·3 |
| **Increase in net cash resources:** | | | | |
| Listed investments | 62·0 | | – | |
| Short term deposits | 35·1 | | 33·8 | |
| Cash at bank and in hand | 6·6 | | ·3 | |
| Decrease in bank loans and overdrafts | 5·7 | | 10·1 | |
| | | 109·4 | | 44·2 |
| | | 280·3 | | 166·5 |

*Fig. 15.1    Statement of Source and Application of Funds*
Courtesy: The Boots Company PLC, from their annual report ending March 31, 1984

Figure 15.1 is a source and application of funds statement taken from a set of published final accounts. It provides a good illustration of how the information can be organized and presented clearly and concisely. The information is taken from the same source as the final accounts illustrated in section C of the last chapter.

## D. RECENT EXAMINATION QUESTIONS

Objective questions **1** and **2** included in this section are on stock turnover. The remaining questions are mainly computational, and test your understanding of the three chapter topics.

Question **3** is on source and application of funds; it also asks you to report on a declining cash balance.

Questions **4** and **5** test your ability to prepare forecast accounts. Question 4 asks for forecast profit; and question 5 involves the preparation of forecast final accounts and a forecast bank account.

Questions **6** and **7** provide you with information from which you have to prepare a series of accounting ratios: both questions also require you to make comments on the results. *Question 7 is answered fully in section F, 'A tutor's answer'.*

Question **8** combines source and application of funds with accounting ratios, and is a comprehensive test of your knowledge of both topics.

### Objective questions

**1** The rate of stock-turn (rapidity of turnover) is found by dividing
. . . . . . by . . . . . .

(Cambridge Board Principles of Accounts O level, Summer 1983)

**2** During the past year a firm's average stock has been £3 000 at cost, the mark-up on cost price has been 50% and sales have been £13 500.
The firm's rate of stock turnover during the past year has been:

A   4.5
B   3.0
C   2.25
D   1.5

(AEB Specimen Accounting O level Paper, 1980)

### Essay and computational questions

**3** James, a sole trader, has been in business for many years. The following series of balance sheets were prepared from his books at 31 December:

|  | 1980 £ | 1981 £ | 1982 £ |
|---|---|---|---|
| Assets: |  |  |  |
| Premises | 10 000 | 10 000 | 20 000 |
| Motor Vans | 15 500 | 11 500 | 18 000 |
| Stocks | 18 250 | 15 300 | 19 750 |
| Cash at bank | 6 600 | 9 850 | 650 |
|  | 50 350 | 46 650 | 58 400 |

| Sources of Finance: | | | |
|---|---|---|---|
| Capital | 35 350 | 19 400 | 29 950 |
| Creditors | 15 000 | 27 250 | 19 450 |
| Mortgage loan | — | — | 9 000 |
| | 50 350 | 46 650 | 58 400 |

*Notes:*
1. James's drawings for each of the last two years were:
   1981   £29 000
   1982   £27 500
2. On 1 January 1982 a motor van was purchased at a cost of
   £11 300 and new premises which cost £10 000 were acquired. The
   purchase of the premises was financed by a mortgage loan of
   £10 000, repayable at the rate of £1 000 per year.

James complains that despite trading profitability the business is short
of cash.

*REQUIRED:*
(a) Statements of Sources and Applications of Funds for each of the
    years 1981 and 1982.
(b) A brief report to explain the decline in the cash balance to James.

(30 marks)
(RSA II Accounting, March 1983)

**4**  A friend of yours, Victor Vague, plans to enter the kitchen
equipment market with a new food processing machine he has
invented. He proposes to sell the machine at £50 and expects his first
year's sales to be 20 000 units ± 20%. His estimates of unit costs are as
follows:

| | £ |
|---|---|
| Direct material | 20 |
| Direct labour | 8 |

Direct material costs, Victor thinks, could vary within 10% of his
estimate and labour costs could increase by 25%.
   Other expenses for the first year are estimated at £140 000 ± 5%.

*REQUIRED:*
Victor has asked you to prepare a Statement showing the approximate
profit for the year and to indicate the maximum and minimum profits
related to his estimates.

(20 marks)
(AAT Numeracy and Accounting, June 1984)

**5**  Barrett Limited, was formed on 1 October 1982 to trade as a retail
outlet. The issued capital was 50 000 £1 ordinary shares and the full
amount was paid into a business bank account. The following
forecasts have been made for the first year's operations.

Purchase of motor vans £7 200.

Rent and rates payable £3 640.

Wages and salaries of employees £15 310.

Depreciation for the year on motor vans £1 440.

All other running expenses (excluding depreciation) £4 360.

Directors' fees £8 250.

Closing stock, valued at cost price, will be £4 000.

Sales, for the first year, will be £192 000. To determine the selling price of all goods, $33\frac{1}{3}\%$ will be added to the cost price.

A dividend of 15 per cent on ordinary shares will be proposed and the remaining profit 'ploughed back' into the business.

At year end there will be no trade debtors, no trade creditors and no prepayments or accruals.

*REQUIRED:*

(a) For the year ended 30 September 1983:

    (i)   the forecasted trading and profit and loss accounts (including an appropriation section); (9 marks)

    (ii)  the forecasted bank account (6 marks)

    *Note:* A forecasted balance sheet is not required.

(b) Name and explain two reasons why firms prepare forecasted accounts. (5 marks)

(AEB Accounting O level, November 1982)

**6** The trading and profit and loss accounts of two separate businesses, engaged in the same trade and of similar size, are given below.

Trading and Profit and Loss Accounts for year ended
31 December 1983:

|  | CORFU Ltd | RHODES Ltd |  | CORFU Ltd | RHODES Ltd |
|---|---|---|---|---|---|
|  | £ | £ |  | £ | £ |
| Opening Stock | 2 600 | 5 300 | Sales | 48 900 | 43 500 |
| Purchases | ? | ? | Less Returns | 900 | 250 |
|  | ? | ? |  |  |  |
| Less Closing Stock | ? | 4 700 |  |  |  |
| Cost of goods sold | ? | ? |  |  |  |
| Gross Profit | ? | ? |  |  |  |
|  | ? | ? |  | ? | ? |
| Total Expenses | ? | ? | Gross Profit | ? | ? |
| Net Profit | 6 000 | 2 500 |  |  |  |
|  | ? | ? |  | ? | ? |

Additional information:

|  | CORFU Ltd | RHODES Ltd |
|---|---|---|
| Capital employed | £20 000 | £20 000 |
| Rate of turnover of stock | 16 | not given |
| Mark up on cost | 50% | 25% |

*REQUIRED:*

(a)  A copy of the above trading and profit and loss accounts, including all the missing figures denoted by question marks.

(8 marks)

(b)  Calculations for each business of
  (i)   gross profit expressed as a percentage of net sales:
  (ii)  net profit expressed as a percentage of net sales:
  (iii) return on capital employed.

(5 marks)

(c)  Consider the information given above and the figures you have calculated and give two reasons why you feel one of the businesses produced a better performance than the other, during the period concerned.

(3 marks)

(d)  Give two other bases of comparison that are frequently used to evaluate the performance of a business.

(1 mark)

(AEB Accounting O level, June 1984)

**7**  You are presented with the following summarized information concerning J. Free:

**J. Free**

*Trading, Profit and Loss Account (Extracts) for the year to 30 April 1982 and 30 April 1983*

|  | 1983 £ | 1982 £ |
|---|---|---|
| Sales (all on credit) | 200 000 | 120 000 |
| Cost of Sales | 150 000 | 80 000 |
| Gross Profit | 50 000 | 40 000 |
| Expenses | 15 000 | 10 000 |
| Net Profit | 35 000 | 30 000 |

**J. Free**

*Balance Sheet (Extracts) at 30 April 1982 and 30 April 1983*

|  | 1983 | | 1982 | |
|---|---|---|---|---|
|  | £ | £ | £ | £ |
| *Fixed Assets* (net book value) |  | 12 000 |  | 15 000 |
| *Current Assets* |  |  |  |  |
| Stocks | 18 000 |  | 7 000 |  |
| Trade Debtors | 36 000 |  | 12 000 |  |
| Cash at Bank | — |  | 1 000 |  |
|  |  | 54 000 |  | 20 000 |
|  |  | 66 000 |  | 35 000 |
| *Capital Account* |  |  |  |  |
| Balance at 1 April | 29 000 |  | 12 000 |  |
| Net Profit for the year | 35 000 |  | 30 000 |  |
|  | 64 000 |  | 42 000 |  |
| *Less:* Drawings | 23 000 |  | 13 000 |  |
|  |  | 41 000 |  | 29 000 |
| *Current Liabilities* |  |  |  |  |
| Trade Creditors | 15 000 |  | 6 000 |  |
| Bank Overdraft | 10 000 |  | — |  |
|  |  | 25 000 |  | 6 000 |
|  |  | 66 000 |  | 35 000 |

*Notes:*
1. There were no purchases or disposals of fixed assets during the year.
2. During 1982/3 Free reduced his selling prices in order to stimulate sales.
3. It may be assumed that price levels were stable.

*REQUIRED:*
(a) Calculate the following ratios for both 1982 and 1983:
　　(i)　percentage mark-up on sales;
　　(ii)　gross profit on sales;
　　(iii)　return on capital employed;
　　(iv)　debtor collection period;
　　(v)　current ratio;
　　(vi)　acid test (or quick) ratio.　　　　　　　　(12 marks)

(b)  Comment upon the apparent effect that the increase in sales has had on profit and cash flow.                                    (8 marks)

(AAT Accounting 2, June 1983)    (Total 20 marks)

**8**  The following information has been extracted from the books of Context, a small trading company, for the two years to 31 October 1982 and 31 October 1983 respectively:

*Trading, Profit and Loss Accounts (Extracts)*

|  | 1982 | | 1983 | |
|---|---|---|---|---|
|  | £ | £ | £ | £ |
| Sales (all on credit) |  | 120 000 |  | 200 000 |
| *Less:* Cost of Goods Sold: |  |  |  |  |
| Opening stock | 15 000 |  | 16 000 |  |
| Purchases | 96 000 |  | 196 000 |  |
|  | 111 000 |  | 212 000 |  |
| *Less:* Closing stock | 16 000 |  | 40 000 |  |
|  |  | 95 000 |  | 172 000 |
| *Gross Profit* |  | 25 000 |  | 28 000 |
| *Less:* Expenses |  | 20 000 |  | 20 000 |
| *Net Profit* |  | 5 000 |  | 8 000 |

*Balance Sheet (Extracts)*

|  | 1982 | | 1983 | |
|---|---|---|---|---|
|  | £ | £ | £ | £ |
| *Fixed Assets* |  |  |  |  |
| Motor Vehicles, at cost | 25 000 |  | 25 000 |  |
| *Less:* Depreciation | 10 000 |  | 15 000 |  |
|  |  | 15 000 |  | 10 000 |
| *Current Assets* |  |  |  |  |
| Stock | 16 000 |  | 40 000 |  |
| Trade debtors | 30 000 |  | 90 000 |  |
| Bank | 2 000 |  | — |  |
|  |  | 48 000 |  | 130 000 |
|  |  | 63 000 |  | 140 000 |
| *Capital* |  |  |  |  |
| Opening balance |  | 40 000 |  | 37 000 |
| Profit | 5 000 |  | 8 000 |  |
| *Less:* Drawings | 8 000 |  | 10 000 |  |

|  |  | (3 000) |  | (2 000) |
|---|---|---|---|---|
|  |  | 37 000 |  | 35 000 |
| *Long-Term Loan* |  | 10 000 |  | 15 000 |
| *Current Liabilities* |  |  |  |  |
| Trade Creditors | 16 000 |  | 72 000 |  |
| Bank overdraft | — |  | 18 000 |  |
|  |  | 16 000 |  | 90 000 |
|  |  | 63 000 |  | 140 000 |

*REQUIRED:*

(a) Prepare a statement of source and application of funds for the year to 31 October 1983. (10 marks)

(b) Calculate the following accounting ratios for the year to 31 October 1982 and 31 October 1983 respectively:

    (i) gross profit on sales;

    (ii) gross profit on cost of goods sold;

    (iii) current asset ratio;

    (iv) quick (or acid test) ratio;

    (v) trade debtor collection period. (10 marks)

(Total 20 marks)

(AAT Accounting 2, December 1983)

---

**E. OUTLINE ANSWERS**

**1 and 2**: these questions test your knowledge of stock turnover. The gaps for question 1 are 'cost of sales' and 'average stock' respectively, and alternative **(B)** is correct in question 2 (if sales are £13 500, cost of sales is two-thirds of this, giving £9 000 divided by £3 000 average stock).

**3** Working capital figures for 1980, 1981 and 1982 require calculating so that the changes in working capital can be identified.

| *Working capital:* | 1980 | 1981 | 1982 |
|---|---|---|---|
| Current assets (stock + bank) | 24 850 | 25 150 | 20 400 |
| Less Current liabilities (creditors) | 15 000 | 27 250 | 19 450 |
| Working capital | 9 850 | (2 100) | 950 |
| Change 1981 (decrease) |  | (11 950) |  |
| Change 1982 (increase) |  |  | 3 050 |

For the funds flow statement, net profit (source of funds) also requires calculating. It can be calculated from the change in the capital balances (an approach explained in detail in the next chapter).

| *Profit:* | 1981 | 1982 |
|---|---|---|
| Closing capital | 19 400 | 29 950 |
| add back drawings | 29 000 | 27 500 |
| | 48 400 | 57 450 |
| Less opening capital | 35 350 | 19 400 |
| Profit for the year | 13 050 | 38 050 |

The sources and applications can now be listed:

| | 1981 | 1982 | |
|---|---|---|---|
| | £ | £ | £ |
| *Sources:* | | | |
| Profit | 13 050 | | 38 050 |
| Depreciation | 4 000 | | 4 800 |
| Mortgage | — | | 10 000 |
| | 17 050 | | 52 850 |
| *Applications:* | | | |
| Drawings | 29 000 | 27 500 | |
| Mortgage | — | 1 000 | |
| Van purchase | — | 11 300 | |
| Premises | — | 10 000 | 49 800 |
| Increase/Decrease | (11 950) | | 3 050 |

The 1981 changes in working capital are:

| | £ | £ |
|---|---|---|
| Increase in cash | | 3 250 |
| Decrease in stock | (2 950) | |
| Increase in creditors | (12 250) | (15 200) |
| Decrease in working capital | | (11 950) |

The 1982 changes are:

| | |
|---|---|
| Increase in stock | 4 450 |
| Decrease in creditors | 7 800 |
| | 12 250 |
| Reduced cash | (9 200) |
| Increase in working capital | 3 050 |

The depreciation figures are calculated like this:

1981, vans at start, £15 500, less vans at close £11 500 = 1981 depreciation figure.
1982, vans at start, add purchase, less vans at close, gives 1982 depreciation figure.

(b)  A cash flow statement could form the basis of your report, along these lines:

|  | £ | £ |
|---|---|---|
| Opening cash balance |  | 9 850 |
| 1982 sources of cash: |  |  |
| Trading profit | 38 050 |  |
| Add depreciation | 4 800 | 42 850 |
|  |  | 52 700 |
| Less 1982 applications: |  |  |
| Van purchase | 11 300 |  |
| Mortgage payment | 1 000 |  |
| Drawings | 27 500 |  |
| Increased stocks | 4 450 |  |
| Decreased creditors | 7 800 |  |
|  |  | 52 050 |
| Closing cash balance, 1982 |  | 650 |

**4**  Your statement of approximate profit should look like this:

|  | £(000) | £(000) |
|---|---|---|
| Sales (£50 × 20) |  | 1 000 |
| Less: |  |  |
| Direct material (£20 × 20) | 400 |  |
| Direct labour (£8 × 20) | 160 |  |
| Expenses | 140 |  |
|  |  | 700 |
| Approximate profit |  | 300 |

The maximum profit and minimum profit calculations are:

|  | Calculation | £(000) | Calculation | £(000) |
|---|---|---|---|---|
| Sales | £50 × 24 | 1 200 | £50 × 16 | 800 |
| Less: |  |  |  |  |
| Materials | £18 × 24 | (432) | £22 × 16 | (352) |
| Labour | £8 × 24 | (192) | £10 × 16 | (160) |
| Expenses | £140 − 5% | (133) | £140 + 5% | (147) |
| Profit |  | 443 |  | 141 |

The principle to use for maximum profit is to maximize sales (revenue) and to minimize expenses; the reverse applies for minimum profit.

**5** In your trading account, sales are credited at £192 000; cost of sales is three-quarters of this total (£144 000) and gross profit is £48 000. If closing stock is £4 000, purchases are £148 000 (closing stock added back to cost of sales).

The expenses – rent/rates, wages, depreciation, other expenses and directors' fees – are debited to P&L, giving a net profit of £15 000 which is brought down to the Cr of the appropriation section. In appropriation, the £7 500 proposed dividend is debited, leaving a balance also of £7 500.

*Forecast bank account of Barrett Ltd:*

|  | £ |  | £ |
|---|---|---|---|
| Capital | 50 000 | Purchase of van | 7 200 |
| Sales revenue | 192 000 | Rent and rates | 3 640 |
|  |  | Wages and salaries | 15 310 |
|  |  | Running expenses | 4 360 |
|  |  | Directors' fees | 8 250 |
|  |  | Purchases | 148 000 |
|  |  | Balance c/d | 55 240 |
|  | 242 000 |  | 242 000 |
| Balance b/d | 55 240 |  |  |

**6**

(a)   Net sales for Corfu (C) and Rhodes (R) are £48 000 (C) and £43 250 (R). Gross profit (C) is one-third of net sales, £16 000, and cost of sales £32 000. Since the average stock of C is £2 000 (rate of stockturn 16 times on a cost of sales of £32 000), closing stock must be £1 400, i.e. £600 less than average stock, because opening stock of £2 600 is £600 more. Purchases for C are therefore £30 800.

For R, gross profit is 20% of the sales; £8 650. Cost of sales will be £34 600 (cost of sales + gross profit = sales), 'opening stock plus purchases' will be £39 300, adding closing stock to cost of sales, so purchases will be £34 000.

Now that the gross profits are known, P&L expenses can be calculated; £10 000 (C) and £6 150 (R).

(b)   Your answer should be:

|  | *Corfu* | *Rhodes* |
|---|---|---|
| G.P.% | $\dfrac{16\,000}{48\,000} \times \dfrac{100}{1} = 33\tfrac{1}{3}\%$ | $\dfrac{8\,650}{43\,250} \times \dfrac{100}{1} = 20\%$ |
| N.P.% | $\dfrac{6\,000}{48\,000} \times \dfrac{100}{1} = 12\tfrac{1}{2}\%$ | $\dfrac{2\,500}{43\,250} \times \dfrac{100}{1} = 5.78\%$ |
| R.O.C.E. | $\dfrac{6\,000}{20\,000} \times \dfrac{100}{1} = 30\%$ | $\dfrac{2\,500}{20\,000} \times \dfrac{100}{1} = 12\tfrac{1}{2}\%$ |

(c) Your answer could include these points:
Corfu is performing the better; a higher R.O.C.E., a higher net profit %; also, much higher stockturn.

(d) A number of bases could be mentioned; for example, expenses as % of sales, sales to current assets, debtors' and creditors' collection periods, working capital and liquid capital ratios.

**8**

(a)

Context

Statement of Source and Application of Funds for<br>the year to 31 October 1983

|  | £ |
|---|---:|
| *Sources of funds:* | |
| Trading profit | 8 000 |
| Add depreciation (15 000 − 10 000) | 5 000 |
| Increase in loan | 5 000 |
|  | 18 000 |
| *Application of funds:* | |
| Drawings | 10 000 |
|  | 8 000 |

| *Changes in Working Capital:* | £ | £ |
|---|---:|---:|
| Increases: | | |
| increase in stocks | | 24 000 |
| increase in debtors | | 60 000 |
|  | | 84 000 |
| Decreases: | | |
| decrease in bank | (20 000) | |
| increase in creditors | (56 000) | |
|  | | (76 000) |
| Net increase in Working Capital | | 8 000 |

(b)

|  | 1982 | 1983 |
|---|---|---|
| GP% | 20.83% | 14% |
| GP/COGS | 26.32% | 16.28% |
| Current ratio | 3:1 | 1.44:1 |
| Acid test ratio | 2:1 | 1:1 |
| Debtor collection | 91.25 days | 164.25 days |

Workings are (£000):

$$\text{GP\%} \qquad \frac{25}{120} \times \frac{100}{1} \qquad\qquad \frac{28}{200} \times \frac{100}{1}$$

|  | GP/COGS | $\dfrac{25}{95} \times \dfrac{100}{1}$ | $\dfrac{28}{172} \times \dfrac{100}{1}$ |
|---|---|---|---|
|  | Current ratio | 48:16 | 130:90 |
|  | Acid test | (48 − 16):16 | (130 − 40):90 |
|  | Debtor collection | $\dfrac{30}{120} \times 365$ | $\dfrac{90}{200} \times 365$ |

---

## F.  A TUTOR'S ANSWER

Question **7** tests your ability to recall and apply the named ratios, as well as your ability to interpret the information. Here is the suggested answer:

(a)  **1983** (£000)    **1982** (£000)

(i)  $\dfrac{50}{150} \times \dfrac{100}{1} = 33\frac{1}{3}\%$    $\dfrac{40}{80} \times \dfrac{100}{1} = 50\%$

(ii)  $\dfrac{50}{200} \times \dfrac{100}{1} = 25\%$    $\dfrac{40}{120} \times \dfrac{100}{1} = 33\frac{1}{3}\%$

(iii)  $\dfrac{35}{41} \times \dfrac{100}{1} = 85.37\%$    $\dfrac{30}{29} \times \dfrac{100}{1} = 103.45\%$

(iv)  $\dfrac{36}{200} \times \dfrac{365}{1} = 65.7$ days    $\dfrac{12}{120} \times \dfrac{365}{1} = 36.5$ days

(v)  $\dfrac{54}{25} = 2.2:1$    $\dfrac{20}{6} = 3.3:1$

(vi)  $\dfrac{54 - 18}{25} = 1.4:1$    $\dfrac{20 - 7}{6} = 2.2:1$

(b)  Free's sales have increased by £80 000, or 66.7%.
This has led to increases of £10 000 (25%) in gross profit and £5 000 ($16\frac{2}{3}\%$) in net profit.
Selling prices have been reduced, resulting in a reduction in mark-up from 50% to $33\frac{1}{3}\%$.
Greater sales appear to have been achieved by allowing an increase in the debtor collection period, from 37 days to 66 days. Free's liquidity position has worsened, although the ratios for 1983 appear to be satisfactory. This worsening is partially due to the increase in debtors. This is potentially serious, and cash flow appears to be a problem.
Although Free may be experiencing cash flow problems, his return on capital employed is extremely high(over 85%), even though this has fallen in 1983.

## G. A STEP FURTHER

Most syllabuses do not specify precisely which ratios we need to study. We have concentrated on the ratios which most frequently appear in examination questions. Ratios, funds flow statements and projected final accounts can, in practice, involve quite complex analyses and calculations. Some of the complexities can be seen by studying the published accounts of companies (referring to their funds flow statements) and also by consulting some of the more advanced textbooks: for example, Wood's *Business Accounting 2* (4th edn) (Longman) contains a chapter on SSAP 10, which concerns the statement of source and application of funds.

Most accounting textbooks contain chapters on funds flow and on ratio analysis. Here is a selection:

(a)  Source and application of funds:

Bright, *Practical Accounts 2* (Pan 'Breakthrough' series). Ch. 9.

Harrison, *Stage One Financial Accounting* (Northwick). Ch. 25.

Wood, *Business Accounting 1* (4th edn) (Longman). Ch. 43

Wood, *Business Accounting 2* (4th edn) (Longman). Ch. 23.

(b)  Interpretation of accounts and accounting ratios:

Bright, *Practical Accounts 2* (Pan 'Breakthrough' series). Ch. 7.

Garbutt, *Carter's Advanced Accounts* (7th edn) (Pitman). Ch. 29.

Simini and Hingley, *Accounting Made Simple* ('Made Simple' series). Ch. 1.

Wood, *Business Accounting 1* (4th edn) (Longman). Chs 32 and 45.

Wood, *Business Accounting 2* (4th edn) (Longman). Chs 37 and 38.

# Chapter 16     Incomplete records

---

**A. GETTING STARTED**

The topic of *incomplete records* is widely found on accounting syllabuses, and is regarded as possibly the most difficult of syllabus topics. The questions that are set on this topic are computational, often involving the calculation of the profit of a business. A list of balances may be provided: from this information, you could be asked to draw up a statement of affairs or full final accounts, making appropriate adjustments. The precise requirements will vary: for example, you may be tested on your ability to adjust given figures in order to arrive at a stock valuation.

To answer these questions successfully, you need to have a detailed knowledge of the accruals (matching) concept, the 'Accounting equation', and the layout and construction of final accounts.

---

**B. ESSENTIAL PRINCIPLES**

**MARK-UP AND MARGIN**

We need to know the nature of, and the arithmetical relationship between, *Mark-up* and *Margin* to answer some of the questions set on incomplete records. This relationship involves *cost price*, *profit* and *selling price*.

If, for example, the selling price of a firm's product is £1.50, and the cost price is £1.20, the 30p profit can be expressed as either a percentage (or fraction) of the cost price, or as a percentage or fraction of the selling price.

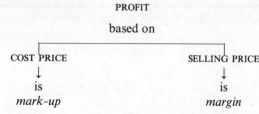

PROFIT

based on

| COST PRICE | SELLING PRICE |
|:---:|:---:|
| ↓ | ↓ |
| is | is |
| *mark-up* | *margin* |

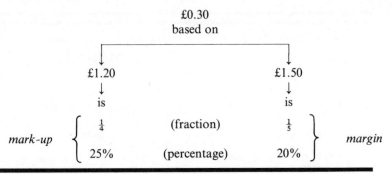

£0.30
based on

£1.20 → is                    £1.50 → is

mark-up { ¼        (fraction)        ⅕ } margin
         { 25%     (percentage)      20% }

## The relationship

If the question gives only one figure (or provides information to calculate only one figure), we can still calculate the other figure. This is because there is a relationship between mark-up and margin which is seen when they are expressed as fractions. The above example hints at this relationship:

| **Mark-up** | **Margin** |
|:---:|:---:|
| ¼ | ⅕ |

The denominator (bottom number) of the margin is greater than the denominator of the mark-up: it is greater by the size of the numerator (top number). In this example, the mark-up's denominator is 4, and the margin's denominator is 5:

4 (denominator of the mark-up)
+ 1 (value of the numerator)
—
5 (denominator of the margin)

If we have calculated that the mark-up used by a business is, say, $\frac{4}{9}$; the margin will be

$$\frac{4}{9+4} = \frac{4}{13}$$

This relationship also works in reverse: if we know the margin, we can calculate the mark-up by altering the margin's denominator. We deduct the value of the numerator from the denominator.
If the margin is $\frac{3}{8}$, the mark-up will be

$$\frac{3}{8-3} = \frac{3}{5}$$

## CALCULATION OF PROFIT

Questions may require us to calculate profit in one of two different ways. The choice of method depends on the type and amount of information given in the question.

1.  The question may provide a list of opening assets and liabilities, together with information on closing assets and liabilities. Profit is

calculated on the basis of the *increase in capital*. A full set of final accounts will not be prepared, because there is not enough information to allow this.

2. A question may provide details of assets and liabilities, and in addition provide other details, e.g. of a cash or bank account. From this information *full final accounts* can be prepared.

**Profit as an increase in capital ('net worth')**

Our first type of question provides details of assets and liabilities. These asset and liability values are given for both the start and the end of the relevant financial period. From this information we calculate the change in capital or *net worth* (assets less liabilities). The question will normally ask for a *Statement of Affairs* (a balance sheet) to be constructed.

How capital increases

There are two ways that capital will increase, and two ways that it will decrease:

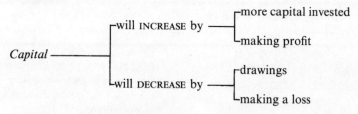

The capital (opening and closing balances) can be calculated by applying the 'Accounting equation':

Assets   =   Liabilities   +   Capital
Capital   =   Assets   −   Liabilities

Calculating profit

Here is an example to demonstrate the steps involved:

1 Jan, assets total £20 000 and liabilities are £4 000.
31 Dec, assets total £22 000 and liabilities are £5 500.
During the year, drawings are £3 500, and £1 000 more capital has been invested.

The steps involved are:

1. Calculate opening capital.
2. Calculate closing capital.
3. Adjust for drawings and any capital invested.

Using the above information:

Step 1: C =   A   −   L
         = £20 000 − £4 000 = £16 000

Step 2: C =   A   −   L
         = £22 000 − £5 500 = £16 500

(a) The increase in capital = £16 500 − £16 000 = £500. If no drawings have been made, nor further capital invested, then this £500 would represent profit for the year.

(b) But drawings have been made; the closing capital has been reduced by the value of the drawings.
(c) Also, capital has been invested during the year, and this has increased the closing capital figure by the amount invested.

These are both 'non-profit' alterations to the capital balance.

|  | | £ |
|---|---|---:|
| Step 3: | Capital increase | 500 |
|  | Add back drawings | 3 500 |
|  | | 4 000 |
|  | Deduct new capital invested | 1 000 |
|  | Profit for the year | 3 000 |

## Profit through construction of final accounts

Our second type of question varies in its precise requirements: but there are two important principles that commonly occur.

1. First, opening capital may not be given in the question. In this situation it must be calculated from opening assets and liabilities.
2. Second, the question may not provide actual purchases or sales totals. These have to be calculated from information which will be given on debtors, creditors, and cash received (from debtors) or paid (to creditors). In addition, a summarized cash or bank account may be provided from which various expenses have to be calculated.

The cash or bank account will probably contain items of capital expenditure, as well as the more typical revenue expenditure items: as we know:

| Revenue expenditure | Capital expenditure |
|:---:|:---:|
| ↓ | ↓ |
| goes to | goes to |
| ↓ | ↓ |
| Trading, Profit and Loss | Balance Sheet |

## Adjustments

Many of the profit and loss items will have to be adjusted, because of the accruals concept. For example, if a question states that £500 has been paid for stationery during the year, that the opening stock of stationery was £45 and that the value of the closing stock is £25, the amount charged to profit and loss will be:

|  | £ |
|---|---:|
| Amount paid | 500 |
| Add stock at start | 45 |
| (used *this* period) | |
| Less stock at close | −25 |
| (paid for this period, but used *next* period) | |
| Stationery cost for P&L | 520 |

Opening or closing prepayments and accruals are often given in these questions: if the amount applies to *this* period we *include* it, but if it does not then we exclude it. Here is a summary of the adjustments made:

Opening prepayment:    paid last period;
                       applies to this period so
                       *add*.

Closing prepayment:    paid this period;
                       applies to next period so
                       *deduct*.

Opening accrual:       paid this period;
                       applies to last period so
                       *deduct*.

Closing accrual:       not yet paid;
                       applies to this period so
                       *add*.

See chapter 8 for further details on the adjustments for prepayments and accruals.

| Calculation of sales and purchases | We use the same principles to calculate sales and purchases figures. We start with the cash received/cash paid totals, and adjust these totals for opening and closing debtor/creditor balances. Opening debtors and creditors will be deducted: cash received or paid by the opening debtors or creditors in *this* period refers to sales or purchases made *last* period. |
|---|---|

The cash or bank amounts will not include credit sales and purchases which have been made this period but for which payment has not yet been received: these credit sales and purchases are represented by the closing debtor and creditor balances, which are therefore added to the cash figure for the period. In summary, cash received/paid, 'LOAN':

L    **Less**
O  = **O**ld balances (opening debtors/creditors)
A    **A**dd
N    **N**ew balances (closing debtors/creditors)

Information on discounts allowed and received may also be given. Discounts plus cash gives the true value of the sale or purchase; we therefore *add* the discount amounts to the relevant cash totals when calculating the true sales and purchase figures.

Discount Allowed              Discount Received
         ↓                             ↓
affects Sales                 affects Purchases
         ↓                             ↓
so *add* to cash              so *add* to cash paid
received total                total

**Calculation of stock figures**

A question may ask you to calculate a stock figure from information provided. There are two common situations:

1.  it is a short time after the end of the financial year: the stock figure at this point in time is given, and it must be adjusted to obtain the closing stock figure for final accounts purposes;
2.  there has been a fire (or other disaster) and records have been destroyed: the value of stock lost in the fire must be calculated from the surviving pieces of information.

*Stock valuation* is particularly important here:

stock is valued at *cost* or *market value*, whichever is *the lower*.

Although this is a slight simplification of the exact position, the important point to remember is that the lowest valuation figure is used.

Sales which have taken place between the end of the financial year and the date in question will have been made at selling price. To calculate the cost price of the stock sold, the selling price must be adjusted. Knowledge of mark-up, margin and their arithmetical relationship when expressed as fractions, will help here.

**C.  USEFUL APPLIED MATERIALS**

The problems associated with the keeping of incomplete records should not arise if a business uses a computerized bookkeeping system.

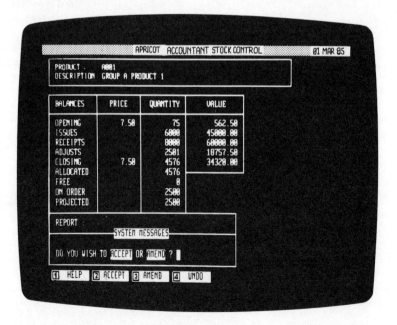

*Fig. 16.1   Computerized stock control*
Courtesy: ACT (U.K.) Ltd

Accurate and up-to-date figures are easily obtained (always assuming, of course, that the input of information has been accurate).

Stock records are often computerized, and this should again avoid problems of inaccurate or incomplete recording. **Figure 16.1** illustrates a typical computer screen layout where a stock control package is being used.

## D. RECENT EXAMINATION QUESTIONS

Questions on the topic of incomplete records tend to be computational rather than descriptive. Question **1**, a multiple choice question, tests whether you can calculate profit from changes in capital. Profit calculation also features in questions **2** and **3**: these questions are computational, and also test your ability to construct ledger accounts and balance sheets from summarized information.

Questions **4** and **5** also involve profit calculation; with these questions, you are expected to construct final accounts to show the net profit figure.

Questions **6** and **7** require stock figures to be calculated from information provided.

*Question 5 is answered in full in section F of the chapter.*

### Objective question

1 A trader prepares balance sheets at the beginning and end of the financial year which show:

| | | |
|---|---|---|
| 1 Jan 1977 | Capital account | £20 000 |
| 31 Dec 1977 | Capital account | £30 000 |

During the year he received a legacy of £11 000 which he paid into the business bank account. His drawings for the year amounted to £8 000.

His profit for the year is:

A £7 000
B £8 000
C £10 000
D £13 000        (AEB Specimen Accounting O level Paper, 1980)

### Computational questions

2 John Boyd is a sole trader who does not keep a full double entry system of bookkeeping. The records he does keep, however, are accurate and they reveal the following information:

| | 28 Feb 1982 | | 28 Feb 1983 |
|---|---|---|---|
| | £ | | £ |
| Bank | 790 | | 870 |
| Stock | 1 470 | | 1 660 |
| Office furniture | | | |
| (VALUATION) | 400 | (VALUATION) | 350 |
| Debtors | 1 960 | | ? |
| Creditors | 1 370 | | ? |

During the year ended 28 February 1983: Credit sales amounted to £6 250; cash received from Debtors was £6 040; Bad debts written off were £110; Discount allowed was £190.

Also during the year ended 28 February 1983: Credit purchases amounted to £4 070; cash paid to Creditors was £3 710; Discount received was £220.

In November 1982, Boyd purchased a delivery van for his business at a cost of £800. At 28 February 1983 this was valued at £720.

John Boyd's drawings during the year ended 28 February 1983 were as follows:

Cash £900. Goods, cost price £50.

*REQUIRED:*
(i)   Calculate Debtors and Creditors as at 28 February 1983.
(ii)  Calculate John Boyd's Capital as at 28 February 1982, and 28 February 1983.
(iii) Calculate John Boyd's Net Profit for the year ended 28 February 1983.

*Note:* Show your calculations.

(25 marks)
(LCCI Elementary Bookkeeping, Winter 1983)

**3**   The balance sheet of Langland's business as at 31 December 1982 was as follows:

*Balance Sheet as at 31 December 1982*

|  | £ | £ |  | £ | £ |
|---|---|---|---|---|---|
| Capital |  | 11 748 | Fixed assets |  | 8 850 |
| Creditors: |  |  | Current assets: |  |  |
| Goods | 2 016 |  | Stock | 2 531 |  |
| Expenses | 102 |  | Debtors | 1 864 |  |
|  |  | 2 118 | Bank | 621 |  |
|  |  |  |  |  | 5 016 |
|  |  | 13 866 |  |  | 13 866 |

The following information about Langland's financial position at 31 December 1983 was extracted from his books:

|  | £ |
|---|---|
| Stock | 3 268 |
| Debtors | 1 932 |
| Bank | 1 246 |
| Creditors: |  |
| Goods | 2 118 |
| Expenses | 84 |

Langland drew £2 400 from his business during 1983 for private purposes. Also during 1983 he received a legacy of £400 which he paid into his business account.

A depreciation charge of 10 per cent on the opening value of fixed assets should be made for 1983.

*REQUIRED:*
(a)  Langland's balance sheet at 31 December 1983.

(10 marks)
(b)  A calculation of Langland's profit for 1983, based on the increase in capital.

(10 marks)

(RSA II Accounting, May 1984)

**4**  On 1 May 1982, A. Jackson opened a photographic studio and paid £14 000 into a business bank account as the commencing capital.

He kept no proper books of account for his first year in business, but the summary given below, covering the year to 30 April 1983, has been prepared from statements supplied by the bank.

| | £ |
|---|---|
| (a)  Payments into the business bank account: | |
| Capital, 1 May 1982 | 14 000 |
| Payments received for photographic work done | |
| (after deducting A. Jackson's drawings and certain | |
| expenses – see below) | 9 554 |
| (b)  Cheques drawn on the business bank account: | |
| Purchase of equipment (furniture and fittings, | |
| cameras, dark-room equipment, etc.) | 11 220 |
| Advertising | 265 |
| Lighting and heating | 656 |
| Rent, rates and insurance | 3 490 |
| Miscellaneous expenses | 214 |
| Payments to suppliers of photographic materials | 2 730 |

Mr Jackson tells you that the total amount received by him for photographic work done was £19 560. He explains that the difference between this total and the amount paid into bank is accounted for by: drawings £8 100, wages of a part-time assistant £1 840, miscellaneous expenses £66.

You are asked to prepare a Profit and Loss Account for the year ended 30 April 1983 and a Balance Sheet as at 30 April 1983, taking the following matters into consideration:

(i)  Unpaid bills from suppliers of photographic materials totalled £525 at 30 April 1983.
(ii)  £950 is to be allowed for depreciation of equipment.
(iii)  At 30 April 1983, the stock of photographic materials is valued at £620.
(iv)  The item above for rent, rates and insurance (£3 490) includes the premium paid (£144) on an insurance policy covering a 12 months' period starting on 1 August 1982.
(v)  Mr Jackson tells you that at 30 April 1983 £2 720 is owing to him for work done. He estimates, however, that only three-quarters of this amount will be collected eventually.

(20 marks)

(Oxford Board Principles of Accounts O level, Summer 1983)

**5** John Lane runs a shop known as the John Lane Emporium, and on 1 January 1983 his total assets and liabilities, including both personal and business items, were, at historical cost less depreciation where appropriate:

|  | £ |
|---|---:|
| Assets: | |
| Business premises | 30 000 |
| House | 20 000 |
| Delivery van | 3 500 |
| Cash float in till | 100 |
| Trading stock | 14 250 |
| Personal bank account | 700 |
| Business bank account | 2 300 |
| Shop fittings | 5 000 |
| House furniture | 2 840 |
| Personal clothes | 740 |
| Premium bonds | 550 |
| Garden greenhouse | 450 |
| Garden shed | 150 |
| Personal car | 2 000 |
| Watch | 40 |
| Liabilities: | |
| Creditors for stock purchases | 1 500 |
| Domestic electricity | 70 |
| Business electricity | 85 |

The business bank account for the year to 31 December 1983 is:

|  | £ |  | £ |
|---|---:|---|---:|
| Balance brought down | 2 300 | Wages | 11 500 |
| Sales | 75 350 | Electricity | 250 |
|  |  | Motor expenses | 750 |
|  |  | Purchases | 52 200 |
|  |  | Drawings | 10 000 |
|  |  | Additional shop fittings | 1 600 |
|  |  | Balance carried down | 1 350 |
|  | 77 650 |  | 77 650 |

You are given the following information:

(a) At 31 December 1983 creditors for stock purchases were £2 000 and £100 was owed for business electricity.
(b) The value of shop fittings at 31 December 1983 was £5 940 and the van was valued at £2 500.
(c) At 31 December 1983 a float of £100 was held in the till, and trading stock was valued at £15 850.

*REQUIRED:*

(i) Prepare the Balance Sheet of the John Lane Emporium at 1 January 1983 to show clearly the capital which John Lane has invested in his business.

(ii) The Trading and Profit and Loss Account of the John Lane Emporium for the year to 31 December 1983 and a balance sheet at that date. The cost of goods sold and gross profit should be identified in the trading account.

(30 marks)

(RSA II Accounting, March 1984)

**6**  Edward Greenwood is a sole trader whose year end is 31 January each year. Owing to pressure of business, he is unable to value his stock in trade at the close of business on 31 January 1984 but he does so on 7 February 1984 when the value, *at cost price*, is calculated at £2 830.

For the period 1–7 February his purchases were £296, of which goods costing £54 were in transit at the time of stocktaking.

Sales for the period 1–7 February amounted to £460, all of which had left the warehouse at the time of stocktaking. Greenwood's gross profit is 20% of sales.

Also during the period 1–7 February, Greenwood took goods costing £38 for his personal use.

Included in the valuation figure of £2 830 given above were goods which cost £120, but which had a *market price* of £97 only at the date of the year end, i.e. 31 January 1984.

*REQUIRED:*

Calculate the figure which should be shown as 'Stock at 31 January 1984' in Greenwood's Trading Account for the year ended 31 January 1984.

*Note:*

Calculations must be shown.

(20 marks)

(LCCI Elementary Bookkeeping, Winter 1984)

**7**  During the night of 17 June 1983 the premises of Match Ltd were damaged by a fire which also destroyed a quantity of stock and all of the company's stock records. The destroyed stock was covered by insurance against loss by fire and the company wishes to calculate the amount to claim. The following information is available:

(i)

|  | On 1 January 1983 | On 17 June 1983 |
|---|---|---|
|  | £000 | £000 |
| Stock at cost | 132 | |
| Trade creditors | 45 | 53 |
| Trade debtors | 39 | 47 |

(ii) The following transactions took place between 1 January and 17 June 1983:

|  | £000 |
|---|---|
| Cash purchases | 17 |
| Payments to creditors | 274 |
| Cash received from debtors | 314 |
| Cash sales | 80 |
| Discounts received | 10 |
| Discounts allowed | 8 |

(iii) A physical stock take carried out first thing in the morning on 18 June 1983 showed the remaining stock to have a cost of £91 000.

(iv) Match Ltd earns a gross profit of 30% of selling price on all of its sales.

*REQUIRED:*

Calculate the cost of the stock destroyed by the fire.

(20 marks)

(RSA II Accounting, June 1983)

---

**E.   OUTLINE ANSWERS**

**1**   This tests your ability to calculate profit from changes in capital. Workings are: Closing capital, add back drawings, deduct legacy, giving £27 000; opening capital is £20 000, so the net profit is £7 000 (A).

**2**

|  |  | £ | £ |
|---|---|---|---|
| Debtors: | Opening balance | | 1 960 |
| | Add credit sales | | 6 250 |
| | | | 8 210 |
| | Less: cash received | 6 040 | |
| | bad debts | 110 | |
| | discount allowed | 190 | 6 340 |
| | closing debtors | | 1 870 |

The calculation of closing creditors follows the same principles: balance + purchases − cash and discount, giving £1 510.

Calculation of capitals:

| | 28/2/82 | 28/2/83 |
|---|---|---|
| | £ | £ |
| Bank | 790 | 870 |
| Stock | 1 470 | 1 660 |
| Furniture | 400 | 350 |
| Debtors | 1 960 | 1 870 |
| Van | — | 720 |
| | 4 620 | 5 470 |
| Creditors | (1 370) | (1 510) |
| Capital | 3 250 | 3 960 |

| Calculation of profit: | | |
|---|---|---|
| Closing capital | | £3 960 |
| Add drawings | | £950 |
| | | £4 910 |
| Less opening capital | | £3 250 |
| Net Profit | | £1 660 |

**3** Your balance sheet should include:

Fixed assets less depreciation;
Current assets as listed in the question (31/12/83);
Current liabilities at 31/12/83;
Capital: opening balance £11 748, add £400 legacy, less drawings £2 400; £9 748. The closing capital balance should be £12 209 (total assets £14 411 less current liabilities £2 202). The difference between the £12 209 and £9 748 represents net profit (£2 461).

**4** You have to calculate the bank balance: total receipts are £23 554 and total payments are £18 575, giving a closing £4 979 balance.
Income: £19 560 + £2 720 owed = £22 280 total.
Expenses: wages £1 840, miscellaneous £214 + £66, provision for bad debts £680 ($\frac{1}{4}$ of £2 720), advertising £265, light/heat £656, rent, etc. £3 454 (£3 490 less $\frac{1}{4}$ of £144 as prepayment), cost of materials £2 730 + £525 − £620 stock = £2 635, depreciation £950. Net profit £11 520.
Balance sheet: capital + NP − drawings = £17 420; creditors (CL) £525; assets of equipment less depreciation, £10 270; stock £620, debtors less provision £2 040, prepayment £36 and the bank balance £4 979 calculated above.

**6**

| | £ | £ |
|---|---|---|
| Stock at cost price, 7 February | | 2 830 |
| Deduct purchases in February | 296 | |
| | − 54 | (242) |
| | | |
| Add sales in February at cost price | | 368 |
| Add goods taken for own use | | 38 |
| Less reduction in value (120 − 97) | | (23) |
| | | |
| Stock at 31 January 1984 | | 2 971 |

You have to work backwards from the stock figure of 7 February; purchases have increased stock in hand, so deduct (other than purchases relating to January); sales have reduced the 31 January stock figure (stock has left the premises during the week 1–7 February), so add back at cost price, i.e. 80% of £460; goods own use have also lowered the stock figure, so add back; finally, the stock figure at 7 February is overstated by the £23 (stock always valued at the lower figure), so deduct.

**7** Stock at start of year: £132.
Stock received:

(i) Purchases (cash) £17.
(ii) Purchases (credit); payments to creditors £274 + £10 discounts, less £45 paid for last year's purchases (opening creditors), add unpaid purchases (closing creditors) £53; total £292.
(iii) Total stock inwards £132 + £17 + £292 = £441.

(iv) Stock sold; £80 cash sales + £322 to debtors (including discounts), less opening debtors £39, add closing debtors (sales this period) £47; total £410. This is at selling price; cost price is 70% = £287.

(v) Stock that should be in hand:
£441 − £287 = £154.

(vi) Stock actually in hand: £91.

(vii) Stock lost: £154 − £91 = £63.

## F. A TUTOR'S ANSWER

Question 5 tests your ability to prepare full final accounts from incomplete information. Here is the suggested answer:

(i)
### John Lane Emporium

*Balance Sheet at 1 January 1983*

| Fixed Assets | £ | £ | Capital | £ | £ |
|---|---|---|---|---|---|
| Premises | | 30 000 | Balance | | 53 565 |
| Fittings | | 5 000 | | | |
| Delivery van | | 3 500 | *Current Liabilities* | | |
| | | ——— | Creditors | 1 500 | |
| | | 38 500 | Accrued expense | 85 | |
| *Current Assets* | | | | | ——— |
| Stock | 14 250 | | | | 1 585 |
| Bank | 2 300 | | | | |
| Cash | 100 | 16 650 | | | |
| | | ——— | | | ——— |
| | | 55 150 | | | 55 150 |

*Workings*

Capital is calculated by Assets (£55 150) less Liabilities (£1 585). All personal items are ignored in the business balance sheet.

(ii)
### John Lane Emporium

*Trading and Profit and Loss accounts for the year to 31 December 1983*

| | £ | | £ |
|---|---|---|---|
| Opening stock | 14 250 | Sales | 75 350 |
| Purchases | 52 700 | | |
| | ——— | | |
| | 66 950 | | |
| Less closing stock | 15 850 | | |
| | ——— | | |
| Cost of sales | 51 100 | | |
| Gross Profit c/d | 24 250 | | |
| | ——— | | ——— |
| | 75 350 | | 75 350 |

| | £ | | £ |
|---|---|---|---|
| Wages | 11 500 | Gross Profit b/d | 24 250 |
| Electricity | 265 | | |
| Depreciation: Van | 1 000 | | |
| Fittings | 660 | | |
| Motor expenses | 750 | | |
| Net Profit | 10 075 | | |
| | 24 250 | | 24 250 |

**Workings**

1. Purchases: cash paid £52 200 − opening creditors £1 500 + closing creditors £2 000.
2. Electricity: cash paid £250 − opening accrued £85 + closing accrued £100.
3. Depreciation: van £3 500 − £2 500; fittings £5 000 + £1 600 − £5 940

### John Lane Emporium
*Balance Sheet at 31 December 1983*

| *Fixed Assets* | £ | £ | *Capital* | £ | £ |
|---|---|---|---|---|---|
| Premises | | 30 000 | Opening balance | | 53 565 |
| Fittings | | 5 940 | Net profit | | 10 075 |
| Delivery van | | 2 500 | | | |
| | | 38 440 | | | 63 640 |
| | | | Less drawings | | 10 000 |
| *Current Assets* | | | | | 53 640 |
| Stock | 15 850 | | *Current Liabilities* | | |
| Bank | 1 350 | | Creditors | 2 000 | |
| Cash | 100 | 17 300 | Accrued expense | 100 | 2 100 |
| | | 55 740 | | | 55 740 |

---

## G. A STEP FURTHER

Some accounting syllabuses will include stock valuation as a topic, requiring you to study the various techniques and methods which are used in valuing stock. A syllabus may also include some other stock-related aspects, such as stock records or stock control. Most accounting textbooks include chapters on stock. Here is a selection (the chapter is on stock valuation unless otherwise stated):

Garbutt, *Carter's Advanced Accounts* (7th edn) (Pitman). Ch. 07.

Glautier, Underdown and Clark, *Basic Accounting Practice* (2nd edn) (Pitman). Ch. 6, Section 5 (on inventory control).

Simini and Hingley, *Accounting Made Simple* ('Made Simple' series). Ch. 7.

Wood, *Bookkeeping and Accounts* (Longman). Ch. 38 (on stock records).

Wood, *Business Accounting 2* (4th edn) (Longman). Ch. 1.

The topic of incomplete records is regarded as a complex and demanding one, and it is therefore advisable to study a range of appropriate examples, illustrations and explanations. Here is a selection of books that you may find useful:

Bright, *Practical Accounts 2* (Pan 'Breakthrough' series). Ch. 5.

Castle and Owens, *Principles of Accounts* (7th edn) (M & E). Ch. 17.

Whitehead, *Bookkeeping Made Simple* ('Made Simple' series). Ch. 25.

Whitehead, *Success in Principles of Accounting* (John Murray). Unit 30.

Wood, *Business Accounting 1* (4th edn) (Longman). Ch. 33.

# Index